FOR FAITH
AND CLARITY

# FOR FAITH AND CLARITY

## Philosophical Contributions
## to Christian Theology

JAMES K. BEILBY, EDITOR

Baker Academic

Grand Rapids, Michigan

© 2006 by James K. Beilby

Published by Baker Academic
a division of Baker Publishing Group
P.O. Box 6287, Grand Rapids, MI 49516-6287
www.bakeracademic.com

Printed in the United States of America

Library of Congress Cataloging-in-Publication Data
For faith and clarity : philosophical contributions to Christian theology / James K. Beilby, editor.
    p.   cm.
   Includes bibliographical references and index.
   ISBN 10: 0-8010-2766-7 (pbk.)
   ISBN 978-0-8010-2766-6 (pbk.)
   1. Philosophical theology.  I. Beilby, James K.
  BT40.F54  2006
  261.5'1—dc22                                   2006000980

Dedicated to Steve

My best friend,
who also happens to be my brother

# CONTENTS

# CONTRIBUTORS

**James K. Beilby** (Ph.D., Marquette University) is associate professor of systematic and philosophical theology at Bethel University in St. Paul, Minnesota. His primary areas of research are religious epistemology and theology and culture. He has published articles in *Faith and Philosophy*, *Religious Studies*, *International Journal for Philosophy of Religion*, and *Philosophia Christi*, among other journals. He is the author or editor of numerous books, including *Epistemology as Theology: An Evaluation of Alvin Plantinga's Religious Epistemology* (Ashgate, 2006); *Naturalism Defeated? Essays on Plantinga's Evolutionary Argument against Naturalism* (Cornell University Press, 2002); and, with Paul Eddy, *Divine Foreknowledge: Four Views* (InterVarsity, 2001).

**David Clark** (Ph.D., Northwestern University) has been professor of theology at Bethel Seminary in St. Paul, Minnesota, since 1988. He also serves as a pastor at Faith Covenant Church in Burnsville, Minnesota. He is especially interested in applying the resources of analytic philosophy to bring insight and resolution to theological concerns. In addition to many articles, he has written or edited eight books, the latest of which is *To Know and Love God: Method for Evangelical Theology* (Crossway, 2003).

**William Lane Craig** (Ph.D., University of Birmingham; D.Theol., University of Munich) is a research professor of philosophy at Talbot School of Theology in La Mirada, California. Before his appointment at Talbot, he spent seven years at the Higher Institute of Philosophy of the Katholike Universiteit in Leuven, Belgium. He has authored or edited more than thirty books, including *The Kalam Cosmological Argument*; *Divine*

9

*Foreknowledge and Human Freedom*; *Theism, Atheism, and Big Bang Cosmology*; and *God, Time, and Eternity* as well as more than a hundred articles in professional journals of philosophy and theology, including the *Journal of Philosophy*, *American Philosophical Quarterly*, *Philosophical Studies*, *Philosophy*, and *British Journal for Philosophy of Science*.

**William Hasker** (Ph.D., University of Edinburgh) is professor emeritus of philosophy at Huntington College in Huntington, Indiana. His main interests in philosophy are philosophy of religion and philosophy of mind. He is the author of *Metaphysics: Constructing a Worldview* (InterVarsity, 1983); *God, Time, and Knowledge* (Cornell, 1989); *The Emergent Self* (Cornell, 1999); and *Providence, Evil, and the Openness of God* (Routledge, 2004), and is coauthor or coeditor of several other volumes. He is president for 2005–2006 of the Society for Philosophy of Religion and editor of the journal *Faith and Philosophy*.

**J. P. Moreland** (Ph.D., University of Southern California) is distinguished professor of philosophy at Biola University and Director of the Eidos Christian Center. In addition to his Ph.D. in philosophy, he has earned three other degrees: chemistry (University of Missouri), theology (Dallas Seminary), and philosophy (M.A., University of California–Riverside). He has authored or contributed to twenty books with publishers ranging from Oxford University Press to InterVarsity. Among them are *Does God Exist?*, *The Creation Hypothesis*, *Philosophical Naturalism*, and *Body and Soul*. He has also published more than sixty articles in journals, including the *American Philosophical Quarterly*, *MetaPhilosophy*, *Religious Studies*, and *Faith and Philosophy*. Dr. Moreland served for eight years as a bioethicist for PersonaCare Nursing Homes.

**Paul K. Moser** (Ph.D., Vanderbilt University) is professor and chair of philosophy at Loyola University of Chicago. He is the author of *Philosophy after Objectivity* (Oxford University Press) and *Knowledge and Evidence* (Cambridge University Press); the editor of *The Oxford Handbook of Epistemology* (Oxford University Press) and *Rationality in Action* (Cambridge University Press); and the coeditor of *Divine Hiddenness* (Cambridge University Press) and *The Rationality of Theism* (Routledge).

**Alan G. Padgett** (D.Phil., University of Oxford) is an ordained Methodist minister and professor of systematic theology at Luther Seminary in Minnesota, where he teaches courses in theology and science. The author or editor of seven books and numerous journal articles, he is well known for his contributions to philosophy of religion, philosophy of science, and systematic theology. His most recent work is *Science and the Study* *of God* (Eerdmans, 2003); he wrote his best-selling book with three other philosophers: *God and Time: Four Views* (InterVarsity, 2001).

**Alvin Plantinga** (Ph.D., Yale University) is John A. O'Brien Professor of Philosophy at the University of Notre Dame, where he has taught philosophy for twenty-two years. He gives seminars in philosophy of religion, metaphysics, and epistemology. Previously he taught at Calvin College for nineteen years. Among his many books are *God and Other Minds*; *The Nature of Necessity*; *God, Freedom, and Evil*; *Does God Have a Nature?*; *Warrant: The Current Debate*; *Warrant and Proper Function*; and *Warranted Christian Belief*.

**Bruce Reichenbach** (Ph.D., Northwestern University) is professor of philosophy at Augsburg College, where he has taught for thirty-seven years. He has received study grants from the National Endowment for the Humanities and the U.S. Department of Education and taught in a university and a seminary in Africa. His primary research interest is philosophy of religion and applied ethics. In addition to more than fifty articles and book chapters, he has published *The Cosmological Argument* (Thomas, 1972); *Is Man the Phoenix?* (Eerdmans, 1978); *Evil and a Good God* (Fordham, 1982); *The Law of Karma* (Macmillan, 1990); *On Behalf of God* (Eerdmans, 1995); and *Introduction to Critical Thinking* (McGraw-Hill, 2001), and coauthored two widely used textbooks in philosophy of religion, including his most recent book, *Reason and Religious Belief* (Oxford, 2003).

**Jay Wesley Richards** (Ph.D., Princeton Theological Seminary) is research fellow and director of institutional relations at Acton Institute in Grand Rapids, Michigan. He is the author of many academic articles in philosophy, science, and theology as well as popular articles and editorial features in publications such as the *Washington Post*, *Washington Times*, *American Spectator*, *Touchstone*, and *Seattle Post-Intelligencer*. He is author of *The Untamed God: A Philosophical Exploration of Divine Perfection, Immutability, and Simplicity* (InterVarsity, 2003); coauthor, with Guillermo Gonzalez, of *The Privileged Planet: How Our Place in the Cosmos is Designed for Discovery* (Regnery, 2004); editor and contributor, with George Gilder, of *Are We Spiritual Machines? Ray Kurzweil vs. the Critics of Strong AI* (Discovery Institute Press, 2002); and editor and contributor, with William A. Dembski, of *Unapologetic Apologetics: Meeting the Challenges of Theological Studies* (InterVarsity, 2001).

**Nicholas Wolterstorff** (Ph.D., Harvard University) taught philosophy for thirty years at Calvin College before he came to Yale as Noah Porter

Professor of Philosophical Theology in the Divinity School. He retired in December 2001. He has written books on metaphysics (*On Universals*), aesthetics and philosophy of art (*Works and Worlds of Art* and *Art in Action*), epistemology (*John Locke and the Ethics of Belief* and *Thomas Reid and the Story of Epistemology*), philosophy of religion (*Divine Discourse*), and political philosophy (*Until Justice and Peace Embrace* and *Religion in the Public Square*). He is working on a book on justice. In the fall of 1993, he gave the Wilde Lectures at Oxford University; in the spring of 1995, the Gifford Lectures at the University of St. Andrews; and in the spring of 1998, the Stone Lectures at Princeton Seminary on political philosophy and theology. He has been president of the American Philosophical Association (Central Division) and of the Society of Christian Philosophers.

**Keith E. Yandell** (Ph.D., Ohio State University) is Julius R. Weinberg Professor of Philosophy at the University of Wisconsin–Madison. He has published *Basic Issues in the Philosophy of Religion* (Allyn & Bacon); *Christianity and Philosophy* (Eerdmans); *Hume's "Inexplicable Mystery"* (Temple); *The Epistemology of Religious Experience* (Cambridge University Press); and *Philosophy of Religion* (Routledge), and edited or coedited *Problems in Philosophical Inquiry* (Holt, Rinehart, & Winston); *Ockham, Descartes, and Hume* (University of Wisconsin Press); *God, Man, and Religion* (McGraw Hill); *Religion and Public Culture* (Curzon); and *Faith and Narrative* (Oxford University Press). He has published articles in metaphysics, epistemology, ethics, Indian philosophy, philosophical theology, and philosophy of religion.

# INTRODUCTION

## The Contribution of Philosophy to Theology

꒷| James K. Beilby |꒦

> Good philosophy must exist, if for no other reason, be-
> cause bad philosophy needs to be answered.
>
> C. S. Lewis

THE RELATIONSHIP BETWEEN THEOLOGY AND philosophy is
akin to the relationship between siblings; they are either the best of
friends or the worst of enemies, depending on the situation and who else
is in the room. Like siblings, philosophy and theology share a common
genetic bond—the search for truth, beauty, goodness, and understanding.
Nevertheless, differences in personality, environment, methodology, and
presuppositions create an aura of suspicion that often emerges when
the two disciplines enter into conversation. I experienced this firsthand
when (in 1995–1996) I applied to Ph.D. programs in systematic theology
and expressed a strong interest in bringing philosophy into conversation with theology. I discovered that the attitudes toward philosophy on
the part of theologians, and theology on the part of philosophers, range
from enthusiasm to disapprobation. Consequently, many of those with
whom I shared my academic goals responded with surprise, some with
skepticism, and a few with thinly veiled incredulity. (I expect my experience would have been similar if I had applied to philosophy programs
with a desire to do work on theological questions.)

13

Fully investigating the causes of this interdisciplinary suspicion is
a complex task and, happily, is not necessary for the purposes of this
volume. Nevertheless, some general observations can be made. Undoubtedly, part of the problem is the fact that theology and philosophy are
two separate disciplines and interdisciplinary work is difficult. But the
roots of the divide run deeper.

Consider the state of affairs characterizing academic philosophy in
the middle third of the twentieth century. During this period, under the
influence of a philosophical movement known as logical positivism, many
philosophers came to view religious statements as not merely false but
meaningless. Logical positivism, with a little help from the Supreme
Court, effectively banished most public expressions of Christian faith
from American academia.[1] The response of theologians to the depreda-
tions of logical positivism varied widely. Many accepted the positivistic
critique of "God-talk" and modified their approach to theological beliefs
accordingly. Others saw in logical positivism a tangible example of Paul's
warning to the Colossians to beware of being taken "captive through
philosophy" (Col. 2:8) and built barriers between the two disciplines.
Similarly, some Christian philosophers responded by rejecting realism
and treating theism as an expression of emotion or value, not a description of reality or a worldview. Theists who maintained their religious
realism increasingly excluded their religious beliefs from their teaching
and publications to avoid ridicule and censure. The relatively few realist
Christians who remained active and vocal in philosophy were like voices
crying in the wilderness.

In the 1960s, a decade that is decried for its hedonism and secular-
ism, the state of affairs in Western academia began to change. The noted
atheist Quentin Smith describes this change:

*Quentin Smith on Plantinga*

The secularization of mainstream academia began to quickly unravel upon
the publication of [Alvin] Plantinga's influential book on realist theism, *God
and Other Minds*, in 1967. It became apparent to the philosophical profes-
sion that this book displayed that realist theists were not outmatched by
naturalists in terms of the most valued standards of analytic philosophy:
conceptual precision, rigor of argumentation, technical erudition, and an
in-depth defense of an original worldview. This book, followed seven years
later by Plantinga's even more impressive book, *The Nature of Necessity*,
made it manifest that a realist theist was writing at the highest qualitative
level of analytic philosophy, on the same playing field as Carnap, Russell,
Grünbaum, and other naturalists. . . . In philosophy, it became, almost overnight, "academically respectable" to argue for theism, making philosophy a

1. Kenneth Konyndyk, "Christianity Reenters Philosophical Circles," *Perspectives* 7/9
(November 1992): 17.

favored field of entry for the most intelligent and talented theists entering academia today. . . . God is not "dead" in academia; he returned to life in the late 1960's and is now alive and well in his last academic stronghold, philosophy departments.[2]

Since the late 1960s, "Christian philosophy" has flourished in remarkable ways. The Society of Christian Philosophers, formed in 1978, now boasts over one thousand members and one of the premier journals in philosophy of religion in the world: *Faith and Philosophy*. Other explicitly Christian philosophical groups—notably the Evangelical Philosophical Society and its journal, *Philosophia Christi*—are seeing similar growth.

The central contention of this volume—indeed, its raison d'être—is that theology can benefit greatly from philosophy. Of course, the reverse is equally true—philosophy can benefit greatly from theology. In fact, a number of the essays in this volume take up the latter theme. Nevertheless, the primary function of this book is to demonstrate some of the ways that philosophy can help clarify theological questions, debates, and issues and thereby demonstrate the existence, viability, and fecundity of a distinctively Christian approach to philosophy.

Discussing the contribution of Christian philosophy to theology raises two deeper questions: (1) what is Christian philosophy, and (2) what are the arenas in which Christian philosophy can contribute to theology? These are weighty questions that cannot be fully explored in any single volume. Although the essays in this volume address these questions at least implicitly, perhaps we can here say something more general and programmatic.

The question "What is Christian philosophy?" can be more effectively restated as "What is it that makes a philosophy *Christian*?" How this question is answered will depend to a significant extent on certain crucial theological and philosophical presuppositions. Nevertheless, I submit that it is not enough to merely be a Christian who does philosophy. There must be something uniquely or distinctively Christian about the philosophy itself. James Ross lists four distinct yet overlapping senses in which a philosophy may be considered Christian: (1) when the philosophy has distinctively Christian insights into a philosophical question, (2) when a philosopher includes Christian revelation as an indispensable source, (3) when the basic issue being discussed cannot be comprehensively framed in a manner that is neutral to the Christian faith, and (4) when the whole system of Christian wisdom—including

Ross

---

2. Quentin Smith, "The Metaphilosophy of Naturalism," *Philo* 4/2 (fall–winter 2001): 2, 3.

doctrines, civilizations, and arts—is compared to or contrasted with other competing philosophies.[3]

Focus on the first of the above senses in which a philosophy might be called Christian—when it has distinctively Christian insights into a philosophical question. It seems clear that a philosophy could be Christian in this sense but contribute to the fields of philosophy or theology in a variety of different ways. In other words, Christian philosophies will vary not only according to the sense in which they may be considered Christian but also according to their purpose or the aspect of theology they discuss.

Alvin Plantinga has discussed four different arenas in which Christian philosophy can contribute to theology.[4] First, Christian philosophy can seek to demonstrate the truthfulness of the Christian faith. This could come in the form of either *negative apologetics* (responding to the various objections that can be raised against the Christian faith) or *positive apologetics* (providing arguments for aspects of the faith).

Second, the Christian philosopher can engage in *philosophical theology*—the task of employing the resources of philosophy in an effort to clarify and deepen our understanding of various facets of the Christian faith. One of the main contributions from philosophical theology—although by no means the only one—is the clarification of theological questions. For example, when Christians ask about God's relationship to time or the nature of divine foreknowledge, what question (or, more likely, questions) are being asked? Theological issues such as these are actually a complex thicket of questions all interrelated in ways that are complex and difficult to discern. One of the services the Christian philosopher can perform for the church is to seek to untangle this thicket.

Third, Christian philosophers, according to Plantinga, can and should engage in what he calls *Christian philosophical criticism*. The purpose of this criticism is to analyze and critique the perspectives, assumptions, and research programs that dominate the intellectual culture in which we live. Many of these run directly counter to fundamental Christian beliefs. This is not to say that Christians have nothing to learn from those who espouse non-Christian worldviews, but neither is it the case that Christians should unthinkingly acquiesce to presuppositions that arise from a worldview directly counter to Christianity.

The fourth and final arena in which Christian philosophy can contribute to the Christian faith is *constructive* or *positive Christian philosophy*.

3. James F. Ross, "On Christian Philosophy: *Una vera philosophia?*" *Monist* 75/3 (July 1992): 354–80.

4. Alvin Plantinga, "Christian Philosophy at the End of the 20th Century," in *Christian Philosophy and the Close of the Twentieth Century*, ed. Sander Griffioen and Bert Balk (Kampen: Kok, 1995), 29–53.

This project is the consideration of philosophical issues from an unapologetic and explicitly Christian or theistic perspective. This includes considering topics not deemed to be interesting or even viable by the broader academic community. But Plantinga argues that the Christian philosopher's primary allegiance must be to the Christian community. This is particularly important when considering philosophical questions that cannot be discussed in a way that is neutral to Christianity. Questions about the nature of personhood and the destiny of human beings certainly fall into that camp. This is a sense in which the Christian philosopher is in the broader academic world but not of it. Ultimately, she or he has a higher calling, a calling to serve the Lord Jesus Christ and the Christian church.

The essays in this volume are all instances of Christian philosophy, in one or more of the senses listed above. The purpose of these essays is to demonstrate some of the ways that Christian philosophy can contribute to theology. Each of them thereby indirectly addresses the topic of the relationship between theology and philosophy. The first essay in this volume, however—"The Relationship between Theology and Philosophy: Constructing a Christian Worldview" by Alan Padgett—addresses this relationship directly. Padgett begins by considering the nature of theology and philosophy. Rightly eschewing the voluminous task of providing a thoroughgoing definition of these disciplines, he shoulders a more modest project. He utilizes prominent historical examples—Anselm and Aquinas, to name just two—and discerns what can be learned about the relationship between theology and philosophy from the approaches of these figures. He argues that philosophy and theology, though separate disciplines, can engage in a fruitful and collegial partnership in the search for truth and in the development of a Christian worldview. He then applies these insights to a concrete example: the debate over the nature and legitimacy of natural theology.

In "General Ontology and Theology: A Primer," J. P. Moreland provides an introduction to a collection of crucial philosophical concepts: existence, essence, identity, substance, properties, and relations. Not only are these concepts fundamental to philosophical discourse; many theological doctrines are articulated in terms of these concepts or assume definitions of these concepts. For example, it is common to talk of God's attributes. But what are attributes and in what sense does God have them? After discussing the nature and usage of these concepts, Moreland provides a few concrete applications of their usage in theological discourse.

In "Reorienting Religious Epistemology: Cognitive Grace, Filial Knowledge, and Gethsemane Struggle," Paul Moser discusses some of the critical presuppositional issues behind religious epistemology, the study of whether religious beliefs are rational, justified, warranted, or intellectually respectable. Moser not only discusses how epistemology affects theology, but he also addresses the issue of how theology should affect epistemology. The fundamental question in religious epistemology, Moser argues, is not "Does God exist?" but rather "What kind of human knowledge would an all-loving God desire humans to possess?" He suggests that if our relationship with God is properly understood as filial knowledge, we will realize that we must attune ourselves to the available evidence of God's self-revelation rather than demand that the evidence of God must fit our preconceived categories.

Following the opening three essays, which address theological methodology/prolegomena, Bruce Reichenbach's "Divine Revelation: Discernment and Interpretation" is the first of two essays addressing the matter of revelation. He discusses its nature and five critical issues attending a theological discussion of revelation: the role of context in revelation, the necessity of revelation, the continuation (or cessation) of revelation, the task of identifying instances of revelation, and the interpretation of revelation.

In "Beyond Inerrancy: Speech Acts and an Evangelical View of Scripture," David Clark discusses the commitment to the doctrine of inerrancy on the part of broadly conservative or evangelical theologians. He argues that J. L. Austin's speech act theory is a fruitful way to explain the core insight behind inerrancy without falling prey to modernistic and fundamentalistic assumptions about the nature of Scripture.

The resurgence in the field of philosophy of religion in the last forty years has led to a philosophical discussion of most areas of theological discourse, but the doctrine of God has undoubtedly received the greatest attention. This volume contains three essays on the doctrine of God. The first is William Lane Craig's "Pantheists in Spite of Themselves: God and Infinity in Contemporary Theology." In this essay, Craig discusses the God-world relationship, and particularly a recent trend on the part of some contemporary theologians toward rejecting theism in favor of panentheism. Theologians such as Wolfhart Pannenberg, Philip Clayton, and LeRon Shults argue that if creation is seen as "outside" or "over and against" God, then God is limited and no longer infinite. Craig locates the roots of this tendency in German idealism and specifically in the metaphysics of G. W. F. Hegel (1770–1831). He argues that once the sense in which God is infinite is properly understood, the impetus toward panentheism is nullified.

Among the divine attributes, one of the most contentious is divine simplicity. Although the assertion of divine simplicity has played a prominent role in church tradition, it is currently widely rejected by Christian theologians and philosophers alike, and it is virtually unknown among ordinary Christians. In "Divine Simplicity: The Good, the Bad, and the Ugly," Jay Richards seeks to disambiguate the sense in which it might be said that God is simple. Depending on how "simplicity" is understood, the various understandings of divine simplicity range from the uncontroversial to the highly contentious and problematic. Richards argues that when the doctrine in its various expressions is properly understood, "much of its underlying motivation, and a good bit of its traditional content, can still be defended."

Another divine attribute that has not received sufficient attention from philosophers and theologians is God's justice. In "Justice of God," Nicholas Wolterstorff addresses the common notion—a theme exemplified in Anselm, Anders Nygren, and Reinhold Niebuhr—that there exists a tension between God's love and God's justice. Wolterstorff argues that the tension between God's love and justice assumes that justice is equivalent to retributive justice, or the "just" response to a wrongdoing of some sort. But such an understanding of justice—called secondary justice—cannot be properly understood apart from the original requirement to avoid wrongdoing—primary justice. If one begins with primary justice, then, according to Wolterstorff, "love is not in tension with justice; love practices justice."

The final three essays consider aspects of God's creation. In "Evolution and Design," Alvin Plantinga discusses the compatibility of "design" and current evolutionary theory. There are two different senses of "design." If "design" is merely understood as "having a function or a purpose," then, there is no incompatibility between evolution and design. To say that an aspect of an organism is designed in this sense is to explain why the mechanisms of evolution selected this aspect rather than another. But there is a "stronger and more interesting sense of 'design,'" a sense that subsumes the weaker notion of design under the plan of an intelligent designer. Plantinga's goal is to investigate the compatibility of design in this sense with evolutionary theory. He argues that evolution, taken by itself, and in spite of the claims of many evolutionary biologists, is perfectly compatible with intelligent design. The appearance of incompatibility is not due to evolution but the metaphysical naturalism that is commonly taken to accompany evolution and the methodological naturalism that is taken to be a necessary component of science.

In "Theology, Philosophy, and Evil," Keith Yandell considers the perennial question of the relationship between God and evil. He discusses the logical and evidential problems of evil against the backdrop of Christian and naturalistic accounts of human destiny, various philosophical distinctions about intrinsic worth, and the dilemma posed for Christian theology in the Platonic dialogue *Euthyphro*. Yandell argues that when these objections are properly understood, none offers a refutation of Christian theism.

The final essay in this volume is William Hasker's "Philosophical Contributions to Theological Anthropology." Hasker focuses attention on the philosophical presuppositions and commitments necessary to maintain certain fundamental theological assumptions about human nature—rationality, moral responsibility, freedom, and immortality, for example. Many contemporary philosophical accounts of human nature are such that these theological assertions are imperiled or denied outright. Hasker considers the challenge of materialism—the notion that human beings are entirely composed of ordinary physical matter and everything about humans is to be explained in material terms—and three different responses available to the Christian: traditional dualism, Christian materialism, and emergent dualism. Hasker suggests that emergent dualism allows for a clear-cut commitment to fundamental theological assumptions about human nature and avoids the pitfalls to which both the other views are subject.

The articles in this volume therefore discuss a range of theological issues: theological prolegomena and the doctrines of Scripture, God, and creation. This is, of course, not exhaustive. Much might be said (and has been) from a philosophical point of view regarding Christology, soteriology, ecclesiology, or eschatology. Space constraints do not permit more comprehensive coverage of theological areas.

The perspective of this volume is circumscribed in another important sense. The contributors all write from an analytic, as opposed to a continental, philosophical perspective. The differences between the two perspectives are labyrinthine and contentious; there is no point in continuing this perennial philosophical debate here. Nonetheless, both have something to offer the Christian faith, and both can contribute to theological discourse, although in very different ways. The stark differences in assumptions, methodology, and style between the two perspectives, however, are such that a volume containing only one of the perspectives is to be preferred over a volume mixing the two.

There are barriers inherent in each perspective. Continental philosophy brings a unique vocabulary and set of idiomatic expressions that often challenge the uninitiated. Analytic philosophers, on the other hand, are accused of being closet mathematicians because their essays are often filled with logical symbols, variables, and other such daunting hieroglyphics. These barriers, however, are not insurmountable. Just as one can learn the language of continental philosophy, one can learn to translate logical symbols into prose. After such translation is accomplished, it becomes possible to see that the "mathematical shenanigans" of analytic philosophers are intended to clarify rather than obfuscate. The use of numbered propositions, for example, is intended to highlight and succinctly state the main points of an argument. If the very same argument were stated in prose, it would require much more space, and a step in the argument would more likely be missed. Although the essays in this volume employ numbered propositions and logical variables, pains have been taken to help the reader understand their meaning and import.

No project such as this comes to fruition without the assistance of many people. Thanks go to Bob Hosack; I cannot conceive of a better editor for this book. In addition to proofreading the entire volume, my teaching assistant, Eric Helleloid, provided an invaluable student's perspective on the content of the essays. My department chair, Mike Holmes, allowed me to structure my teaching load so as to maximize research and writing time, for which I am appreciative. Finally, I owe an immeasurable debt of gratitude to my wife, Michelle, and to my children, Sierra, Madeline, Zachary, and Malia. They bring joy to each and every one of my days and serve as a constant reminder of God's love and grace.

# PART I

# METHODOLOGICAL
# ISSUES

# I

# THE RELATIONSHIP BETWEEN THEOLOGY AND PHILOSOPHY

## Constructing a Christian Worldview

❧| **Alan G. Padgett** |❦

## THEOLOGY AND PHILOSOPHY AS COLLEAGUES

Tertullian once asked this famous question: "What indeed has Athens to do with Jerusalem? What concord is there between the Academy and the Church?"[1] Whereas the great rhetorician and second-century apologist meant this as a rhetorical question, I propose in this chapter to take it seriously as an open one: what role does the academy play in the church, and the church in the academy? To focus this large question down to a smaller topic, we will let philosophy, the love of wisdom, stand in for the academy. Theology, the study of God, will likewise stand in for the church. So our question now is this: what concord is there between philosophy and theology?

1. Tertullian, *Prescription against Heretics (De praescriptione haereticorum)* §7.

To give things away just a bit, we are going to find an answer different from the one Tertullian did. Tertullian thought that once we find Christ, we have no more need for philosophy. Perhaps he had in mind the verse from Colossians where Paul warns the church, "See to it that no one takes you captive through philosophy and empty deceit, according to human tradition" (Col. 2:8). In this chapter I will argue that theology and philosophy should be colleagues, and will spell out some specific areas where they should work together in the quest for truth.[2]

We might begin with a better understanding of Paul's point in Colossians. Paul was one of the first great intellectuals of the church. He valued wisdom, understanding, and knowledge, but he grounded the quest for truth in Christ. This becomes clear if we take the time to read his whole chapter. He begins chapter 2 telling the church that he wants them to be "encouraged and united in love." Why? "So that they may have all the riches of assured understanding and have the knowledge of God's mystery, that is, Christ himself, in whom are hidden all the treasures of wisdom and knowledge" (Col. 2:2–3). The problem in Colossae was that some believers were being led astray by heretical, anti-Christian teachings. This is what Paul is objecting to: not the love of wisdom itself but any human reasoning that sets itself up against the lordship of Christ (Col. 2:6–8). The lesson we learn should be this: knowledge is good but can be corrupted by sin. Wisdom is a good thing, and so is the love of wisdom, but loving the Lord our God with all our mind is greater still (see Matt. 22:37). If Paul is right, then Tertullian must have been wrong. Or was he?

### What Are Philosophy and Theology?

To speak of the relationship between philosophy and theology would seem to call for a definition of both—but none is forthcoming. There are no accepted definitions of these two disciplines. Let me say some generally accepted things about them, however, before I go on to hazard a working definition for our present purposes.

First of all, although theology and philosophy are both rigorous academic disciplines, they also speak to that which is beyond academics. Theology here means Christian doctrine, what is sometimes called dogmatics or systematic theology. The origin of Christian teaching lies in faith and worship of Jesus Christ and therefore also of the triune God. When Christians worship together, their hymns, prayers, liturgies, and

2. Many of the working assumptions and perspectives upon which this chapter is based are worked out in Alan G. Padgett, *Science and the Study of God: A Mutuality Model for Theology and Science* (Grand Rapids: Eerdmans, 2003).

sermons already contain a good deal of Christian doctrine. Theology is not made up in the seminary but already found in the Christian way of life. Christian doctrine is caught up in Christian practice, in the Christian way of being in the world, both as individual believers and also as a community of the Spirit. For the most part, however, our focus will be on theology as an academic discipline, that is, academic theology. Theology is the study of God, and Christian doctrine is a discipline that studies God and other things in their relationship to God. It seeks the truth about God and the world on the basis of revelation from God, which finds its center in Jesus the Messiah: the way, the truth, and the life (John 14:6). Other religions will thus have different theologies, based upon differing understandings and starting points.

Philosophy, too, points to that which is already larger than the academy. Every person has a basic way of looking at the world, themselves, and other people that informs their day-to-day activities. We could call this a philosophy of life or a worldview. A worldview is, broadly, our understanding of who we are and of the world we live in, including our system of values and our religious beliefs (if any).[3] I use "worldview" in a broad and flexible way and allow that various communities of faith will develop differing worldviews. Indeed, people within the same broad worldview will have important differences among them. The point is that any functioning adult human operates with some philosophy of life or worldview, however implicit.

One task of philosophy is to make our worldviews clear and to criticize them on the basis of reason and experience. People outside the academy can do this well. Philosophers are not limited to colleges and universities! Still, for the most part, in this chapter we will be speaking of philosophy as an academic discipline. As such, philosophy seeks the truth. It does so based upon our common resources as humans, especially reason and experience. Philosophy seeks to answer the larger questions of life, the big questions.[4] It does not concern itself with details about factual matters, which it is happy to leave to the natural and human sciences. Rather, philosophy seeks truth about issues of meaning, interpretation, value, beauty, and existence as a whole, but always with

3. For more on worldviews, see ibid., 74–77; see further David Naugle, *Worldview: The History of a Concept* (Grand Rapids: Eerdmans, 2004).

4. The Chinese philosopher Fung Yu-Lan defines philosophy "very briefly" as "systematic, reflective thinking about life." He then goes on to describe what he means by "systematic" and "reflective," also noting that "Life is an all-inclusive whole." The activity of philosophy he calls "the inner-directed development of the human mind." See Fung Yu-Lan, *A New Treatise on the Methodology of Metaphysics* (Beijing: Foreign Language Press, 1997), 1–2. Cf. Edward Craig, *Philosophy: A Very Short Introduction* (Oxford: Oxford University Press, 2002), who writes about "some very general picture of what the world is like" and three basic philosophical questions—value, reality, and knowledge (p. 1).

an eye to rationality, clarity, evidence, and argument. Philosophy thus reflects upon the methods and findings of the other disciplines without seeking to establish or refute their results. It does so not on the basis of faith in Jesus but on the basis of common human reason and experience. In this way philosophy is common to all human cultures. Alvin Plantinga has rightly argued that Christian philosophers should begin their philosophical work on the basis of Christian faith; but philosophy as a discipline does not.[5]

Second, each academic discipline seeks rational knowledge. Both theology and philosophy seek the truth. They both pursue good arguments, logical clarity, fair argumentation, and sound conclusions. And they are both concerned with the larger questions of life. But the focus, goals, and methods of these two disciplines are quite distinct. Theology's goal is to glorify God with our minds and seek the truth as it is in Jesus (Eph. 4:21). As Paul rightly said, scholars of Christian doctrine are not interested in abstract truth but in seeing everything from the perspective of faith in Christ. Philosophy, as a truth-seeking community, is not committed to Christ but seeks the truth on the grounds of our common humanity and life in the world. The rationalities in these different approaches means that conversation between theology and philosophy is bound to be complicated.

Finally, we can agree that there are no pure, eternal, and essential forms of either philosophy or theology. It is important to note the various philosophical schools, for they differ in their approaches, methods, and forms of rationality. In thinking about theology and philosophy, it is important to realize that different disciplines have different traditions, with slightly different understandings of what counts as good evidence and argument. Differing approaches have different background assumptions too, which they will bring to bear in making arguments, setting up questions, and discussing rival theories. All of this means that Christianity can never encounter philosophy pure and simple but always only the philosophy of a particular time, culture, and school of thought. For example, neo-Confucian philosophy in China and Korea is a very different philosophical tradition from, say, Hegel and idealism in Europe. Yet Christianity has encountered both schools and been in very different dialogues with them over the centuries. Philosophy can never encounter a pure and eternal Christian theology either, for there are varying schools

5. The evidence for this is the obvious fact that many perfectly good philosophers are not Christians. We should note that Plantinga's criteria for warranted Christian belief are person-relative. He typically writes about what a Christian can or should or may think, not about what philosophy as a discipline is up to. See Alvin Plantinga, *Warranted Christian Belief* (New York: Oxford University Press, 2000), ch. 11.

and approaches in the tradition of Christian doctrine as well. Suddenly things are looking complex.

### Christian Scholarship

To bring things down to earth somewhat, I am going to suggest some historical examples that will provide us with models of the ways in which theology and philosophy can interact. To further limit the discussion, I will focus on the ways in which theology responds to and uses philosophy. The other side of the coin is just as important. I am certain that theology has important roles as dialogue partner and colleague for philosophy. This is because I believe that a mutuality model best describes the proper relationships between academic disciplines, including theology. But for our purposes in this book, we will focus on just one side of the coin: theology's encounter with philosophy.

For the most part, we will be speaking of academic disciplines, not individuals, when we talk about this encounter. As many philosophers of science have argued in recent times, the rationality of academic disciplines is a learned induction into a community and tradition of scholarship. By a discipline we mean any of the academic traditions of the university, any of the arts or sciences (natural or social). Becoming a scholar in a particular discipline is like being an apprentice in a guild or union: certain assumptions, practices, narratives, and values should be absorbed and mastered not merely by conceptual learning but also by doing. Following Thomas Kuhn, we can call these paradigms.[6] A paradigm is, roughly, a set of practices and beliefs that guides research, theory-making, and evaluation within a tradition of academic and/or scientific inquiry. They can also be called research programs or traditions of inquiry. Paradigms are functional, practical, communal, and traditional. They are not eternal absolutes, nor are they the property of any individual. Such research programs are not all-inclusive, and they make assumptions that call for further philosophical investigation. Thus, *research programs can be shared by people with differing worldviews*. This is a crucial point for understanding the character of Christian scholarship.

The tradition of inquiry I am calling Christian doctrine seeks the truth about God and about other things in relationship with God. For this reason, Christian scholarship is important for the goal of Christian theology. In order to rightly see all things in relationship to God, theologians as a community of scholars need a big-picture view of the truth about crea-

---

6. Kuhn in turn borrowed the term from Wittgenstein. See Thomas Kuhn, *The Structure of Scientific Revolutions*, 2nd ed. (Chicago: University of Chicago Press, 1970). For Wittgenstein's use of this term, see Ludwig Wittgenstein, *Philosophical Investigations* (Oxford: Blackwell, 1953), 50–57.

tures—all creatures. But theology cannot and will not, on its own, find the truth about these matters. For this we depend upon experts in other fields, especially the experts who are willing to interpret the findings of their science or discipline for the larger task of general human understanding (e.g., for the construction and evaluation of worldviews). Thus, theology relies upon experts in all the academic disciplines, many of whom will themselves be believers, who can rightly interpret the results of these other arts and sciences. Only in this way can theology come to see the truth about God and the world made and sustained by God. Creation, sin, providence, Christology, church, eschatology: all of the standard topics of Christian theology touch upon realities outside theology in the strict sense. For example, theologians say that human beings are created in the image of God. What does this mean for our understanding of human nature today? How does this touch upon psychology, anthropology, and sociology? The theologian cannot be an expert in all of these fields. We depend upon others in order to fulfill our vocation.

Fortunately for us, a tradition of Christian scholarship or Christian learning already seeks to understand all of reality from the perspective of a Christian worldview.[7] Each branch of science and the humanities maintains its own standards of good reason, evidence, and argument, but the Christian approaches his or her scientific paradigm from a perspective of faith. In other words, Christian scholars accept the tradition of inquiry or paradigm of their specialty and are willing to be the best philosophers, sociologists, or biologists they can be. But they understand this communal rationality in a larger context. This helps in three ways: (1) a Christian worldview funds and founds the metaphysical, epistemological, and value commitments of a disciplinary paradigm without imposing itself or prejudicing outcomes of investigation; (2) a Christian worldview provides a broad horizon in which the results of research can be interpreted for the larger culture; and (3) when the believing scholar is confronted with theories that are a matter of intense debate within a discipline, a Christian worldview may sometimes guide the scholar in a temporary preference of one theory over the other, subject to further review, evidence, and argument. The Christian will be guided toward the rival theory that best fits with his or her larger worldview, just as any rational being would. This is because we are finally seeking truth, and we expect our truths to all fit together some day (perhaps not in this life). It may be that in the long run, our worldview will need to change

7. For some brief introductions to the idea of Christian scholarship, see Arthur Holmes, *All Truth Is God's Truth* (Grand Rapids: Eerdmans, 1977); *The Idea of a Christian College* (Grand Rapids: Eerdmans, 1975); Nicholas Wolterstorff, *Reason within the Bounds of Religion*, 2nd ed. (Grand Rapids: Eerdmans, 1984); and George Marsden, *The Outrageous Idea of Christian Scholarship* (New York: Oxford University Press, 1997).

to fit new facts and theories. On the other hand, Christian truth may require that elements of accepted "fact" need to be questioned again. The direction of revision cannot be determined a priori.

## Models from History

After considering Christian scholarship in general terms, it is time to focus more specifically on philosophy. We will look at historical examples of the ways in which theologians have encountered and worked with philosophy, not in purely historical terms but as models or types of relationship.[8]

### Anselm of Canterbury: Theology Seeks Philosophy

Anselm (1033–1109), one of the greatest theologians of his age, was a philosopher, monk, abbot, and eventually archbishop of Canterbury. He wrote a number of central and influential works in theology, which helped to establish the scholastic tradition in the High Middle Ages. In an extended prayer to God that is also a meditation on who God is (his *Proslogion*), Anselm comments that our Christian faith is a faith that is seeking understanding (*fides quaerens intellectum*). This conception of Christian thought as beginning with faith in Jesus and then seeking larger understanding through philosophy has become the most common understanding of theology's method and approach in our time. The Anselmian model, then, starts with faith.

### Thomas Aquinas: Philosophy Leads to Theology

The greatest mind of the Middle Ages was the philosopher and theologian Thomas Aquinas (1224/5–1274). He developed a complex understanding of the relationship between faith and reason, in dialogue with the best philosophy and science of his time, which were based upon Aristotle. He authored the most important of the ancient systems of Christian theology, his famous *Summa theologiae*. For Aquinas, all things come from and lead back to God. Faith and reason call out to each other. Rightly understood (and this part cannot be ignored), philosophy leads to

8. I borrow the notion of such a typology from H. Richard Niebuhr, *Christ and Culture* (New York: Harper & Row, 1951). We cannot do justice to each scholar in this brief typology. For good introductions to each theologian, see G. R. Evans, *Anselm* (London: G. Chapman, 1989); Brian Davies, *Aquinas* (New York: Continuum, 2002); G. G. Scorgie, *A Call for Continuity: The Theological Contribution of James Orr* (Macon, GA: Mercer University Press, 1988); James A. Nestingen, *Martin Luther: His Life and Teachings* (Philadelphia: Fortress, 1982); and two articles on Bowne by Rufus Burrow: "Borden Parker Bowne," *Methodist History* 36 (1997): 44–54; and "Borden Parker Bowne's Doctrine of God," *Encounter* 53 (1992): 381–400.

and supports faith. Philosophy acts as a *praeambulum fidei*, a journey that leads toward theology. At the same time, philosophy itself seeks to be completed by theology; that is, it seeks to know that which is above and beyond nature by means of a *desiderium naturale*, a natural desire to know the answer to our deepest longings. This intellectual quest can find its true rest only in God. In his *Summa contra gentiles*, Thomas shows how this method can work. The method begins with philosophical exposition and critique, setting the basis of a Christian worldview, but concludes with biblical and theological truths that complete it.

### Martin Luther: Theology in Tension with Philosophy

A German monk turned Protestant reformer and Bible professor, Martin Luther (1483–1546) is remembered as the father of the Reformation. Because of his powerful emphasis upon the word of God as the highest court of appeal in Christian life and thought (and so the basis for the reform of the church), Luther was suspicious of the pretensions and arrogance of human reason. All of God's good gifts to human beings, including our reason, have become corrupted by sin and stand in need of redemption through Christ. Luther thought that philosophy was fine as long as it stayed in its own domain and out of theology or the church. In theology the word of God reigns supreme, and philosophy is a humble handmaid at best (a tool of the devil at worst). He was often critical of philosophy and of theologians who relied too heavily upon it.

### James Orr: Theology Transforms Philosophy

The Scottish theologian and apologist James Orr (1844–1913) stands in here for the tradition of John Calvin, Luther's contemporary in Switzerland. The Reformed tradition that stemmed from Geneva, and of which Orr was a part, agreed with the doctrine of sin that Luther preached but had a different model of the way in which theology and philosophy can relate. Philosophy on its own may well be a tool for the devil. But for the Reformed tradition, faith can provide the basis for rethinking and reinterpreting the academic disciplines, including philosophy. Orr was a prolific evangelical scholar and a pastor and professor, contributing to numerous works, including magazines, dictionaries, encyclopedias, and books. His series of lectures on the Christian worldview was eventually published as *A Christian View of God and the World* (1893). Orr is a good historical example of one who believed that faith in Christ provides us with a light that can and should illumine our understanding of all reality.

## Borden Parker Bowne: Theology Becomes Philosophy

The Methodist philosopher and theologian Borden Parker Bowne (1847–1910) represents our last model, that of liberal Protestant thought. Trained in the German tradition of idealist philosophy, Bowne believed that the Christian faith needed to be defended and revised in keeping with modern culture. A contemporary of James Orr and William James, he founded a school of personalism at Boston that was very influential in its day. At the beginning of the twentieth century, he was the foremost Methodist scholar in America, but he was charged with heresy (and acquitted). Like Hegel and James, he saw philosophy as taking up and almost absorbing the truths of theology into a larger and more complete whole. The parts of traditional theology that did not fit with modern philosophy and science would need to be revised in order to save the rationality of the Christian faith. Like most liberals, Bowne was a real believer in intellectual and cultural progress.

### *Philosophy as Partner and Colleague*

Each of these models has something to teach us. Luther is right that theology must maintain its ultimate allegiance to special divine revelation, that is, to Jesus Christ and the word of God. To give these up is to cease being *Christian* theology. At the same time, both Anselm and Aquinas are surely right that theology seeks out philosophy as its colleague and helper. Theology needs the clarity and rationality of philosophy and has always used philosophy as a tool for expounding and defending the Christian faith. Finally, the Calvinist tradition makes an important point: Christian faith can provide a basis or perspective from which we do philosophy. But we cannot accept the notion of Bowne, that theology must be based upon (and thus finally absorbed by) the right kind of philosophy. Theology and philosophy can cooperate and be partners only when each maintains its own proper autonomy as a distinct tradition of inquiry. This cautionary tale is our most important lesson from the liberal experiment.

Philosophy and theology are colleagues together in the creation of a Christian worldview (or, better, worldviews, for many different ones have been constructed over the millennia). In this task they work with all the academic disciplines, as understood by Christian scholarship. Neither should dominate or be subservient to the other. In its own domain, with respect to its own goals for understanding and seeking the truth, each is autonomous. Within this autonomy, however, there can and should be partnership. This partnership has been fruitful, especially for theology. The following examples should illuminate the central claim here, that theology and philosophy can and should be colleagues.

*Critical dialogue.* Philosophers have been critical of Christianity for centuries and no doubt will continue to be so. There is much to be learned here about problems in the church, in our ethics, and in our understanding of the faith. Philosophy provides Christians with a valuable service when it is critical of Christianity. More intellectuals in the church should be listening.

*Understanding culture and diverse viewpoints.* The gospel is proclaimed and lived in a variety of cultures all over the globe. Philosophy gives expression to the deepest insights, questions, struggles, and values of human experience. The study of philosophies in various cultures can be a rich source for understanding differing cultures and worldviews, including one's own.

*Standards of reason and logic.* One task of philosophy is to study good reasoning in general, that is, formal and informal logic. Like other academic disciplines, theology seeks clarity and truth, using human reason to come to conclusions about its central doctrines. Philosophy can assist theology in this quest, especially if we are careful and humble about our arguments and conclusions.

*Developing theological concepts and theories.* All Christian theologians depend upon key philosophical concepts in order to develop their theories. Like other academic disciplines, theology draws upon paradigms, which include philosophical understanding. Theology must use philosophical ideas, but critically. The criterion of this critique is the revelation of God in Christ Jesus. No system of philosophy, no metaphysical analysis, can be accepted as the only proper Christian view. Theology uses philosophy, but it should do so with a light touch, always seeking to ground itself in divine revelation rather than merely human wisdom.

*Explaining and defending the Christian faith on philosophical grounds.* Philosophy is obviously necessary in areas of thought that combine theology and philosophy. Three of them are *apologetics*, which is the rational defense of the Christian faith; *philosophy of religion*, which is a branch of philosophy concerned with any and all religions; and *philosophical theology*, which explores philosophical issues within a particular theology. Thus a Christian philosophical theology is philosophy of religion applied to Christian theology. Each of these areas has a slightly different approach and purpose, but they are also quite similar. Whatever name we wish to use, the point is that these are necessarily interdisciplinary tasks. Explaining and defending the Christian faith on philosophical grounds will always draw from both philosophy and theology.

*Constructing a Christian worldview.* The task of constructing a Christian worldview belongs to all the disciplines of the university, as interpreted through Christian scholarship. Philosophy and theology have important roles to play, but not the only ones. Systematic theology (Christian doctrine) does not of itself create a Christian worldview. In fact, theology cannot do its task without the help of the other disciplines, founded and interpreted by the community of Christian scholarship.

The academic discipline of Christian theology seeks to know and love God, as revealed in Christ and the Christian scriptures. Philosophy proves to be a very helpful dialogue partner and colleague in this process. Especially important is conversation with philosophers who are Christian scholars. Both academic disciplines represent noble communities and traditions that seek after the truth. Problems arise in this collegiality, however, when one partner seeks to control the other. Theology should not seek to control philosophy's quest for truth or prejudice its conclusions for or against the faith.[9] Individual philosophers may well begin with Christian faith, but the discipline of philosophy as a community of rationality will question all authority, including the authority of Jesus Christ. For this reason theology can never become philosophy, and philosophers as a community (Christian and non-Christian) must always be free to question faith. In theology, Jesus Christ alone is Lord; but Jesus is also the servant. The word of God made flesh is our friend and not only our master. He who is the author of all truth and the creative ground of freedom desires true freedom of inquiry for all people. The triune God is eternal love. Eternity can afford to be patient with the academy.

Theology and philosophy can and should be colleagues. They can work together to help us create Christian worldviews, but neither discipline should simply absorb the other, nor do their methods and results become one in the long run. A right understanding of the independence and partnership of both disciplines can go a long way in helping us seek the truth.

## THE PROBLEM OF NATURAL THEOLOGY

Having argued that theology and philosophy are mutually beneficial traditions of inquiry, we proceed to a concrete example—natural theology—to demonstrate and illuminate the points just made. Natural theology, its nature and legitimacy, has been a lively question since the theologian Karl Barth attacked this field. But the objections of Barth and the philosopher Alvin Plantinga can be overcome when we pay

9. As George Marsden rightly notes, "No matter what commitments one brings into one's academic work, one would have to argue for one's scholarly interpretations on the same sorts of publicly accessible grounds that are widely accepted in the academy" (*Outrageous Idea*, 52).

careful attention to the differences between the two research programs
of philosophy and theology.[10]

Among Christian theologians today, natural theology has fallen on
hard times. We are told that natural theology is bad for us: it leads to
atheism, to a reduction or rejection of the Christian God, or to an aban-
donment of the Christian gospel.[11] The term "natural theology" (*theologia
naturalis*) is highly ambiguous, especially in the hands of its critics. Even
a proponent of natural theology such as James Barr can use the term
in so many ways that it becomes difficult to follow his argument.[12] Two
senses of the term *theologia naturalis* are particularly important: natural
theology in the strict sense, and a theology of nature.[13] Distinguishing
between these two is important for a clear understanding of the current
debate surrounding natural theology.

One simple sense of "natural theology" refers to philosophical arguments concerning the existence and nature of a god. These appeal, like
all philosophy, to general characteristics of our world ("nature") and are
based upon human reason. The word "god" is lowercase here because it
is not necessarily the Western God that is in view. The character of this
god is also open to philosophical reflection and critique. Alvin Plantinga
is thus overly narrow in defining natural theology as "the attempt to
prove or demonstrate the existence of God."[14] Philosophy of religion is
rightly concerned not only with the existence of god but also with the
nature of this god, as known through philosophical inquiry. Here Stephen Davis and Richard Swinburne are on firmer ground; both of these
natural theologians provide philosophical arguments about the nature
*and* existence of god.[15]

10. The arguments made here are developed in more detail in Alan G. Padgett, "Theologia Naturalis," *Faith and Philosophy* 21/4 (October 2004): 493–502.

11. See, e.g., Karl Barth, "No!" in E. Brunner and K. Barth, *Natural Theology*, trans.
Peter Fraenkel (1946; repr., Eugene, OR: Wipf & Stock, 2002); Michael J. Buckley, *At the
Origins of Modern Atheism* (New Haven: Yale University Press, 1987).

12. James Barr, *Biblical Faith and Natural Theology* (Oxford: Clarendon, 1993), 1–7.

13. For a different taxonomy, see George L. Murphy, *The Cosmos in the Light of the
Cross* (Philadelphia: Trinity Press International, 2003), 8–25. Murphy puts together into
one category, "dependent natural theology," what I wish to distinguish as natural theology
versus a theology of nature.

14. See Alvin Plantinga, "Reason and Belief in God," in *Faith and Rationality*, ed. Alvin
Plantinga and Nicholas Wolterstorff (Notre Dame, IN: University of Notre Dame Press,
1982), 63. See, more recently, Plantinga, *Warranted Christian Belief*, 171n, 179n.

15. See Richard Swinburne, *The Coherence of Theism* (Oxford: Oxford University Press,
1977); *The Christian God* (Oxford: Oxford University Press, 1994); *The Existence of God*,
rev. ed. (Oxford: Oxford University Press, 1991); Stephen T. Davis, *Logic and the Nature of
God* (Grand Rapids: Eerdmans, 1983); *God, Reason, and Theistic Proofs* (Grand Rapids:
Eerdmans, 1997).

Natural theology, thus understood, is a part of philosophy. It appeals to a knowledge of god derived from reason and nature and makes no central appeal to special revelation. For the purposes of clarity in discussing the nature and province of natural theology, let us use the term "natural theology" in this strict sense to denote an aspect of the philosophy of religion. So when William Alston defines natural theology as "the enterprise of providing support for religious beliefs by starting from premises that neither are nor presuppose any religious beliefs," we need to understand that his definition of natural theology places it with the discipline of philosophy: natural theology thus understood is a *philosophical* enterprise.[16]

"Theology of nature," on the other hand, here designates an essential aspect of Christian doctrine. George Hendry places this question at the heart of such a theology of nature: "What is the place, meaning, and purpose of the world of nature in the overall plan of God in creation and redemption?"[17] *Theologia naturalis* understood as a theology of nature is part of a Christian doctrine of creation, grounded in the revelation of God in Scripture and supremely in Jesus Christ. Because the doctrine of creation is an essential part of the task of Christian doctrine, a theology of nature is essential to Christian doctrine rightly understood. Even Karl Barth developed a doctrine of creation at great length in his *Church Dogmatics*.[18]

It is important to distinguish these two senses of *theologia naturalis* (natural theology in the strict sense and a theology of nature) in order to appreciate the debates surrounding natural theology today. For example, when James Barr states (in criticism of Karl Barth) that "the natural theology of the Bible *is* built into the revelational and salvific material [in Scripture]," we can only accept this conclusion when we realize that Barr means a theology of nature, and not natural theology in the strict sense.[19] Barr is noting that the Bible's theology of nature is built into the biblical witness concerning human salvation and divine revelation. Another example of this tendency to confuse natural theology and a theology of nature comes from the recent work of Alister McGrath. In defending the purpose and place of natural theology for Christian doctrine today, McGrath claims that "it is perfectly possible to frame a natural theology in such a manner that it does not involve such an in-

16. William P. Alston, *Perceiving God* (Ithaca, NY: Cornell University Press, 1991), 289.

17. G. S. Hendry, *Theology of Nature* (Philadelphia: Westminster, 1980), 11.

18. Karl Barth, *Church Dogmatics*, ed. and trans. G. W. Bromiley and T. F. Torrance, 4 vols. in 13 (Edinburgh: T. & T. Clark, 1936–1975). Volume 3 is *The Doctrine of Creation*.

19. Barr, *Biblical Faith*, 190n; his emphasis.

tention to prove God's existence."[20] When McGrath goes on to describe such a natural theology, it becomes clear he is describing a theology of nature, not natural theology in our sense.

These different senses of *theologia naturalis* arise from their placement in different disciplines. As mentioned, it is impossible to give a generally accepted definition of either philosophy or Christian doctrine. Yet we can insist that they are not the same academic discipline without having a universally accepted or necessary definition of either. As argued above, all the disciplines of academia (including philosophy and theology) are best understood in the light of Christ as distinct but interconnected and equally important colleagues, whose task is the development of a Christian worldview for the church today. Each discipline can, under certain circumstances, rationally influence the other, but each remains distinct with respect to its main goals and methods of inquiry. Thus, to understand the character and nature of *theologia naturalis*, we need to grasp its placement in the distinct academic disciplines of philosophy and Christian doctrine.

### Objections to Natural Theology: Plantinga and Barth

As this collection of contributions demonstrates, Christian philosophy has an important role to play in the development of a Christian worldview for our times. Most Christian intellectuals are rightly interested in the rational assessment of religious claims, the relationship between faith and reason, and the extent to which reasons can be given for our Christian faith. Philosophers of religion investigate all of these questions, and natural theology (as part of a philosophy of religion) seems to be essential to these investigations. Yet even when we pay attention to the different senses of *theologia naturalis* as natural theology in the strict sense (in philosophy) and a theology of nature (in Christian doctrine), there are still scholars who will object to the aims and methods of natural theology in philosophy of religion. Although we cannot here examine all such criticisms, two Reformed thinkers are particularly prominent: Plantinga and Barth. We will focus upon their objections.

Plantinga's objections to natural theology are spelled out in several essays. In a central paper, "Reason and Belief in God," his major objection to natural theology is that it is a form of evidentialism and rationalism—that is, classical foundationalism. The natural theologian appears to hold that belief in God is not epistemically adequate without evidence and argument. In "rejecting natural theology," Plantinga asserts that

20. Alister McGrath, *A Scientific Theology*, vol. 1, *Nature* (Grand Rapids: Eerdmans, 2001), 266.

"the propriety or rightness of belief in God in no way depends upon the success or availability of the sort of theistic arguments that form the natural theologian's stock in trade."[21] In other words, Plantinga's main objection to natural theology is the apparent assumption that faith needs evidence and argument in order to be rationally acceptable or philosophically legitimate.

I agree with Plantinga that belief in God can be and often is perfectly legitimate and proper without any philosophical arguments. In other words, Christian faith does not depend upon the practice of philosophy (specifically natural theology) but rather upon more direct, immediate, and spiritual sources of the knowledge of God. Nevertheless, as a specialty within philosophy of religion, natural theology will indeed be based upon reason, nature, evidence, and argument. This is because natural theology, as a philosophical enterprise, will use the standard methods of philosophy to achieve its aims. In his essay, Plantinga allows for this possibility, stating that "the natural theologian" may engage in philosophical debate with unbelievers but at the same time point out that "belief in God is not based upon its relation to the deliverances of reason."[22] In his more recent Gifford lectures, Plantinga goes so far as to admit, "Of course it doesn't follow [from his position] that theistic belief can't get warrant by way of argument from other beliefs; nor does it follow that natural theology and more informal theistic argument is of no worth in the believer's intellectual and spiritual life."[23] We can see from these comments that Plantinga allows for a natural theology that is a part of philosophy but in no way provides a philosophical foundation for Christian faith or the necessary epistemic warrant for Christian belief understood in general terms. My only caution is that a natural theologian need not be a believer.

Plantinga's objections to natural theology are not decisive. On the contrary, they help us to see that natural theology is best understood as a part of the philosophy of religion. Natural theology should not be confused with religion itself or with a doctrinal theology based upon religious faith and practice. Yet as Christian scholars interested in the development of a Christian worldview, we will want this intellectual activity (natural theology) to be grounded in Christian learning, just as we would any intellectual discipline. A Christian philosopher may well be very interested in natural theology, but he or she should not suppose that the viability and epistemic justification of Christian faith is dependent upon natural theology. On the other hand, as a philosopher, a Christian

21. Plantinga, "Reason and Belief," 72.
22. Ibid., 71.
23. Plantinga, *Warranted Christian Belief*, 179n.

natural theologian will need to give some reason and evidence for his or her beliefs and conclusions. Here Richard Swinburne, perhaps the world's leading natural theologian, has a point. Rational belief *within the discipline of philosophy* (including rational religious belief) requires rational explication and explanation, including some evidence and argument, even if those beliefs are not *based upon* evidence and argument.[24] Plantinga, after all, does give many *arguments* for the beliefs he accepts in philosophy of religion. He provides logical explication and explanation of them as well. I am not here talking about a return to classical foundationalism but about the kind of things philosophers do in the normal practice of their research program.

Objections of a different type to natural theology come from the work of Karl Barth. First we need to understand Barth's definition of *theologia naturalis*, and then we can begin to grasp the heart of his objection. In his famous debate with Brunner, Barth defined natural theology as

> every (positive or negative) *formulation of a system* which claims to be theological, i.e., to interpret divine revelation, whose *subject*, however, differs fundamentally from the revelation in Jesus Christ, and whose method therefore differs equally from the exposition of Holy Scripture.[25]

Here Barth's notion of *theologia naturalis* is quite different from either of the senses developed in this essay. Natural theology as he uses the term is first of all a kind of theology, that is, a type of Christian doctrine that seeks "to interpret divine revelation." Second, it is not so much an argument or philosophical inquiry as the "formulation of a system," that is, a systematic theology. Barth's objection to natural theology, then, is his objection to any so-called Christian theology or dogmatics that is done independent of the revelation of God in Jesus Christ, made known in the witness of the Old and New Testaments, the work of the Holy Spirit, and the witness of the church. Again, in his *Göttingen Dogmatics*, Barth argues that "if God does not speak, then it is not God that we hear in those supposed voices of God but a voice from this world, from this unredeemed world, from the contradiction of our existence." For this reason he seeks to "take the one part of the material world that has been mentioned by what is called natural theology and include it at once in the true Christian theology that is called supernatural, that is, in revelation."[26]

24. See Richard Swinburne, *Faith and Reason* (Oxford: Oxford University Press, 1981). What Swinburne calls "belief" in this book I interpret as *rational* belief.
25. Barth, "No!" 74.
26. Karl Barth, *The Göttingen Dogmatics*, trans. G. W. Bromiley (Grand Rapids: Eerdmans, 1991), 92.

Barth's objection to natural theology, then, is an objection to any Christian doctrine (systematic theology) that is not based primarily and essentially on special, supernatural revelation, that is, the word of God. Natural theology denotes, for him, "a theology which makes a great show of guaranteeing the knowability of God apart from grace and therefore from faith."[27] For Barth, the words "natural theology" point to the attempt of sinful, disobedient, and arrogant "natural man" to control god, to put the knowledge of god at our own disposal, and therefore to "know" a false god.[28] For this reason Barth objects to any natural theology that pretends to be a philosophical foundation for faith in the Christian God, "so that the establishing of his knowability in the natural sphere, in the sphere of the human life-endeavour, will in fact mean a preparation for the establishing of His knowability in His revelation."[29] Barth objects to any theology that seeks to control, found, or guarantee the word of God.

Barth, and Luther before him, have powerful truths to declare about the pretensions of human reason and the ability of sin to turn even our best and highest cultural expressions into evil, idolatry, and death. Even so, does this mean that any and all types of *theologia naturalis* are minions of Satan? There is plenty of room in Barth's theological method for a theology of nature, as he himself develops later in *Church Dogmatics*. But by the term "natural theology," Barth always means something in opposition to the knowledge of God found in God's own revelation in Jesus Christ. For Barth, natural theology is liberal or modernist Christian theology, of the type exemplified by Borden Parker Bowne.

Barth did not object to a theology of nature grounded in the word of God, which he developed in his doctrine of creation. But what about the philosophical attempt to know God; that is, what about natural theology in our strict sense, as a discipline of philosophy of religion? Here Barth seems to shout once again, *Nein!*[30] What he fails to consider seriously is the idea that there might well be a *Christian philosophy* that does not confuse the God of Abraham and Sarah with the god of the philosophers.[31] Indeed, Søren Kierkegaard (whom Barth often quotes and/or borrows from) should be understood exactly as such a Christian philosopher.

27. Barth, *Church Dogmatics*, 2/1:85.
28. See ibid., 86–87.
29. Ibid., 89.
30. *Nein!* is the German title for the booklet Karl Barth wrote against Brunner; the English translation is Barth, "No!"
31. See, e.g., Karl Barth's rejection of a Christian worldview, based upon his fallacious equation of Christian learning with the triumph of Christendom, in *The Holy Spirit and the Christian Life* (Louisville: Westminster John Knox, 1993), 37–38.

Though rejecting the idea of a Christian philosophy in explicit terms, in an important essay, "The First Commandment as an Axiom for Theology," Barth comes close to considering such a possibility. Here he considers what it would mean to add the little word "and" to revelation so as to include other sources of truth in theology, for example, revelation *and* reason.[32] In this essay, dedicated to avoiding idolatry in Christian theology, Barth gives three cautions to those who would add "and" to revelation, as a basis for the knowledge of God. First, we must speak of revelation "with a notably heightened seriousness and interest, and by speaking of that other criterion only secondarily and for the sake of revelation" (p. 73). Second (and this sounds very much like what I am calling Christian scholarship), theology expresses its commitment to the first commandment by "interpreting those other things according to revelation and not the other way around" (74). Third, theology must permit "no possibility . . . of intermixing, exchanging, or identifying the two concepts in this relation" (75). All these cautions are well taken. Yet *pace* Barth, there is plenty of room here for a Christian philosophy that takes Christian faith and revelation seriously but nevertheless engages in philosophy *as philosophy* (not exchanging one for the other or mixing them up). Indeed, it is only by not mixing up the disciplines of philosophy and theology that we can avoid the objections of both Barth and Plantinga to *theologia naturalis*.

To avoid the Barthian objection, natural theology must keep its place within a strictly philosophical domain. It cannot and should not become a kind of substitute for revelation—a more acceptable means (to the arrogance of Enlightenment rationalism) of the knowledge of God, a means independent of, and laying the foundations for, the word of God. That humans can know God through nature, reason, and philosophy is not in question. Whether such a god is Yahweh or Baal is the real theological point of Barth's objection. By rejecting the Enlightenment call to provide a sure, rational foundation for faith, natural theology can avoid this objection.

Second, though a part of Christian scholarship and therefore willing to own its Christian presuppositions without apology, a Christian natural theology should do its work according to the highest and most rigorous philosophical standards, in dialogue and debate with other philosophers in a pluralistic academy. That is, natural theology should maintain itself as good philosophy and not short-circuit philosophical debate by appeals to special revelation, religious faith, or other particularities of the

32. Karl Barth, "The First Commandment as an Axiom for Theology," in *The Way of Theology in Karl Barth*, ed. H. M. Rumscheidt (Allison Park, PA: Pickwick, 1986).

Christian religion as a means of settling arguments. The best natural theologians already practice their art in just this manner.

I have proposed that we accept two distinct senses of *theologia naturalis*: natural theology in the strict sense (in philosophy) and a theology of nature (in Christian doctrine). By paying attention to these differences, we can overcome the objections to natural theology brought by Plantinga and Barth. Thus understood, natural theology continues to have an essential role to play in both Christian philosophy and Christian doctrine. This provides a concrete example of my main point: theology and philosophy are distinct traditions of inquiry, yet they should work together at many levels. Indeed we can go so far as to claim that the collegiality of theology and philosophy depends upon their being distinct methods and traditions of academic study.

### Some Objections Considered

Several proponents of natural theology have argued that Christian doctrine itself should include natural theology;[33] in other words, Christian doctrine must always include philosophy as part of its work. I have argued that natural theology should keep its place in philosophy instead. Does this mean philosophy has no place in theology? By no means. Christian doctrine uses the methods of many other disciplines, including rhetoric, literature, history, philology, and philosophy. But since natural theology eschews any basis in special revelation and depends upon broadly philosophical bases for its arguments, its disciplinary home is philosophy and not doctrinal theology. Christian doctrine should listen to and engage natural theology, but theologians must test the conclusions of natural theology according to the standards of truth and reason found within Christian doctrine.

Another objection might be that theology and philosophy are being treated as if their aims, boundaries, and methods were fixed for all time. Such is not the case. Some attention to real differences among the current mix of disciplines within the flux of academia is also important. Take politics as an analogy. The differences between political entities such as nations, states, counties, and cities are equally open to revision, historical change, and social construction. But knowing the difference between the United States and Canada, or Delhi and Delphi, is still important. The fact that things are in flux does not imply that all differences and distinctions are irrelevant. For our purposes, it is best

33. One example would be the somewhat neglected work of Richard Rice, *Reason and the Contours of Faith* (Riverside, CA: La Sierra University Press, 1991), especially the two chapters on natural theology.

that the distinction between philosophy and doctrinal theology be clarified. Other chapters in this book develop their similarities and provide
fruitful topics for interdisciplinary dialogue.

One final objection: it might seem that I am seeking to seal off Christian doctrine from intellectual attack or at least from the rigor of philosophical argument and public debate. But again, such is not the case.
Christian doctrine does its work in public and is open to public scrutiny.
Its arguments, evidence, and rationality are open for all to examine. This
does not imply that we must give up our belief in special revelation as
the heart and soul of Christian doctrine. For the aim of Christian doctrine is to know and love God—not just any god but the God and Father
of our Lord Jesus Christ—and to know other things in relation to the
blessed Trinity. To say that Christian doctrine is rational and public does
not imply that Christian doctrine should be done as if the Father had
not spoken in his word, as if Jesus Christ were not the incarnation of
the living Logos, and as if the Spirit had not inspired the prophets and
apostles in their written witness. Such a denial of basic Christian commitment would not only alter but also undermine the two-thousand-year
tradition of inquiry that is Christian doctrine.

We are now in a better position to answer Tertullian's question: what
concord is there between philosophy and theology? The answer we have
found, *pace* Tertullian, is a rich and fruitful collegiality between two distinct communities and traditions of rational inquiry. Both theology and
philosophy seek the truth, but as academic disciplines their methods and
interests differ. Understanding their differences as academic disciplines
can open the way to new avenues for cooperation and dialogue.

# 2

# GENERAL ONTOLOGY AND THEOLOGY

## A Primer

## ✴| J. P. Moreland |✴

METAPHYSICS HAS HAD A LONG, distinguished history, boasting some of the greatest thinkers of all time: Plato, Aristotle, Augustine, Aquinas, Descartes, Leibniz. And metaphysics has been the long-standing friend of theology. Many of the greatest metaphysicians have been and are Christians. And many of the great Christian pastors and thinkers throughout church history have studied metaphysics. John Wesley advised pastors, "Do I understand metaphysics; if not the depths of the Schoolmen, the subtleties of Scotus or Aquinas, yet the first rudiments, the general principles, of that useful science? Have I conquered so much of it, as to clear my apprehension and range my ideas under proper heads?"[1]

Christians have been interested in metaphysics because theology makes claims that are inextricably connected to metaphysical issues.

Wesley ✓

1. John Wesley, "An Address to the Clergy," delivered February 6, 1756, in *The Works of John Wesley*, 3rd ed., 7 vols. (Grand Rapids: Baker, 1996), 6:217–31.

45

Christians affirm a realm of reality that is neither sense perceptible nor physical and, for many, is not located in space and time. How are we to understand these affirmations? Classic theology holds that God is a substance with various attributes. What is a substance and how is God a substance? What are attributes and in what way does God have them? In some sense Jesus is God but in another sense he is not, since the Triune God and Jesus are not the same thing. What is involved in trinitarian and christological assertions? Is the mind reducible to the brain? If so, what does this mean? And so on.

For our purposes, metaphysics may be characterized as the philosophical study of being or reality. To help clarify this, let us consider the following sentences:

(1) Socrates is real.     *Being*
(2) Socrates is the teacher of Plato.     *Identity*
(3) Socrates is human.     *Essential Predication*
(4) Socrates is white.     *Accidental Pred.*
(5) Socrates is skin and bone.     *Constitutional (Part/Whole Is)*

Each sentence uses a different sense of the word "is." Metaphysical investigation seeks to distinguish these different senses and say something helpful about each one of them. Sentence 1 uses an "is" of *being* or *existence*. It asserts that Socrates exists. This sense of "to be" raises these questions: What is it to exist or not exist? What is it about something that accounts for its existence? Sentence 2 uses an "is" of *identity*. It says that Socrates is identical to, is the very same thing as, the teacher of Plato. This raises these questions: What does it mean for some thing x and some thing y to be the same thing? What is it for something to be identical to itself and different from everything else?

Sentence 3 employs an "is" of *essential predication*. It says that being human is the very essence of Socrates. This raises these questions: What does it mean to say that something (being human) is the essence of something else (Socrates)? Do things really have essences and, if so, what are they? Sentence 4 contains an "is" of *accidental predication*. It says that Socrates has a property, being white, that is "present in" him. This raises these questions: Do properties exist and, if so, what are they? Is there a distinction between essential and accidental properties? Does humanness relate to Socrates in a way different from the way whiteness relates to Socrates? Finally, sentence 5 uses an "is" of *constitution*, sometimes called a *"part/whole"* is. It says that Socrates is a whole with skin and bones as parts. Socrates is constituted by these parts. This raises these questions: Are parts different from properties? Can something lose parts and still be the same thing?

Issues associated with these five sentences form the basic area of metaphysical investigation. Philosophical reflection on them has led to some widely accepted subbranches of metaphysics, the most important of which for our purposes is general ontology.

## GENERAL ONTOLOGY

There are three main tasks that make up general ontology. First, general ontology focuses on the nature of existence itself. What is it to be or exist? Is existence a property that something has? Does nothingness itself exist in some sense? Is there a sense of being such that fictional objects, for example, the unicorn Pegasus, have being even though they do not exist?

    (1) Existence

Second, in general ontology we study general principles of being, general features that are true of all things whatsoever. Medieval philosophers used the term "transcendentals" to stand for all the features that characterize all the different kinds of entities that exist. Some have taken the notions of existing, unity, true, and goodness to be examples of a transcendental. Everything that is—a carbon atom, a person, a number, the property of being green—is such that it exists, is a unity (i.e., is one entity in some sense), and is true and good. Below we will investigate one such feature of reality—the nature of identity. Everything whatsoever is identical to itself and different from everything else. The study of identity can be classified as part of general ontology in that identity is a transcendental feature of all entities that exist.

    (2) Transcendental

Third, general ontology includes what is called categorial analysis. It is possible to classify or group, in various ways ranging from very specific to very broad types of classification, things that exist. For example, consider a light brown dog, Spot, standing to the left of a desk. The dog itself can be classified in broader and broader ways according to the following scheme: an individual dog, a mammal, an animal, a living thing, a substance. The color of the dog can be classified in this way: light brown, brown, a visible property, a property. The relationship between Spot and the desk can be grouped as follows: to the left of, a spatial relation, a relation.

    (3) Categorial Analysis

In the example just mentioned, the ultimate categories used are those of substance, property, and relation. A set of categories is a collection of the ultimate, broadest classifications of all existent entities whatsoever such that (1) each entity will fit into a specific category and (2) the categories taken as a group will allow us to classify all entities. A set of categories is a set of mutually exclusive and exhaustive classifications of all entities. A set of categories is mutually exclusive in that a given category will have a distinguishing feature that sets off entities in that category and makes them distinct from the entities in the other categories. A set of categories is exhaustive in that all entities (except the transcendentals) will fit into one of the categories.

In what follows, we will briefly look at core issues in general ontology: the nature of existence, identity, and three categories (substance, property, relation). Space forbids us to apply these explicitly to topics in theology. Because ministers and those working in theology and biblical studies seldom receive exposure to general ontology, this chapter aims to place these ideas clearly before the reader, to whom I leave the responsibility of application.

## THE NATURE OF EXISTENCE

Suppose we have before us a real, live horse named Fury. Now think about something that is not real, for instance, the unicorn Pegasus. There are many things true of Fury: he is black, a horse, and so on. But the most fundamental thing true of Fury is that Fury exists. If we compare Fury with Pegasus, clearly there is something different between them: Fury exists and Pegasus does not. This difference is as real as the difference in color between a brown and a blue billiard ball. How are we to account for this difference between Fury and Pegasus? A theory of existence tries to answer this and related questions.

### Five Characteristics of an Adequate Theory of Existence

A good theory of existence ought to have five traits. First, it needs to be consistent with and explain what actually does and does not exist. Second, it needs to be consistent with and explain what could have existed but either does not exist or is not believed to exist (perhaps falsely) by the person advocating a given view of existence. Even though unicorns do not, in fact, exist, they could have existed. God could have made a world where Pegasus exists in the same sense that Fury exists. Physicalists do not believe the soul is real, but even if they are right, surely existence is such that souls *could have* existed.

Third, a theory of existence must allow for the fact that existence itself exists. To put the point differently, it must not be self-refuting. For example, if someone claims that to exist is the same thing as being inside space and time (existence itself is being spatiotemporally located), then, in at least some views, space and time would not themselves exist, since they are not inside space and time. Whatever existence amounts to, one thing is clear—it makes a real difference in the world, and it must itself exist to make such a difference. If existence itself does not exist, then nothing else could exist in virtue of having existence.

Fourth, a justified theory of existence must not violate the fundamental *But cf.* laws of logic—the laws of identity (P is identical to P), noncontradiction *Cusa* (P cannot be both true and false at the same time in the same sense), *on ∞* and excluded middle (P must be either true or false). Contradictory states of affairs, for example, a square circle or its simultaneously raining in Grandview and not raining in Grandview, do not exist. Moreover, something must either exist or not exist, and nothing can exist and not exist at the same time.

Fifth, a theory of existence must allow for the existence of acts of knowing. Since a theory of existence is a theory, it will depend for its rational acceptability on knowledge that people have. Now, an act of knowing something is, among other things, a conscious act of a person. Thus, any theory of existence that denies the existence of conscious persons who know things is false. It has been said, not unfairly, that some versions of strict physicalism (the view that human beings are simply physical objects) suffer from this problem.

### Different Theories of What Existence Itself Is

Someone might think that Christian theology has a fairly straightforward answer to the question "What is existence?": to exist is to be created by God or to be God. Now it is certainly true that everything other than God has been created. But this answer will still not do. Why? Because it is circular. Suppose we want to know what it means to say, "x exists," and we answer, "x is created by God." If we now ask what this statement means, we will answer, "For God gives x existence." Thus, "x exists" will amount to "x is given existence by God," and we have made no progress. We want to know exactly what God does when God creates something. To answer this, we need a theory of existence.

Several theories of existence have been offered. Here are some that are inadequate. To exist is to (a) be located in space and time; (b) be physical; (c) be causally efficacious, that is, be capable of being an efficient cause (that by means of which an effect is produced) or of being acted on by an efficient cause; (d) be an event or a bundle of events; (e) be perceived or be a perceiver; (f) be a property; (g) be a property of properties (e.g., to be a second-order property of first-order properties).

We will not apply each of the five features of a theory of existence to each view of existence, although it would be a good exercise to do so. A few remarks, however, should give you a feel for how to use the five features listed above to evaluate different views of existence. Feature 3 (existence itself exists) would seem to rule out theories a and c. Space and time are not themselves located in space and time; when an efficient cause produces an effect, the cause and effect enter into a causal relation, and that relation itself is not causally efficacious, yet it exists.

Feature 2 (what could have existed but does not exist or is not believed to exist) counts against theory e (which was held by George Berkeley [1685–1753]). Surely, mountains and dinosaurs could exist even though no one is looking at them; and even though God constantly looks at mountains even if humans do not, it is not God's gaze that gives mountains being but God's creative act of speaking them into existence and continually holding them in being. Moreover, one could be "seeing" a mountain in a hallucination, and it would not follow that a real, extramental mountain existed. Feature 2 also counts against theory b (as well as others on the list) because disembodied existence is surely metaphysically possible even if it is not real, and theory b rules out the very *possibility* of disembodied existence since it would not be physical existence. It also makes God's existence metaphysically impossible—quite a strong claim.

Feature 1 (what actually does and does not exist) eliminates theories b and d if minds, God, values, and abstract objects exist, since they are neither events, groups of events, nor physical entities. It also rules out theory g. If theory g is true, then existence is a second-order property of properties. That is, existence is something that truly applies only to properties—for example, to being red, to hardness, triangularity, humanness. But we all know that, in addition to properties, various individuals exist as well—for example, a specific red ball. If existence is a feature only of properties, then individuals could not have existence; since they do, in fact, have existence, theory g must be false.

The point here is to illustrate ways that features of a theory of existence can be used to evaluate alternative proposals for existence itself. So far, nothing has been said about theory f: existence is a property. Throughout the history of philosophy, many thinkers (e.g., Plato and Descartes) have held that existence is a property in the same sense that redness or being square is a property. For a ball to be red is for it to have the property of redness; for it to exist is for it to have the property of existence. Now at first glance, something seems right about this proposal. We do say, quite appropriately, that the ball *has* redness and that it *has* reality as well. In some sense, then, things can be said to have or not have existence.

But something seems wrong with this proposal also. Existence is simply not a normal property like redness. Immanuel Kant (1724–1804) made this point in *Critique of Pure Reason* (A 600/B 628):

> By whatever and by however many predicates [properties] we may think a thing—even if we completely determine it—we do not make the least

addition to the thing when we further declare the thing is. Otherwise, it would not be exactly the same thing that exists, but something more than we had thought in the concept; and we could not, therefore, say that the exact object of my concept exists.[2]

Kant's point can be understood in this way. When you think of a ball, to be told that it is red adds to your conception of the thing. But to be told that it exists does not add to your conception of the ball. Put differently, saying that a ball is red tells us something about the character of the ball. But saying that it is real says that the ball, with all of its properties, does in fact exist. Thus, existence does not relate to the ball like being red does.

Kant seems right here; nevertheless, saying that the ball is real does add something because there is, in fact, a real difference between existence and nonexistence. Can we shed more light on what this difference is? Perhaps so. Consider the statement "Tigers exist." This appears to assert the following: (1) The property of being a tiger (2) belongs to something (an individual tiger, let us say Tony). This "belonging" relation has gone by several names: *exemplification, predication,* and *instancing.* The claim that tigers exist is the claim that the essence of being a tiger (the *what* of being a tiger) is actually exemplified by, or belongs to, something (the ground for the *that* or *fact* of an individual tiger existing).

Note that when "Tigers exist" is broken down into the two aspects above, (1) referring to the essence or nature of being a tiger and (2) expressing reality or existence, we learn two things. First, there is a difference between a thing's essence and its existence. Knowledge of what a tiger is does not tell us that tigers exist. There is a fundamental difference between essence (whatness) and existence (thatness).

Second, existence is not a property *that* belongs; it is the *belonging of* a property. Existence is the entering into the predication or exemplification relation, and in general, the following characterization of existence seems to fit the five features of a theory of existence: *existence is either the belonging of some property or the being belonged to by a property or, more simply, the entering into the nexus of exemplification.* In the case of Tony the tiger, the fact that the property of being a tiger belongs to something and that something has this property belonging to it is what confers existence.

How does this view square with the five features of a theory of existence? It seems to account for everything that does or could exist and that does not or could not exist. Things that exist have properties. When

2. Immanuel Kant, *Critique of Pure Reason*, trans. N. K. Smith (New York: St. Martin's Press, 1965), 505.

something such as Zeus fails to exist, there is no object Zeus that actually has properties. Since unicorns could have existed, this means that the property of being a unicorn could have belonged to something. It would also account for existence itself existing because the belonging-to (exemplification, predication) relation is itself exemplified (a nonfictional, real tiger named Tony and the property of being a tiger both enter into this belonging relation) and the belonging-to relation exemplifies other features (e.g., it has the property of being a relation that belongs to it). Finally, this view of existence does not violate the fundamental laws of logic, nor does it rule out the existence of acts of knowing.

Even if someone rejects this as a definition of existence, it still seems adequate as an expression of the truth conditions for existence. That is, even if one rejects this as an adequate characterization of what existence itself is, it still seems true that for any entity e, e exists if and only if e enters the nexus of exemplification (e has properties or is a property that is had).[3]

In sum, we have learned three things from our brief discussion of existence: (A) There is a genuine difference between existing and not existing. (B) This difference is not a normal property like the property of being red. (C) Existence is not part of the essence or whatness of ordinary entities; that is, for ordinary entities there is a difference between essence and existence.

### Final Observations about Existence

There are two further remarks to be made about existence. First, our characterization of existence will allow us to specify some other notions: *coming-to-be* and *perishing*. Since we already have an idea of what existence itself is and since coming-to-be and perishing involve gaining and losing existence, then the latter notions can be understood in terms of our general theory of existence itself.

> *E comes into being* = $_{df}$ There is at least one property that is such that E has that property, and there is no property that is such that E had that property.
>
> *E perishes* = $_{df}$ There was at least one property that was such that E had it, and there is no longer any property that is such that E has it.

When something comes into existence, there must be at least one property that belongs to that thing. When a human being comes-to-be, then the property of being human belongs to that individual at that

3. See William Vallicella, *A Paradigm Theory of Existence* (Dordrecht: Kluwer, 2002).

moment. When something ceases to be, it no longer has any properties whatever. Coming-to-be and perishing should be kept distinct from what philosophers call *alteration*. An example of an alteration is an apple's going from sweet to sour. Alterations are types of change. Before change is possible, two things must be true: (1) the thing that is changing must exist, and (2) the thing that changes must exist at the beginning, during the process, and at the end of change. In the example above, the apple exists and continues to exist while it is sweet, during the time it changes to being sour, and while it is sour. An alteration is a case where a thing changes in the properties it has; it is not a case where something changes with respect to existence itself. Alterations presuppose and therefore cannot be the same thing as a change in existence itself.

A second remark about existence is this: nothingness is just that—nothing. Nothingness has no properties whatsoever. Things that do not exist have no properties. The winged horse Pegasus has no properties, and that is what his nonexistence amounts to. You may think that he has the property of being a winged horse. But that is not true. Our *concept* of Pegasus (which is in our minds when we are thinking of Pegasus) is a concept *of* something that would have the property of being a winged horse if it existed. But Pegasus does not exist and he, along with all other cases of nothing, has no properties. It should also be said that one's concept of Pegasus exists, it is in the mind of the person knowing the concept, and it does not have the property of being a winged horse.

Many philosophers also hold that negative properties do not exist either. An apple may positively possess the property of being red, sweet, and round, but if negative properties exist, then the apple would also have the properties of not-being-green, not-being-square, and indeed, the apple would have an infinite amount of negative properties (e.g., of not-being-an-elephant). However, it is more natural to say that the apple *fails* to have the property of being green, instead of claiming that it *has* the property of being not-green. In general, when it is not the case that x is F (the apple is not green), we can explain this as a case where x fails to have F, rather than asserting the positive existence of negative properties—for example, as a case where x has not-F.

## THE NATURE OF IDENTITY

### Four Crucial Questions

When philosophers talk about the problem of identity, usually one of these four issues is in mind:

1. When x and y are contemporaneous, what is it for x to be identical to (be the same entity as) y? In general, what is it for anything to be identical to itself?
2. When x and y are noncontemporaneous, what is it for x to be identical to (be the same entity as) y? Are there continuants? Do things remain the same through change, and if so, how are we to understand what accounts for this?
3. What kind of evidence or criteria are there that enable us to know that a given x and y are identical?
4. What are the different kinds of identity statements? How are we to understand sentences that contain two or more linguistic expressions that refer to the same thing?

Questions 1 and 2 are basic metaphysical questions. Question 2 focuses on sameness through change and is central to the metaphysics of substance and topics in personal identity. Question 1 is the most basic metaphysical question about identity, and it will be the subject of investigation shortly. Question 3 is basically an epistemological question, not a metaphysical one. Finally, question 4 is a matter of the philosophy of language. Its main concern is not identity itself but identity *statements*, that is, linguistic expressions that assert identity. Given the space limitations, our study of identity will be limited to question 1.

### *The General Nature of Identity Itself*

Suppose you wanted to know whether J. P. Moreland is identical to (is the same thing as) Eileen Spiek's youngest son. If "they" are identical, then in reality there is only one person: J. P. Moreland who *is* (identical to) Eileen Spiek's youngest son. If they are not identical, then there are two people, not one. There is a general law of identity known as *Leibniz's law of the indiscernibility of identicals*:

Leibniz's Law of the indiscernability of Identicals

$$(x)(y)[(x = y) \Rightarrow (P)(Px \Leftrightarrow Py)]$$

This principle states that for any x (e.g., the person who is J. P. Moreland) and for any y (the person who happens to be Eileen Spiek's youngest son), if "they" are identical to each other ("they" are, in reality, the very same entity), then for any property P (being 5'8", being human), P will be true of x (J. P. Moreland) if and only if P is true of y (Eileen Spiek's youngest son). In general, everything is what it is and not something else. Everything is identical to itself and thus shares all properties in common with itself. This implies a test for nonidentity or difference: if

[Leibniz's law implies that] The fact that something is identical to itself is a necessary feature of everything.

GENERAL ONTOLOGY AND THEOLOGY                                        55

we can find one thing true of x not true of y or vice versa, then x is not identical to y.

We can gain further insights about identity if we think about how it applies to events. Let us assume what is called the *property exemplification view* of an event: an event is the coming-to-have, continued possession, or ceasing-to-have of a property by a substance at or through a time. A leaf losing greenness at noon would be an example of an event where a substance (the leaf) loses a property (greenness) at a time (noon). If E, S, P, and t refer to an event, a substance, a property, and a time respectively, then Leibniz's law of the indiscernibility of identicals, applied to events, becomes this:

*Property Exemplification View of an Event*

$$(E_1 = E_2) \Rightarrow [(S_1 = S_2) \& (P_1 = P_2) \& (t_1 = t_2)]$$

If $E_1$ and $E_2$ are identical, then the substances, properties, and times constituting "those" events will be identical as well. If the latter are not identical, then the events are different. For example, a case where $S_1$ is different from $S_2$ would be where two apples become red simultaneously; a case where $P_1$ is different from $P_2$ would be where a specific apple became red and sweet at the same time; a case where $t_1$ and $t_2$ are different would be when an apple became sweet at noon, turned sour overnight, and became sweet again the next day.

Leibniz's law of the indiscernibility of identicals implies another insight about identity:

$$(x)(y)[(x = y) \Rightarrow \Box(x = y)]$$

For all x and y, if x is identical to y, then necessarily x is identical to y. There is no possible world where the thing that is x is not identical to the thing that is y. For example, a cat may happen to be yellow and twenty pounds, but it does not just happen to be identical to itself. It is necessarily identical to itself. The fact that something is identical to itself is a necessary feature of everything. Suppose the person who is J. P. Moreland and the person who is Eileen Spiek's youngest son are different but both are 5'8". Then, in the actual world, they do not differ in height. But if it is just possible for them to differ in height—if there is a possible world where one is 5'8" and the other is 6', then they are not identical.

Again, if disembodied existence is metaphysically possible—if there is a possible world with disembodied existence—then a person cannot be identical to his or her body because there is no possible world where the person's body exists and is disembodied. Since it is possible for a person to exist disembodied but it is not possible for a body to exist

*Personal existence is poss (not merely disembodied existence)*

disembodied, then a person is not identical to his or her body. Why? Because something is true of the person (the possibility of disembodied existence) and not true of his or her body.

The identity relation is a relation that everything has to itself and to nothing else. This relation should be kept distinct from three other notions with which it is sometimes confused: *cause-effect, coextensionality*, and *inseparability*. If A causes B, then A is not identical to B. Smoke causes fire as its effect, but smoke is not identical to fire. Further, two things can be coextensional—that is, one obtains if and only if the other obtains. For example, the property of being triangular is coextensive with the property of being trilateral. One obtains if and only if the other obtains; no object has one without the other. But the two properties are not identical because the property of triangularity has something true of it, namely, being an angle, not true of the property of being trilateral.

Finally, two entities can be parts of some whole, and be inseparable either from each other or that whole, yet still not be identical. For example, the individual white instance of color in a sugar cube cannot be separated from the individual square instance of shape in that cube and still exist, just as the leg and back of a chair can be separated from each other or from the chair taken as a whole. But the instance of whiteness in the cube is an instance of color and its instance of shape is not; thus, they are not identical. Again, a person's emotions cannot be separated from the person or from the person's beliefs and placed in different locations of the room as the hand and leg of his body can. But one's various emotions and beliefs are all distinct and not identical to other emotions or beliefs.

## SOME IMPORTANT CATEGORIES

This section briefly looks at three important categories: substance, property, and relation.[4]

### *The Traditional View of Substance*

A *substance* is an entity, such as an acorn, a carbon atom, a dog, or an angel. Substances have a number of important characteristics. First, substances are particular, individual things. A substance, such as a particular acorn, cannot be in more than one place at the same time.

---

4. See J. P. Moreland and Scott Rae, *Body and Soul* (Downers Grove, IL: InterVarsity, 2000), ch. 2.

Second, a substance is a continuant—it can change by gaining new ②
properties and losing old ones, yet it remains the same thing throughout
the change. A leaf can go from green to red, yet the leaf itself is the same
entity before, during, and after the change. In general, substances can
change in some of their properties and yet remain the same substance.
The very leaf that was green is the same leaf that is now red.

Third, substances are basic, fundamental existents. They are not *in* ③
or *had by* other things. The dog Fido is not had by something more
basic than him. Rather, properties (and parts) are in substances that
have them. For example, Fido has the property of brownness and the
property of weighing twenty-five pounds. These properties are in the
substance called Fido.

Fourth, substances are unities of parts, properties, and capacities (dis- ④
positions, tendencies, potentialities). Fido has a number of properties,
such as the ones already listed. He also has a number of parts—four legs,
some teeth, two eyes. Further, he has some capacities or potentialities
that are not always actual. For example, he has the capacity to bark even
when he is silent. As a substance, Fido is a unity of all the properties,
parts, and capacities had by him.

Finally, a substance has causal powers. It can do things in the world. ⑤
A dog can bark; a leaf can hit the ground. Substances can cause things
to happen.

### Properties and Relations

In addition to substances, there are also entities that exist called *properties*. A property is an existent reality, examples of which are brownness, triangularity, hardness, wisdom, painfulness. As with substances,
properties have a number of important features.

One feature is that a property is a general feature that can be in more ①
than one thing at the same time. Redness can be in a flag, a coat, and
an apple at once. The very same redness can be the color of several particular things all at the same time. Another feature of properties is their
immutability. When a leaf goes from green to red, the *leaf* changes by
losing an old property and gaining a new one. But the property of redness does not change and become the property of greenness. Properties
can come and go, but they do not change in their internal constitution
or nature.

Moreover, properties can, or perhaps must, be in or had by other things ②
more basic than they. Properties are in the things that have them. For
example, redness is in the apple. The apple has the redness. One does not
find redness existing all by itself. In general, when we are talking about
a property, it makes sense to ask the question "What is it that has that

property?" That question is not appropriate for substances, for they are among the things that have the properties. Substances have properties; properties are had by substances.

It certainly seems that properties exist. Indeed, one of the most obvious facts about the world is that it consists of individual things, such as dogs and cars, that have properties. A dog could have the property of being brown, or a car, red. It seems that several objects can have the same property—for example, that several cars can possess the same shade of red. The problem of universals is actually a set of related issues involving the existence and nature of properties (where a property is just a quality of some sort that a thing can have). But both the existence and the nature of properties have long been a matter of dispute, and *the problem of universals* is the name for the issues central to this debate.

Historically, the problem of universals has been closely connected to what is called the problem of the "one and the many" (a.k.a. "one over many," "one in many"), which calls for giving an account of the unity of natural classes. To illustrate, consider the following words: RED, RED, BLUE. How many words are in the sequence? Two answers seem possible: either two or three words. There seem to be two word types and three word tokens, where a type is something that can "show up" or be instanced in different places and a token is a specific instance of a type. If we form a set containing the first two tokens {RED, RED}, the unity of the set seems to be grounded in the fact that both tokens have the same word type (both are examples of RED and not BLUE) in common.

What distinguishes a class of members that form a real natural set from a contrived set? What is the basis for set membership in natural sets? The obvious answer is that the members of a natural set literally have something in common—all seven balls are red—but this isn't true of the members of a contrived set. So the problem of the one and the many is this: how is it possible to group together a number of individual things that all share something in common, thereby forming one natural set of those things? The problem of universals includes the issues and options surrounding the one and the many. But since the problem of universals is about the existence and nature of properties, it goes beyond the one and the many and includes these questions:

(1) Do properties exist?
(2) If properties exist, are they universals or particulars?

Realists affirm both the reality of properties and the fact that they are universals. In one way or another, different forms of nominalism deny that properties are genuine universals.

Relations are (arguably) universals that require two or more entities *Relations* (e.g., properties, particulars) in order to be exemplified. Put differently, a relation is any real, discernible aspect of two or more things *taken together*. Relations obtain between or among entities. Examples are "being to the left of" between two balls or "being lighter than" between two colors. Relations are what constitute the structure of the other things that exist. There are various kinds of relations that exist: part/whole relations, causal relations, spatiotemporal relations, the laws of mathematics and logic, and so forth.

An important subcategory of relation draws a distinction between *Internal* internal and external relations. To understand this distinction, suppose *Relations* we have two entities, a and b, that are standing to each other in some relation R. There are two things true of internal relations as they are usually construed. First, if the R of a to b is internal to a, then anything that does not stand in R to b is not identical to a. If the relation "brighter than" between yellow and purple is internal to yellow, then anything that is not brighter than purple cannot be the color yellow. Second, internal relations are not primitive but, rather, are grounded in the natures of the entities they connect. D. M. Armstrong has defined an internal relation as a relation that is logically determined by the nature of the related terms.[5]

Armstrong goes on to point out that we can explain why internal relations are such that given two internally related entities a and b, there is no possible world in which the objects remain unaltered but in which the internal relation fails to obtain; we do this by recognizing that internal relations are derived from and grounded in the natures of the entities so related.[6] Indeed, the reason internal relations are called internal is that they actually enter into the being of, they partly constitute, the entity to which they are internal. If the relation between a heart and a living human body is internal to the heart, then at least part of what it is to be a heart is to stand in certain relations to the circulation system and, indeed, to the organism as a whole. If the heart ceases to be so related to the organism, it is no longer a heart, strictly speaking.

External relations are those that are not internal. If two entities, a and b, stand in external relation to each other, then a and b can cease to stand in that relation to one another and still exist. For example, the relation "to the left of" between a desk and lamp is external to both. The lamp can be placed on top of or to the right of the desk—indeed,

5. D. M. Armstrong, *Universals and Scientific Realism*, vol. 2, *A Theory of Universals* (Cambridge: Cambridge University Press, 1978), 172.

6. D. M. Armstrong, *Universals: An Opinionated Introduction* (Boulder: Westview, 1989), 43–44, 55, 100. Cf. J. P. Moreland, *Universals* (Montreal: McGill–Queen's University Press, 2001).

the lamp can be destroyed—and the desk can still exist and be identical to itself. These relations are called external because they do not enter into the very being of the entities they relate to in that those entities (e.g., the desk) can exist and be themselves whether or not they enter into the external relation.

## Why Care about General Ontology?

Life is short and we are all busy, so you might be thinking, "Who cares if properties exist and are universals? What difference does any of this make to my life? Isn't this far too abstract to have any real practical importance? Does all this really matter?" These are fair questions, and the short answer to them is "Yes, it does!" The issues of general ontology are extremely important. To illustrate this, let us consider the practical importance of what may seem at first glance to be the least practical issue of those mentioned in this chapter, the problem of properties and universals. Following are three examples of how important the debate about properties and universals really is.

Several years ago the Christian theologian Bernard Ramm argued that one reason for the breakdown of the family was the rise of nominalism. Why think that one cause for the breakdown of the family was a rejection of universals? According to Ramm, a realist says that the class of all families literally has certain properties in common, certain universals (having a father, a mother) which in turn have certain important properties in common (being nurturing) such that a group is not a family just because we say it is but rather because it exemplifies the same properties at all times and in all places. Nominalists claim that there is no such universal attribute to a family and thus feel free to define a family in relativist terms. Advocates of homosexual "marriage," claims that being a good father is whatever one believes sincerely this is, denials that there are true, universal moral properties all involve a rejection of certain universals relevant to the topics in question.

As a second example, consider love. This is a property—being loving—that people and their actions may or may not exemplify. It is a real property—not just a word—and it is a universal that is present in all and only individual acts of love or loving people. Indeed, since being loving is a real universal, being loving itself has further properties that we could discover. What are these second-order properties that the first-order property being loving has? Paul describes some of them in 1 Corinthians 13—patience, kindness, and so on. Since love and its properties are real universals, passages such as 1 Corinthians, in their descriptions of love, are describing reality as it is in all cultures. These descriptions give us true knowledge of reality—in this case, of properties understood as universals.

Finally, debates about postmodernism concern the acceptance or rejection of universals. As a philosophical standpoint, postmodernism is primarily a reinterpretation of what knowledge is and what counts as knowledge. More broadly, it represents a form of cultural relativism about such things as reality, truth, reason, value, linguistic meaning, the self, and other notions. All such notions are social constructions, arbitrary creations of language that are relative to different cultures.

*(handwritten margin note: iffy reading)*

Postmodernists deny the existence of universals. Remember, a universal is an entity that can be in more than one place at the same time or in the same place at different, interrupted time intervals. Redness, justice, being even, and humanness are examples of universals. If redness is a universal, then if one sees (the same shade of) redness on Monday and again on Tuesday, the redness seen on Tuesday is identical to, is the very same thing as, the redness seen on Monday. Postmodernists deny such identities and claim that nothing is repeatable, nothing is literally the same from one moment to the next, nothing can be present at one time or place and literally be present at another time or place. Thus, postmodernists hold to some form of nominalism.

*(handwritten margin note: Maybe, maybe not)*

Because postmodernists reject universal properties, they also reject essentialism. According to essentialism, some things have essential and accidental properties. A thing's essential properties are those such that if the thing in question loses them, it ceases to exist. A thing's essential properties answer the most fundamental question, "What sort of thing is this?" For example, being even is an essential property of the number two, being human is essential to Socrates, being omnipotent is essential to God, being $H_2O$ is essential to water. An accidental property is one such that a thing can lose it and still exist. For example, being five feet tall is accidental to Socrates.

According to postmodernists, there is no distinction in reality between essential and accidental properties. Rather, this division is relative to our interests, values, and classificatory purposes, and as such, the division is itself a social construction that will not be uniform throughout social groups. For example, if a group's definition of birds includes having a beak, then, assuming for the purpose of illustration that everything that has a beak has feathers, having a feather is an essential property of birds. If the group defines birds so as to include bats, having a feather is an accidental property. Thus, what is essential to birds is not a reflection of reality; it is a construction relative to a group's linguistic practices. It should be clear that postmodern nominalism, if widely accepted, would have a disastrous impact on the objective existence of important universals relating to truth, values, and Christian teaching.

Instead of providing illustrations of the practical importance of other topics addressed in this chapter, it may be more useful to provide a sort of homework assignment. See if you can use the material in this chapter to shed light on the following.

Have you ever had a conversation like this?

Believer: Have you heard of the Four Spiritual Laws?

Unbeliever: I'm not interested.

Believer: How come?

Unbeliever: 'Cause you Christians are crazy! You believe some pretty weird things.

Believer:  Like what?

Unbeliever: You say that moral values are real. But if something is real, you've got to be able to see it, to locate it somewhere. Cleveland is real. You can see it and I can tell you where it is. But who's ever seen a moral value, and where are these things anyway?

Believer: Love's real, isn't it?

Unbeliever: It's just a word, an idea in people's heads, but while we're on the subject of love, it brings up another crazy thing you Christians believe.

Believer: Sounds like I walked into a trap.

Unbeliever: Trap or no trap, here's the problem. You say that God is love, but how can that be true? Love's just an idea, or maybe it's an attitude or action, but love isn't alive. You can't pray to it. If your God is real, then he would be alive, but he sure isn't the same thing as an attitude or action. So it's nuts to say that God is love.

Believer: Well, Jesus still died for your sins, and you have to decide what you are going to do with that fact.

Unbeliever: The topic of Jesus raises another problem. If the president of the United States in 2003 is the same thing as George Bush and if Laura Bush's husband is the same thing as George Bush, then the U.S. president in 2003 is the same thing as Laura Bush's husband.

Believer: So what?

Unbeliever: Well, if Jesus is the same thing as God, and the Holy Spirit is the same thing as God, then Jesus is the same thing as the Holy Spirit. But you Christians believe that they're different. How can that be?

This dialog brings up a number of issues and exhibits several confusions. Can you spot those issues and identify and solve the confusions they involve? This much should be clear. Existence, identity, and the categories of substance, property, and relation are all relevant to forming a vibrant Christian worldview. By supplying insights on these topics, studies in general ontology serve the theologian in his or her craft.

# 3

# REORIENTING RELIGIOUS EPISTEMOLOGY

*Cognitive Grace, Filial Knowledge, and Gethsemane Struggle*

### ✴| Paul K. Moser |✴

WHAT IF THE GOD AND Father of Jesus, the Jewish outcast, really is God, the true God, the Maker of heaven and earth? What if, in particular, the true God really is cognitively subtle, morally challenging, and perfectly loving toward us humans? In that case, we may have to rethink our lazy preconceptions regarding appropriate evidence of God's reality. We may then have to recast our standards for evidence of God's reality to fit God's sometimes unsettling but nonetheless loving ways. This would call for a kind of cognitive modesty rare among philosophers and people in general.

"What if?" questions loom large in philosophy, past and present. They figure prominently in philosophical efforts to formulate best available explanations of relevant data. For instance, in metaphysics, some philosophers look at how we ascribe truth and ask, What if truth bearers are abstract propositions rather than sentences? In epistemology, some philosophers look at how justification accrues to empirical beliefs and ask, What if perceptual experiences, rather than beliefs, are the ulti-

65

mate justifiers of empirical beliefs? The general explanatory strategy is straightforward and is captured by this question: *what if* reality is actually *this* way? Does the assumption that reality is *this* way shed explanatory light otherwise unavailable? Does it make sense of relevant data needing illumination? Such explanation-seeking questions underlie the familiar pattern of inference to a best available explanation in philosophy, in the sciences, and in everyday life.[1]

What about human knowledge of the reality of God? Do "What if?" questions figure in the assessment of this matter? If so, how? This essay pursues these issues. It contends that the reality of the true God is cognitively accessible in a way that depends on human openness to cognitive grace, filial knowledge, and the moral struggle exemplified by Jesus in Gethsemane.

## ATTUNEMENT AND AGAPE TRANSFORMATION

Let us use the term "God" as a title connoting a being who is worthy of worship and is thus morally impeccable. (Use of such a title, of course, leaves open whether a titleholder actually exists.) Let us suppose, then, that a divine titleholder must be a God of corrective love who seeks to save people from their unloving ways. In being loving, God must refrain from coercing or intimidating people into accepting divine commands. God thus must allow people to reject the divine invitation to be saved from unloving ways. In addition, God must not be arbitrary in loving people. God must love *all* people at *all* times with *full* love. God must be, in this respect, *all*-loving. The true God, in being all-loving, would seek to encourage and teach all people how to become loving toward God and other people *as God is loving*. God would seek to accomplish this by means of our acquiring and sustaining a loving relationship with God. We may call this a *filial* relationship, whereby God becomes our loving Father and we become loving children of God. This filial relationship would *personalize* the process of our learning how to love others. It would teach us to be loving by communion and fellowship with a perfect personal Lover who is our Father. The process would thus go beyond moral injunction to personal acquaintance, interaction, and challenge in relationship with God as our Father.

1. On inference to a best explanation, see William G. Lycan, "Explanation and Epistemology," in *The Oxford Handbook of Epistemology*, ed. Paul Moser (New York: Oxford University Press, 2002), 408–33. I have discussed the role of inference to a best explanation in empirical knowledge in Paul Moser, *Knowledge and Evidence* (New York: Cambridge University Press, 1989).

REORIENTING RELIGIOUS EPISTEMOLOGY

Let us develop an analogy for illustration. I own a Uniden police band and aircraft scanner, a scanning radio that searches for active frequencies between 29 and 956 MHz. This range includes communications by police and fire departments, aircraft, the National Weather Service, ambulances, railroads, buses, taxis, some TV stations, and even ham radio operators. My scanner also picks up older cell phones and mobile phones in the area; so, if you care for your privacy, it is a good idea to replace such phones with newer ones. My scanner enables me to listen in on pretty much every radio communication going on in my part of the world. Of course, we cannot see, touch, taste, or smell the various frequencies, but they are nonetheless real and valuable. Indeed, many of the frequencies are crucial to the communication system underlying a stable society. Without police radio communication, for instance, we would all be in big trouble indeed.

My scanner has a telescoping antenna that can be pointed in different directions for improved reception. If I adjust the antenna in a certain way, I can block the reception of some frequencies. My scanner also enables me to skip undesired frequencies, for instance, the banter of ham radio operators. What is more, my scanner comes with "search delay." I can delay at will the search for new frequencies. So I have remarkable control over the frequencies received by my scanner. I am, we might say, the lord of my scanner.

The most excitement by far occurs on the police frequencies. They offer exciting car chases, foot chases, and other police cases that are the stuff of TV detective shows. I can select which Chicago police district to monitor, and I can switch between districts with ease. Moreover, with the turn of a dial or the push of a button, I can silence the police department dispatcher. I am indeed the lord of my scanner's reception. I am able and often willing to tune in or tune out the frequencies I choose.

The *reality* of the frequencies activating my scanner does not depend on my tuning in to them. The frequencies are real even if I am asleep at my scanner. We are bombarded with radio waves at all hours even if we are unaware of them. Similarly, the *available evidence* of the reality of the radio waves is independent of my tuning in to them. (My not actually having evidence does not mean that it is not available to me.) My failure to turn on my scanner or to adjust its antenna properly may leave me with no evidence of the reality of, say, the ham radio transmissions in my neighborhood. Even so, the distinctive evidence of ham radio activity can be acquired by all who seek it properly. To acquire the evidence, one need only turn on a suitable scanner, raise its antenna, and adjust the scanner to receive the appropriate frequency. In other words, one must tune in to the desired frequency, and this requires some careful decision making, focusing, and maneuvering. People who do not tune in will lack a certain kind of evidence that is nonetheless readily available to them. Radio waves can carry good news, but if we are not attuned (tuned in), we will miss out on the good news. The good news can be available to us but nonetheless not actually received by us.

Let us extend the analogy a bit. All of us are on a sinking desert island, alone with our personal scanners. Our food and water supplies are dangerously low. Our relationships with one another are frayed and have resulted in selfish factions and fights. We are even willing to sacrifice the well-being of others for our own selfish good. Genuine community has broken down, and in the absence of a rescuer, we will all soon perish. Our island is sinking, and we are too. Successful scanning for a rescuer is our only hope. Will we connect with a rescuer? Will we survive?

Turning to our real-life shared predicament, we are all on a planetary island facing moral breakdown and final death. Any daily newspaper will confirm this unfortunate human situation with war stories and obituaries. Our access to the reality of God is analogous to our access to frequencies on my scanner. We need somehow to tune in to the reality and the available evidence of God. God is, after all, an invisible Spirit with definite character traits and purposes. We need, accordingly, to point our scanner's antenna in the right direction. The right direction, relative to an all-loving God, does not automatically match the direction of our own lives. God, in being all-loving, has a character and purposes significantly different from our own. God's direction thus differs from our own.

The desert islanders should not expect themselves to have control or authority over which frequency a rescuer uses. If they stubbornly insist on such authority, they may very well overlook the frequency occupied by a rescuer. They should at least ask, Who is entitled to choose the rescuer's frequency for communication—the islanders or the rescuer? Once we ask such questions, we see that the islanders have no authority to demand how the rescuer is revealed. Their expectations of the rescuer should be conformed to the character and purposes of the rescuer and not vice versa. Likewise, we should not expect God to appear on the evening TV news or even a Sunday talk show if this would be at odds with God's all-loving character and purposes.

Our starting question, then, is not so much whether God exists but rather what the character and purposes of an all-loving God would be. In addition, we should ask at the start, What kind of human knowledge of God would an all-loving God seek? The most direct answer is that God would seek the kind of knowledge that advances God's kind of love among human knowers. In particular, an all-loving God would seek *filial knowledge of God*, whereby humans become loving children of God and thus know God, in sacred relationship, as their loving Father. This is the lesson of the Jewish scriptures and the Christian scriptures (see, e.g., Isa. 63:16, 64:8–9; Jer. 31:9; Rom. 8:15–16; John 1:12), although the Christian scriptures, under the influence of Jesus, stress this lesson more than the Jewish scriptures do.[2]

Suppose that I tune in to just self-indulgent frequencies, devoting my life exclusively to what advances my own selfish purposes. I might be the kind of islander who cares only about my own rescue, on my own selfish terms, even at the expense of other islanders. In this case, I would be nowhere near the available evidence of the reality of an all-loving God. I would then have my antenna pointed in the wrong direction for purposes of receiving evidence of God's reality. An all-loving God would communicate on a frequency available to all people who are open to divine rescue on God's terms. God's frequency is not the exclusive possession of the educated, the physically strong, the wealthy, or any other group that automatically excludes others. An all-loving God would seek all-inclusive community under the umbrella of God's genuine love. Such a God would desire that everyone be rescued from destruction, even the most pathetic and repulsive among us and even all of our enemies, including God's enemies. This is not, of course, a typical human desire, but it would be integral to an all-loving God. God's ways differ from our selfish ways.

Failure to apprehend evidence of God can result from my looking for God under a misguided conception of God. I might portray God as grudging, vindictive, excessively restrictive, or harmful to my identity. In this case, my scanning for God might find a frequency reflecting me, but I will not find an all-loving God who is worthy of worship. Alternatively, I might conceive of God as offering only pampering, pandering love that does not challenge us to be morally good as God is. In this case, my scanning for God would yield mere noise, not an intelligible frequency. I would then fail to tune in to the true God worthy of worship. I would then be looking in the wrong direction. My attention would be directed toward a convenient idol of my own making.

We sometimes try to avoid God out of self-protective fear. We fear that God will rob us of something good for us or at least something we rightfully want. As a result, we refuse to take seriously the available evidence of God's reality. We might even completely shut down some frequency ranges on our scanner, thereby trying to suppress the issue whether there is available evidence of God's reality. Many people do just this. Our self-protective fear sometimes yields even antipathy toward

2. Regarding Jesus and the New Testament on God as Father, see Bernard Cooke, *God's Beloved* (Harrisburg, PA: Trinity, 1992), 1–24; Neil Richardson, *God in the New Testament* (London: Epworth, 1999), 9–38; and Marianne Meye Thompson, *The Promise of the Father* (Louisville: Westminster, 2000).

God. Thomas Nagel candidly reports his fearful hope that God does not exist. He avowedly wants a universe without God. Nagel has a "cosmic authority problem" with God.[3] A highly educated atheist acquaintance of mine has a similar attitude toward God. When asked how he would respond if after death he met God directly, he replied that he would immediately kill himself. These are sad cases of our self-protective fears banishing God from human lives. All humans may suffer from this problem to some degree. It is the problem of ultimate authority for our lives. We typically want to be, or at least to appoint, the ultimate authority for our lives, as if we had a right to this. We thereby deceive ourselves, blinding ourselves from the supreme reality and authority over our lives. We end up looking in the wrong direction, in a place where God is not allowed to be God.

The needed attunement with God's self-revelation requires more than a good thought or even a good system of beliefs. This self-revelation, constituting God's "frequency," manifests God's forgiving love of the kind demonstrated by the cross of Jesus (cf. Rom. 5:8). The needed attunement is, then, *the proper reception of his love* rather than just a new belief. Since this love announces forgiveness, it also pronounces judgment on us. Our being offered forgiveness presumes that we are in the wrong and thus in need of forgiveness. This means that my will is in the wrong and in need of correction by God's will. The proper reception of God's forgiving love requires that I subject my faulty, selfish will to God's perfect, loving will. This reception is an ongoing struggle and not just an intellectual commitment. It cuts to the core of my intentions and desires, the attitudes that motivate me. It is thus a power struggle between God and me.

Divine love comes to us, then, in the merciful judgment of forgiveness, and our receiving it entails a revolution in our wills relative to God's will. It thus requires a new life-direction, motivated by the obedient resolve shown by Jesus in Gethsemane toward his Father: "Not what I want, but what you want" (Mark 14:36; cf. Matt. 26:39; Luke 22:42). This life-direction begins with acknowledgment of our inadequacy before God relative to God's all-loving character. In this respect, we come under divine love's judgment, owing to our failure to meet the expectations

3. See Thomas Nagel, *The Last Word* (New York: Oxford University Press, 1997), 130. For an explicit acknowledgment of volitional resistance to commitment to God's reality, see Mortimer Adler, *Philosopher at Large* (New York: Macmillan, 1977), 315–16. For discussion of the role of the human will in knowledge of God and its bearing on divine hiddenness, see Paul Moser, "Cognitive Inspiration and Knowledge of God," in *The Rationality of Theism*, ed. Paul Copan and Paul Moser (London: Routledge, 2003), 55–71; "Cognitive Idolatry and Divine Hiding," in *Divine Hiddenness*, ed. Daniel Howard-Snyder and Paul Moser (New York: Cambridge University Press, 2002), 120–48.

REORIENTING RELIGIOUS EPISTEMOLOGY

its morally transforming effects.[4] His experience of being God's Son is clearly expressed in his prayers (including the Lord's Prayer and the conflicted prayer in Gethsemane). Indeed, Jesus seems to have regarded filial prayer toward God, in response to God's amazing love, as an ideal avenue to filial knowledge of God. Such prayer is primarily a matter of asking and hearing what God as our loving Father wants from us rather than what we want from God. This kind of humble prayer figures importantly in the issue of what kind of available evidence of God we should expect and pursue.

Filial knowledge of the true God is irreducibly person-relational. We come to know other human persons by actively relating to them in personal interaction with them. Likewise we come to know God through personal interaction whereby we become personally accountable to God as our loving Father. Through moral conscience, for example, we can be personally convicted on moral grounds by the personal will of God. We could not responsibly apprehend the reality of a parent's or a spouse's love for us apart from a genuine personal relationship with that parent or spouse. An analogous point holds for our responsibly apprehending the reality of God's love. Given that the true God is inherently loving, we know of this God's reality only through our apprehending the reality of God's merciful love. So filial knowledge of God is irreducible to knowledge that a particular object in the universe exists. It is irreducible also to knowledge that the premises of an argument are true.

The required filial knowledge, in keeping with God's preeminent personal character, requires that we know God not as a mere object but as the supreme personal subject who is Lord of all, including our own lives. Knowledge of this kind results from *cognitive grace*, from God's gracious self-revelation of God's loving character, and not from human ways that are self-crediting, manipulative, or selfishly exclusive. The true God first loved us and sought us, before we sought and came to know God. This God graciously inaugurates covenants of unconditional love with people in order to bring them into filial relationship with God.[5]

For our own good, we cannot know God on our self-serving terms. Instead we must conform to God's terms for filial knowledge, and this requires genuine humility and personal commitment on our part toward

---

4. On Jesus's experience of God, see James Dunn, *Jesus and the Spirit* (London: SCM, 1975), 37–40; Cooke, *God's Beloved*, 1–24; and T. W. Manson, *The Teaching of Jesus*, 2nd ed. (Cambridge: Cambridge University Press, 1935), 89–115. Regarding Jesus on knowledge of God, see Paul Moser, "Jesus on Knowledge of God," *Christian Scholars Review* 28 (1999): 586–604.

5. On the nature of divine covenants, see James Torrance, "Covenant or Contract?" *Scottish Journal of Theology* 23 (1970): 51–76; "The Covenant Concept in Scottish Theology and Politics and Its Legacy," *Scottish Journal of Theology* 34 (1981): 225–43.

God. It challenges our supposed cognitive autonomy and calls for the yielding of our own wills, in faithful obedience, to God's will. We must receive, enter into, and participate in a loving filial relationship with God in response to God's first drawing us toward himself through conscience and other means. This exceeds intellectual assent to, or acceptance of, a proposition. It demands that we put the true God at the center of our lives, in terms of what and whom we value, love, trust, and obey. This calls for a revolution in our cognitive lives and in our moral lives as well. There is no coming to know the true God without resulting personal agape transformation through the reception of God's self-giving, forgiving love.

Given God's all-loving purposes toward us, God must be careful to have his self-manifestation to us elicit from us a freely given response of humble love rather than fear, indifference, or arrogance. In promoting divine love, God cares mainly about what and how we love, not just what we believe. For our own good, God aims that we (a) love God above all else, by subjecting our wills to God's all-loving will, and (b) thereby live out God's sacrificial love toward all people. Our filial knowledge of God requires that God's own love be experienced and received by us. We must ask for it, receive it, and yield to it sincerely and repeatedly. This is the constant struggle of Gethsemane, a struggle won by Jesus and now shared by his followers.

Our transformation toward God's kind of sacrificial love and reconciliation is noncoercive but still difficult, owing to obstruction from our wills. The needed transforming lessons must be shown to us in action and in relationship rather than simply stated to us in sentences or arguments. We must learn such lessons in obediently living them rather than merely thinking them, because the lessons concern who we are and how we exist, not just what we think. This bears on the needed role of God as the loving source of our personal transformation. God motivates the needed agape transformation by offering and promoting forgiving love. Accordingly, the sacrificial crucifixion of Jesus as God's unique Son offers a noncoercive demonstration of God's self-giving love toward humans.

Given the crucial reality of human free will (a requirement for genuine love), a demonstration of love has no guarantee whatever of full success in being received even when God is its perfect source. Not even the true God, having supreme power and knowledge, can force or otherwise guarantee genuine loving reconciliation with people. The will of the person loved always plays a crucial role, and some people evidently do not accept God's love. Divine love, then, carries the risk of human rejection. Otherwise it would be coercion and not genuine love.

In response to God's typically subtle call, we must attune ourselves to available evidence of divine self-revelation, the revelation of God's forgiving love. Failure to receive some evidence stems from psychological facts of the intended recipients, not from flaws in the available evidence itself. People whose receptive attitude is closed to God's call to renewal by self-giving, sacrificial love may be blinded from the available evidence for the reality of the God of sacrificial love. The blinding comes from human attitudes opposed to divine love. If we filter all our evidence through our own self-serving grids, with no openness to God's call to receive and promote unselfish love, we will obscure real evidence of the God of sacrificial love. Such filtering will cloud not only the supreme value of God's sacrificial love but also available evidence of God's reality.

The evidence of God's reality may be readily available, but we need a suitable scanner that attends to the needed frequency, God's forgiving love. We need appropriate "ears to hear and eyes to see" the available evidence. We need a change of receptive attitude to apprehend the available evidence in the right way. This change concerns the intended direction of our lives, including our settled priorities. It requires our sincerely receiving God's sacrificial, forgiving love toward us as the motivational and normative basis for our lives. This demands a renunciation of our supposed independence of God regarding lordship over our lives. It also demands, as noted, that we acknowledge our being under the judgment of divine love. It thus requires that we subject our wills to God's will, our lives to God's life of unselfish love.

In resisting transformation toward God's character of sacrificial love, we may be blinded by our own counterfeit "intelligence" and "wisdom." We will then lack the kind of humility and filial obedience appropriate to relating to God cognitively, morally, and otherwise. We will then have assigned the authority appropriate to God to ourselves or to some other part of creation. In this case, we would be guilty of idolatry, the mistake of exchanging God's rightful authority for a misplaced authority. We commit *cognitive* idolatry when we demand a certain sort of knowledge or evidence of God inappropriate to a morally transforming filial relationship with God. We thus refuse to receive knowledge of God on God's terms. This is a failure on our part to let God be God, particularly in the area of our knowing God. We thereby run afoul of God's rightful authority in the cognitive domain. We become cognitive rebels against the true God, the original Knower and Lord of all. Our idolatry isolates us from the true God, for it repudiates the true God.

## LOVE, HUMAN TRANSFORMATION, AND GOD

Two kinds of knowledge have figured in our discussion: (1) *propositional* knowledge that God exists and (2) *filial* knowledge as one humbly, faithfully, and lovingly stands in a child's relationship to God as the righteously gracious Father. Filial knowledge of God logically requires propositional knowledge that God exists, but it goes beyond such knowledge. One can know that God exists but hate God. Indeed, some people testify to being in such a state. Propositional knowledge is thus insufficient for filial knowledge. Even the demons believe (and know) that God exists but shudder, according to the Epistle of James. Filial knowledge of God, in contrast, includes our being reconciled to God (at least to some extent) through a loving filial relationship with God (or at least the start of such a relationship). It requires our entrusting ourselves as children to God in grateful love, so that we are significantly transformed in who we are and in how we exist, not just in what we believe. Such knowledge inherently transforms us toward God's loving character.

Filial knowing of God is knowing God as Father and Lord in the second person, that is, as supreme "You." Divine lordship entails supreme personal *moral leadership*, and such moral leadership entails a call to personal moral accountability and direction. When self-centered humans are the recipients of God's call, the call is for moral redirection and transformation toward God's character of sacrificial love. We stand under the judgment of divine love owing to our unloving ways. Knowing God as Lord requires my submitting my will to God in the manner noted previously: "Not my will but yours be done" (Luke 22:42). Filial knowing of God thus encompasses the spirit of Jesus in Gethsemane, on the way to the cross, in that it depends on our volitional sensitivity and obedience to the will of God. Such knowing requires a genuine commitment to obey God's call even if the call is to give up one's own life in sacrificial love on a criminal's cross. We thus come to know the true God not in our prideful cognitive and moral strength but rather in our own volitional weakness relative to the priority of God's call and will. God's love calls us up short and seeks to change us for the better via filial knowledge of God.

This question arises: are we *entitled* to know God? Specifically, are we entitled to know that God exists without knowing God as Father and Lord, as the morally supreme agent for our lives? Some people uncritically assume an affirmative answer, but this distorts God's status relative to humans. A prior question is this: who is entitled to decide how one may know God—we humans or God? Given our complete inferiority relative to God, can *we* reasonably make demands on God in favor of *our* preferred ways of knowing God, in opposition to God's ways of being known? The question answers itself: no.

God does not owe us any kind of impersonal confirmation of God's reality whereby we are unchallenged by God's personal character of merciful, forgiving love. In fact, God owes us nothing beyond faithfulness to his loving character and to God's promises stemming from such a character. We see, on reflection, that we have no right to make cognitive demands of God beyond such faithfulness. Nothing requires that God allow propositional knowledge that God exists to be our due apart from our filial knowledge of God. An all-loving God would promote the two together. In knowing that the true God exists (rather than, say, the God of deism or "mere theism"), we have knowledge of God's character of merciful love toward us and are thereby profoundly challenged for our own good to abide in filial knowledge of God. An all-loving God can supply evidence of his existence in a manner sensitive to a person's receptivity to filial knowledge of God. God need not offer evidence of his reality susceptible to our trivializing God by not being challenged to undergo transformation toward filial knowledge. The true God, being a God of merciful love, does not settle for mere reasonable belief that God exists. God, being all-loving, seeks to have us become loving as God is loving. God's self-giving love seeks to foster love in us, even in our knowing God.

Many people have objected that God's reality is too unclear to merit reasonable acknowledgment. God, they suggest, owes us more miraculous signs and wonders, whatever God's aims for humans. God, they claim, should present us with some decisive manifestations of awesome divine power. This would not cost God anything, and it would (allegedly) vanquish nagging doubts about God's existence. God's redemptive purposes, many critics will object, do not exonerate God from the charge of negligent restraint in self-revelation. God, if real, is altogether blameworthy for inadequate self-revelation. N. R. Hanson, for instance, comments on the absence of observable happenings that would establish God's existence: "There is no single natural happening, nor any constellation of such happenings, which establishes God's existence. . . . If the heavens cracked open and [a] Zeus-like figure . . . made his presence and nature known to the world, *that* would establish such a happening."[6] Hanson claims that nothing like the Zeus event has ever occurred in a way that recommends theism to all reasonable people. He concludes, then, that theism lacks adequate warrant for universal acceptance.

6. N. R. Hanson, *What I Do Not Believe and Other Essays* (Dordrecht: Reidel, 1971), 322.

By way of reply, let us consider that miraculous signs come in two forms: *agape-impotent* and *agape-potent* miraculous signs. Agape-impotent miraculous signs can astonish people, but they are not intended to transform a person to become more loving. In contrast, agape-potent signs are intended to reveal love and to elicit love; in particular, they are intended to change a person toward God's character of merciful love. The miracles of Jesus should be viewed as agape-potent, intended to elicit agape transformation. People often seek stimulation and entertainment from visible phenomena, but God seeks our personal transformation toward divine love, at the deepest level of our being.

The true God, as perfectly loving, is not in the entertainment business regarding our coming to know God. This God complains about the ancient Israelites that "Day after day they seek me and delight to know my ways, as if they were a nation that practiced righteousness and did not forsake the ordinance of their God" (Isa. 58:2). Our seeking God without obeying God's loving demands is pointless. The New Testament likewise discourages our seeking after agape-impotent signs from God (see Matt. 12:38–39). Hanson's aforementioned example falls short of being agape-potent. In addition, contrary to Hanson's suggestion, it would not "establish God's existence." The realization of his Zeus example is perfectly compatible with the nonexistence of an all-loving God and even with the improbability of the reality of an all-loving God. Hanson's Zeus-like figure could very well be a moral tyrant.

The New Testament promises a personally transforming sign to all seekers actively open to change toward God's character of merciful love. The needed sign is a salient indicator from the God of morally serious love. So we should expect it to manifest the character of God, namely, God's morally serious, merciful love. The New Testament confirms this expectation in no uncertain terms. Paul, for example, observes, "hope [in God] does not disappoint us, because God's love has been poured into our hearts through the Holy Spirit that has been given to us" (Rom. 5:5). This "pouring out" of God's love is inherently *personal*, owing to the ineliminable role of God's personal Spirit. It involves a new filial relationship, as Paul notes: "When we cry, 'Abba! Father!' it is the Spirit [of God] himself bearing witness with our spirit that we are children of God" (Rom. 8:15–16 RSV). (See 1 Cor. 2:4–16 on the role of God's Spirit in Paul's pneumatic epistemology.)[7] As we respond to God's love with filial acceptance, we become transformed into children of God, and God's love emerges as the central motivation of our lives. God's love begets our love in filial relationship.

7. On this topic in 1 Corinthians, see Alexandra Brown, *The Cross and Human Transformation* (Minneapolis: Fortress, 1995).

The presence of God's transforming love is the key *cognitive* foundation for filial knowledge of God. This experienced love is a foundational
source of knowledge of God (cf. 1 Cor. 8:2–3; Eph. 3:17–18; Col. 2:2) and
is salient *evidence* of God's reality and presence. Such love is a matter of
personal intervention by God and is the stable basis of a filial relationship
with a personal living God. So filial knowledge of God rests on divine
love that produces a loving character (at least to some extent) in genuine
children of God, even if at times they cloud God's transformation toward
love. This agape transformation happens to a person, in part, and thus
is neither altogether self-made nor simply the byproduct of a self-help
strategy. We need the phrase "in part" owing to the role of human free
will in responding and tuning in to God.

The supernatural sign of divine love is available at God's appointed
time to anyone who calls on God with due moral seriousness. The clause
"at God's appointed time" respects the fact that God has a privileged
position in identifying when one is duly serious and ready to respond
appropriately to God's presence. Receiving the presence of God's love at
the opportune time transforms one's will to engender gratitude, trust, and
love toward God and unselfish love toward other humans, even enemies.
Thus, "we *know* that we have passed from death to life because we love
one another. . . . Whoever does not love does not know God, for God
is love" (1 John 3:14; 4:8; italic added). We need, then, to learn how to
apprehend, and to be apprehended by, God's love for all of us, not just
truths about God's love. This is often a slow, difficult process of agape
transformation, given our self-centered ways. Neither God nor God's
love, being irreducibly personal, is a proposition or an argument. God
and God's love are much deeper and much more powerful and thus can
underwrite durable hope, healing, and rescue for us as persons.

The evidence of God's reality offered by profound agape transformation cuts much deeper, at least in its grateful recipients, than the com-
paratively superficial evidence found in entertaining signs, wonders,
visions, ecstatic experiences, and philosophical arguments. We could
consistently dismiss any such sign, wonder, vision, ecstatic experience,
or argument as illusory or indecisive, given certain alterations in our
beliefs. In contrast, profound transformation toward God's love does
not admit of easy dismissal by its transformed recipients. It bears directly on who one really is, specifically, the kind of person one actually
is. Such transformation goes too deeply against our natural tendencies
toward selfishness to qualify as a self-help construct. It constitutes firm
evidence of God's reality, evidence resisting quick dismissal, at least by
its changed and changing recipients.

An all-loving God would make his personal reality available to humans
at God's appointed time. God's self-revelation, however, need not exceed

the presence of God's morally serious love or be available apart from morally serious inquiry and seeking. Specifically, God's self-revelation need not include miracles irrelevant to transformation toward God's character of love, even though God may use such miracles to get our wayward attention. A perfectly loving God can properly make confident knowledge of his reality arise simultaneously with filial knowledge of his reality. As a result, God is absolved from the charge of negligently refraining from performing entertaining signs, so long as God reveals his personal reality to anyone suitably receptive. Hanson's aforementioned use of the Zeus example overlooks these considerations and trivializes God's actual redemptive aim for humans. As all-loving, God aims to bring naturally unloving people to love God and others, even others who are avowed enemies.

God's self-revelation of transforming love takes its recipients beyond mere historical and scientific probabilities to a foundation of *personal acquaintance* with God. As we noted from the apostle Paul, in our sincerely crying out "Abba, Father" to God (note the Jesus-inspired filial gist of this cry), God's Spirit confirms to our spirits that we are indeed children of God. We thereby receive God's personal assurance of our filial relationship with him. This assurance is more robust than any kind of theoretical certainty offered by the arguments of philosophers or theologians. It saves a person from dependence merely on speculation, hypothesis formation, probabilistic inference, or guesswork about God. The personal assurance of God's Spirit yields a distinctive kind of grounded confidence in God unavailable elsewhere.[8] God thus merits credit even for proper human confidence in God (cf. Eph. 2:8). Humans who boast of their own intellectual skills in knowing God therefore have misplaced boasting. Such boasting erects a cognitive barrier (not unlike the golden calf of Exod. 32) between humans and God.

## KNOWING GOD AND EXPLAINING GOD

The reality of the true God is testable now in a morally serious manner. In addition, God's reality *should* be tested now by every capable person. Each person must test by seeking God with due sincerity, humility, and moral seriousness. Pride and indifference automatically blind us from seeing God and our genuine need of God. The appropriate test requires one's willingness to forsake all diversions for the sake of the required

8. On the experience of God's Spirit and the Spirit's relation to the cross of Jesus, see Michael Gorman, *Cruciformity* (Grand Rapids: Eerdmans, 2001), 50–62. See also Charles Cosgrove, *The Cross and the Spirit* (Macon, GA: Mercer University Press, 1988); and James Dunn, *The Theology of Paul the Apostle* (Grand Rapids: Eerdmans, 1998), 413–40.

relationship with God, including personal transformation toward God's character of love. Filial knowledge of God is by grace rather than by earning, and this cognitive grace is available (at God's appointed time) to all who call on God with sincere humility and due moral seriousness. The true God wants to give all humans lasting gifts, but we often cling, selfishly and self-destructively, to lesser goods. Even our own lives and our knowledge can become idols blocking reception of the true God.

One's *having adequate evidence of God's reality* is not the same as one's *having a comprehensive explanation of God's ways and means*. We thus need to distinguish between

(a) when you seek God properly, you will find God's self-revelation,

and

(b) when you seek God properly, you will find a comprehensive explanation of why God acts as he does.

The promise of statement (a) regarding God's self-revelation does not depend for its correctness or warrant on our understanding all God's intentions and thus does not underwrite a theodicy. So statement (a) does not entail statement (b). The promise of statement (a) regarding God's self-revelation concerns one's acquiring evidence of God's reality, not one's acquiring a comprehensive explanation of God's ways.

In demanding human seeking, God upholds the supreme value of divine revelation, thereby saving it from being cheapened by naturally selfish humans. God aims to have humans supremely value divine love and to be personally transformed by it, not just to think about it. Still, human seeking, even when accompanied by one's finding God, does not yield a theodicy because it does not produce a comprehensive explanation of God's ways with his creation. Even when one's seeking God delivers evidence of God's reality, the seeker who has experienced God can lack understanding of the specific intentions motivating God's actions at times. This should be no surprise, given the notable differences, cognitive and otherwise, between God and humans. Our lacking a comprehensive explanation of God's ways, however, does not challenge anyone's having good evidence of God's reality and love. (The closing chapters of the book of Job confirm this.) We should not be timid, then, about our lacking a theodicy. In addition, people who hope to find God should not delay their search on the ground that they lack a theodicy. Finding God is not necessarily finding a theodicy. The real and needed treasure is finding the all-loving God of all creation.

Our seeking for and then properly receiving God's self-revelation will change us toward God's love in a morally profound manner. Having undergone the experience of such change, one may then report a personal acquaintance with the Maker of heaven and earth. In addition, one may then report that God figures crucially in the best available explanation of who one really is. One will then be a person who has begun to love as the living God loves. The world actually looks as if it is the kind of place where we are to begin learning humbly to love as God loves. It certainly is not the kind of place where we are to receive either maximal pleasure or maximal pain.

If we are properly attuned to available evidence of God's reality, including God's self-giving love, God will be clear enough. We need, then, proper eyes to see and ears to hear the reality of God. To this end, we must call on the Lord, who alone can empower our cognitive and moral appropriation of the things of God. Ultimately, God's personal Spirit enables us to apprehend the things of God; we cannot do it on our own (1 Cor. 2:11–12). At the opportune time, the true God of love answers our call in his love. All things then become new under God's powerful transforming love. We all do well, then, to seek and to appropriate the available evidence of God's reality, however morally challenging the process is. Our adventure of learning to love as God loves will then begin and never fail. God's love, once received by grace, never fails. Let us, then, taste and see.

PART 2

# REVELATION
# AND SCRIPTURE

# 4

# DIVINE REVELATION

## Discernment and Interpretation

≫| **Bruce Reichenbach** |≪

$I$F PHILOSOPHY IS TO ASSIST theology as it addresses critical questions of revelation, it will best do so by attending to the fundamental questions it asks of all subjects. Philosophy's tasks are multiple but include (though are not restricted to) determining the meaning of key concepts, the clarification of the questions to be asked or issues to be raised, and the development and careful assessment of justifications given for truth claims. In what follows, I want to apply these three tasks to the topic of revelation, beginning first with understanding what is meant by revelation.

## WHAT IS REVELATION?

Before attending to the features of revelation, we need to note the ambiguity of the term. "Revelation" can stand for the *act* of revealing something that was hidden ("His revelation of his role in the swindle brought tears to his eyes"), for *what* is revealed ("God's revelation to

Moses contained the instructions that he should return to Egypt"), and the *means* by which what is revealed is conveyed ("The Scriptures are God's revelation to Christians on how to be reconciled with God"). In this the word "revelation" is not unique; it is similar to "production," which likewise is ambiguous between the act of producing, what is produced, and the means by which the product is conveyed (production line). As we proceed, it will be important to bear in mind these different uses—act, content, medium—of the term.

Let us begin with delineating eight important features of revelation. *First*, although it plays a central role in the three major Western religions, revelation is not strictly a religious concept. "Revelation" or "reveal" can be used in many contexts.

(1) John revealed to the investigator that he was the person who robbed the bank.
(2) The bloodstain on his trousers revealed to the investigator that John was involved in the bank robbery.

As we will observe, the theologian can learn a great deal about revelation by observing how the term and its cognates are used in secular or ordinary contexts. Identifying God as the revealing agent adds stronger truth content to the ordinary concept of revelation.

*Second*, revelation in general is the disclosure of something that was hidden. One should be careful to delineate from whom what was revealed had been hidden. If revelation is to occur, what is revealed must be hidden from the revealee; the revelation must be about something the revealee did not yet know. At the same time, this prior ignorance about what is revealed need not be a general ignorance. In statement 1, it is possible that others, e.g., John's compatriots in the crime, knew that he robbed the bank; it becomes a revelation only to the investigator who did not know this fact. Or consider this:

(3) The moral lapse revealed Jane's true character.

Jane's friends might already have known what her character was like; it becomes a revelation only to someone who did not know this fact. Hence, although the revealee should be ignorant of what is revealed, the revelation need not convey new information per se. This has theological import not only in allowing for continuing revelation but possibly by providing a test for the authenticity of continuing revelation. If one has an accepted past revelation, one might compare current revelation claims with that past revelation to establish their reliability or genuineness. The new revelation (as content) need not be new to everyone, but it might not have been known to the revealee who received it. We will return to the significance of this point for theology later on when we address the question of whether revelation (act) is ongoing.

*Third*, statements 1 and 2 show that revelation as an act can be formulated in various ways. For example, statement 1 might be generalized to this:

(4) B revealed r to C, where B and C are persons and r is something revealed (content).

We will term this *agent revelation* because in this type of case the agent, or revealer, is indicated or specified.

Statement 2 might be generalized to this:

(5) e revealed r to C, where e is some thing, place, act, or event.

The term e might be a document ("The Pentagon Papers revealed the extent to which the Johnson administration misled the American people in the Gulf of Tonkin affair"), a state of affairs ("The brown, dying leaves hanging from the branches revealed that the tree had fallen prey to oak wilt"), statistics ("The most recent census data on home ownership reveal the extent to which the Hmong have become integrated into American society in the last twenty-five years"), a place ("Turning a corner, he encountered a dead end, which revealed that he had taken a wrong turn somewhere in the town"), or an event ("The pattern of explosives placed in the rural mailboxes revealed that the bomber was creating a happy face"). We will call this *manifestational revelation.*[1]

The Christian theologian has in Scripture both agent and manifestational revelation. For a case of agent revelation, the theologian might focus on Jesus's statement in response to Peter's confession that Jesus is the Christ, the Son of the living God: "This was not revealed to you by man, but by my Father in heaven" (Matt. 16:17 NIV).

Another example of statement 4 is this:

(6) The Father revealed to Peter that Jesus is the Christ, the Son of the living God.

An instance of statement 5—manifestational revelation—is found in Romans 1:17, "In the gospel, a righteousness from God is revealed" (NIV):

---

1. George Mavrodes, *Revelation in Religious Belief* (Philadelphia: Temple University Press, 1988), ch. 3.

(7) The gospel reveals the righteousness of God.

One might note several differences between agent and manifestational revelation. First, whereas it is clear in agent revelation—statement 4—that an agent brings about the revelation, whether there was an agent in manifestational revelation is not necessarily germane to the revelation. Consider this statement:

(8) The garish tie and cut of his suit revealed his poor taste in clothes.

The clothes were not the agent of the revelation but the occasion for it. This is not to say that no agent was involved or that the agent might not be important. In revelation that manifests God, as we will see, we can readily translate manifestational revelation accounts into agent revelation.

A second difference concerns the matter of intentionality. In agent revelation the question of intention arises; the revealing may be intentional (the revealer wants the revealee to know) or unintentional (the revealer may reveal something to the revealee by a slip of the tongue, as in this:

(9) The double agent revealed his duplicity to his contact by absent-mindedly telling her secret information about the war plans.

It may be quite important to the revealee to discover whether the revelation was intended or accidental. The intentional utterance of the code word might have an entirely different significance from the unintentional slip of the spy. The question of intention does not arise, however, in manifestational revelation, since agent actions are unspecified. Whether the wearer intended to reveal his poor taste is unspecified and not a part of the revelational content. Rather, emphasis is placed on the thing or event as the occasion for the revelation. Intention would come into play only if we translated manifestational revelation into agent revelation.

Indeed, in manifestational revelation the emphasis might be more rightly placed on the revealee, for the revealee takes the event as a revelation. That is, since the revealee understands the event as revealing something, manifestational revelation can be interpreted as a case of seeing-as, as in "Judy saw the inkblot as a pair of birds." Interpreting manifestational revelation as seeing-as does not remove the possibility that such events can be translated into agent revelation language, but doing so shifts the focus from the interpreter (the one who sees it as) to the originator and, usually, the intender. Both involve interpretation, but in different modes. Interpretation in manifestational revelation inquires whether the seeing-as is a proper and justified account of the event; interpretation in agent revelation inquires whether the revealee has properly understood and interpreted the revealer. We will return to interpretation in the second part.

A third difference can be found in Wolterstorff's suggestion that the difference between agent and manifestational revelation is located in the means used in the revelation. Whereas manifestational revelation requires that the means be a natural sign (indicator, symptom) of what is revealed, agent revelation does not. Wolterstorff does not tell us what he means by "natural sign," but one might infer that it refers to some kind of relationship (causal, symbolic) that connects the sign with what is revealed.

Wolterstorff calls revelations akin to statement 4 propositional revelations, in that although the means of revelation might not employ propositions or assertions, this kind of revelation "cannot occur without propositions being entertained and transmitted."[2] The reason for this is that agent revelation, as revelation often intended by the revealer, proceeds through the knowledge or understanding of the revealer. As such, it is "knowledge-transmitting revelation." One might, however, reply that it is not the employment of propositions that distinguishes between agent and manifestational revelation. In manifestational revelation the revealee often can formulate what is revealed in terms of propositions. Further, most but not all agent revelation is transmitted or entertained through propositions. As Gracia writes, "What is revealed is always expressible in a proposition, although there are two exceptions to this: (i) when the aim of revelation is not to produce understanding but some other effect on the receiver, such as an emotion; and (ii) when revelation is deemed to be beyond intellectual grasp, as happens with mystical experiences."[3]

*Fourth*, agent revelation appears to include a triadic relation: a revealer, a person to whom the revelation is made, and that which is revealed. (Manifestational revelation likewise is triadic, but of a different sort: the event, the revealee, and what is revealed.) So understood, agent revelation partakes of the pattern found in acts of communication, where there is a communicator, one communicated to, and something communicated. In this respect, agent revelation differs from other modes of discourse, such as asserting or promising, that may or may not involve communication. For example:

2. Nicholas Wolterstorff, *Divine Discourse* (Cambridge: Cambridge University Press, 1995), 28.

3. Jorge J. E. Gracia, *How Can We Know What God Means?* (New York: Palgrave, 2001), 4; propositions in quote renumbered to avoid confusion.

(10)  George W. Bush asserted that Iraq had sought to procure material for weapons of mass destruction from an African country.

(11)  She promised that she would be a better mother to her children.

It might seem that an act of asserting or promising is triadic, and normally this is the case. We usually assume that when someone makes an assertion or a promise, the assertion was heard or promise made to someone. In statement 10, however, it is possible that the president was practicing his speech alone in the Oval Office or wrote it on a piece of paper. In such a case, there is no necessity that the sentence has an indirect object regarding to whom, if anyone, he made the assertion. Likewise, in statement 11 the woman might have made a promise to no one in particular or only to herself. So, although these forms of acts are generally transitive (someone actually comes to know or believe something by means of the assertion or the promise), there is no necessity that they be such. That is, they can be intransitive.

Can agent revelation be intransitive? Can an agent reveal without a revealee coming to believe something by means of the revelation? Wolterstorff suggests that "reveal" might have two uses or senses. "According to one of these, a condition of properly predicating 'has revealed X' of some agent is that someone actually [has] come to know X by means of the agent's disclosing it; according to the other, what's necessary is only that the agent make X knowable to appropriately qualified observers, not that anyone actually [has] come to know it by means of the disclosure."[4] He suggests the following as a proper use of "reveal":

(12)  "The old man revealed the location of the jewels in a document he wrote just before his death; but by then his hand was so unsteady that none of us has yet been able to decipher what he wrote."[5]

Two questions in this discussion need to be distinguished: (a) does an act of revealing require a revealee, and (b) must the revealee think or believe that a revelation has taken place for there to be a revelation? Clearly, an affirmative response to question b presupposes an affirmative response to question a. But in revelation can one have an affirmative response to question a without affirming question b? One might consider three possibilities:

4. Wolterstorff, *Divine Discourse*, 31.
5. Ibid., 299 n. 10.

- Revelation can occur without a revealee: the answer to question a is no, such that agent revelation need not be triadic.

- Revelation needs a revealee but does not require that the revealee have any beliefs brought about by the revelation: the answer to question a is yes, but revelation can be intransitive.

- Revelation needs both a revealee and a recognition or belief about the revelation on the part of the revealee: the answer to question a is yes, but revelation must be transitive.

Let us address question a first. Consider a slight revision of statement 2:

(13) The bloodstain on his trousers revealed that he was involved in the bank robbery.

The manifestational revelation found in statement 13 does not provide a clear answer to question a or b. But consider a further modification of statement 2:

(14) The bloodstain on his trousers revealed that he was involved in the bank robbery, though no one took any notice, and he passed off into the night.

The bloodstain on the trousers could be considered a natural sign that he was involved in the crime, and there is no objection that he did not intend to reveal the stain, since this is a case of manifestational revelation. Manifestational revelation, it would seem, can occur without anyone realizing it or entertaining beliefs because of it. This seems consistent with a quote from Isaiah, "Every valley shall be raised up, every mountain and hill made low; the rough ground shall become level, the rugged places a plain. And the glory of the LORD will be revealed, and all mankind together will see it" (40:4–5 NIV). What is interesting is that the last sentence has two independent clauses: the first affirms that a revelation has taken place; the second, that it will be observed. The structure of the sentence seems to allow that the first could occur without the second. It is at least possible that these events could occur without humans taking any notice of their significance as revealing God's glory.

Something similar can be said about agent revelation. Consider a revision of statement 1:

(15) John revealed that he was the person who robbed the bank.

It might happen that John reveals that he is the robber but no one believes him because they all know him to be an upright fellow. It might even happen that he shows them the money but they do not pay attention to his revelation, taking it for a prank. In effect, it is possible that A reveals something to B but B either pays no attention to the revelation or does not believe what A revealed. Consider the following:

(16) God revealed to Moses that he had appointed him to a specific task.

Such a statement is possible without Moses understanding or believing that he was called to the task (which in fact Moses did not believe at first). The revelation to Moses might be too esoteric or ambiguous, or it might be contrary to what Moses believes is his vocation in life. In such a case, one could say that a revelation (an act) had taken place—God revealed something to Moses—but that Moses was not receptive and hence failed to recognize that a revelation had occurred.[6]

Something seems odd about the claims that manifestational and agent revelation can be intransitive. The puzzlement seems clearest with manifestational revelation. If no witness attached any significance to the manifesting event, there would be no seeing of the e (the event) "as," which we noted to be a central feature to manifestational revelation. For the garish tie in statement 8 to reveal the wearer's poor taste, someone must take it as revealing poor taste. Otherwise it is a mere fact that he is wearing a garish tie. Similarly with the glory of God; unless someone sees these events as revealing God's glory, it is difficult to see that God's glory has been revealed or manifested.

Agent revelation is even trickier. Perhaps one way of addressing the problem is to ask whether "reveal" is being used as an "act" verb or a communication verb. A verb such as "assert" is an "act" verb; it requires neither an audience nor any response on the part of a listener. Return to statement 10 above. Bush can successfully assert, by uttering, the relevant sentences regarding Iraq. But from his uttering the sentences it does not follow that he communicated with anyone. Only if someone heard and understood the assertion can we affirm that communication between Bush and his hearer took place. "Inform," however, is a communication verb. And here is where the ambiguity arises. On the one hand, it seems that we can use "inform" as an act verb:

6. Roderic A. Girle, "The Concept of Revelation," *Australasian Journal of Philosophy* 65/4 (1987): 470–82.

(17)  The sergeant informed his lieutenant over the radio that civilians were still in the village, but the lieutenant didn't understand the transmission.

Here "inform" is being used in the sense of an act verb; it is an act that the sergeant performed with respect to his lieutenant. It is not, however, functioning as a communication verb, for the receiver of the information did not understand what was communicated. For communication to occur, to be successful, the communicator must address a communicatee, and the communicatee must understand something of what the communicator is communicating, that is, be able to form some belief on the basis of the communication. Hence, one might distinguish between attempted communication (an act verb only) and successful communication. To be a successful communication (as over against an attempted communication), revealing requires transitivity.

It seems that "reveal," as used in agent revelation, can be used like "inform." When used merely as an act, the agent discloses something that is hidden, but it is at best an attempted communication. To be successful, revelation must be a communication, whether intentional or unintentional—the double agent communicated something even though he did not intend to. If the revealee cannot decipher the revelation, so that what was to be revealed remains hidden, then we have a disclosure from an agent who *attempted* a revelation but not a *successful* revelation. As such, successful agent revelation—as distinct from attempted agent revelation—is, like other forms of communication, triadic and transitive. Where no communication occurred, one would best say that the agent revealed (as an act)—or, better, attempted to reveal—something.[7]

In sum, then, we have two senses of "reveal." "Reveal" can be used like "exhibit," as in statement 12, where one can exhibit something that was hidden but without communication occurring; in this context, revelation can be intransitive. When one is concerned with agent revelation as a form of communication, it must be treated transitively. Theologically, God can reveal his glory (as an act), but unless humans perceive it, no divine communication has occurred.

*Fifth*, what things might be revealed? Observe the following:

7. Obviously this solution in terms of distinguishing successful from attempted revelation will not work with manifestational revelation. This is why I resolved the latter in terms of the notion of "understanding-as." For example, one can make a statement such as statement 17 only because someone (a third party?) understands it as a revelation. If no one understood it thus or so interpreted it, statement 17 could not make a great deal of sense, for it would claim that it was a revelation, but no one understood it as a revelation.

(18) In the vision Jesus revealed to Paul that he should go to Damascus and wait for someone to visit him with important information.

(19) The magician pulled the curtain aside to reveal a woman in a box sawed in two.

(3) The moral lapse revealed Jane's true character.

(20) Jesus's glance at Peter revealed that Jesus knew that Peter had denied him.

Obviously a great many things can be revealed: propositions as in statement 18 (A might make statements to B that reveal certain truths), persons as in statement 19, states of affairs as in statement 3, and items of knowledge as in statement 20. These should not be taken as mutually exclusive, for one could make propositional claims about the woman revealed in the box (that she was sawed in two). The important point here is that although diverse things can be revealed and although the revelation might not itself be propositional, what is revealed usually can be described by propositions. At the same time, it is possible that some things might be revealed that are not propositional. For example, as we noted above, God might be revealed in mystical experience that is too profound to be expressed propositionally. The important point here is the fact that the revealee's inability to describe propositionally what was revealed does not count against the fact that it might have been a revelation.

*Sixth,* what is the medium of revelation? Theologians distinguish between general revelation and special revelation. In general revelation, where God communicates himself to all persons at all times and places, the medium is usually conceived to be nature ("The heavens declare the glory of God; the skies proclaim the work of his hands. Day after day they pour forth speech; night after night they display knowledge" [Ps. 19:1–2 NIV]; "For since the creation of the world God's invisible qualities—his eternal power and divine nature—have been clearly seen, being understood from what has been made" [Rom. 1:20 NIV]) or history (which reveals God's power to control the destinies of the nations). These would be appropriate instances of manifestational revelation. In special revelation, God communicates to particular persons at particular times or places. Here the media may be historical events (the exodus from Egypt), special experiences (Saint Theresa sensing God's presence as she sat in the chapel), or specific messages or communications (Scripture).

Much twentieth-century theological ink was spilled over the question whether the Bible was itself a propositional revelation, communicating divine truth, or rather the medium of revealing God himself in the person of Jesus Christ. The former view, held by orthodoxy, led to the emphasis on believing and affirming truths about God and God's purposes and actions. The latter, advanced by neoorthodox theologians, stressed that revelation was to bring us to a divine encounter and from there to trust and commitment. Neoorthodoxy held that Scripture is a means, a locus, where we encounter God. Neoorthodoxy did not deny truths, but it held that they were not divinely communicated. Rather, they grow out of the relationships or encounters we have with God. The Bible is the fallible witness to these revelatory encounters in the past and the locus for contemporary personal encounters with God.

There is no need to treat the options disjunctively. Consider the following:

(21) In her novel the author revealed that she had a great love for animals.

How might one learn of her love? She might have said so in the novel, where autobiographical statements are allowed. Or one might infer this from the detailed descriptions the author gives of animals and their care, or from the connotations where language was used to disparage persons who abused animals. Or one might, through the novel, meet the author herself. The author's personality is revealed through the novel in such a way that reading the novel is the medium by which we encounter her. In fact, all these are simultaneously possible because the "or" is not exclusive. That is, the novel can be considered propositionally a revelation of her and at the same time a means or locus for encountering her. Similarly with the Scriptures. The text can be considered a propositional revelation and at the same time the locus wherein we encounter God in Jesus Christ. Indeed, it seems that both aspects are critical for properly understanding divine revelation, for without propositions we have no way of making sure that our doctrines are correct. Even the great proponents of nonpropositional revelation, such as Karl Barth, write volumes in which they cite Scripture for their purposes. And without the living Word, the objective words can become mere items of knowledge and not lead to conviction and commitment.

This leads to a broader question that in particular addresses the status of Scripture. The question concerns whether Scripture is merely a record of revelation to particular individuals in the past—Moses, Isaiah, Paul, Peter—so that by reading it we discover the revelations made to others. Because we have the Scriptures today, we do not need any additional, personal revelation from God. We can read about the experiences of these biblical greats and glean from them what God wants us to know about salvation and Christian living. "We can share their beliefs without sharing their experiences."[8] Or is personal revelation necessary for us today to encounter God, for, since the Bible is specific about the events that it addresses directly, it cannot provide guidance "particularized enough to the specificities of [our] own circumstances to serve [our] spiritual needs"?[9] We need new revelation from God to let us know what God wants us to do here and now. The Bible and other writings thus become the occasion for God speaking to us. God speaks to me just as he spoke to the biblical greats. The Bible, other writings, and events are the media of revelation.

Here again we might think of rejecting this disjunctive way of thinking. One might hold that the Scriptures are the record of revelation to particular persons—a record from which we can glean truths for formulating doctrine and principles for living—and at the same time conceive of Scripture as the medium that God uses to reveal himself to individuals. It might, for example, be a tool used by the Holy Spirit to guide us in revelatory fashion in particular ways. The latter presupposes that revelation is ongoing (see the second section of this chapter).

*Seventh*, since revelation is at times propositional, revelation is connected with truth and hence with knowledge. Consider the following claims:

(22) B revealed to me that Jesus will come again, but I don't believe he will come again.
(23) B revealed to C that Jesus will come again, but I don't believe he will come again.

Now compare statements 22 and 23 with these:

(24) B asserted to me that Jesus will come again, but I don't believe he will come again.
(25) B asserted to C that Jesus will come again, but I don't believe he will come again.

Whereas statements 22 and 23 are paradoxical and puzzling, neither statement 24 nor statement 25 is paradoxical. That is, C can accept that B has asserted something without C accepting or knowing it as true. Accepting the assertion does not commit C to anything. But if C accepts that B has revealed something, then C has affirmed the grounds for ad-

8. George Mavrodes, "Revelation and the Bible," *Faith and Philosophy* 6/4 (1989): 402.
9. Ibid., 406.

mitting that what is revealed is true. That is, provided what is revealed is true, C, in accepting that a revelation has occurred, has knowledge. C could, of course, deny that B revealed anything; C could claim that B was simply making it up or lying. But should C accept B as making a revelation, to deny that what is revealed is true is paradoxical.[10]

The point here is that revelation is a way or means of knowing the truth of a proposition. C might not know the truth of the proposition r in the same way as B knows r (B might not know it on the basis of revelation), but if C accepts that B is making a revelation about r, then, provided that r is true and C had not known r before, C now knows it on the basis of revelation. Successful revelation, consequently, can be a source of knowledge.

A very important caveat, however, is necessary. It does not follow from this insight that C understands r in the same way that B understands r. That B has revealed r to C does not guarantee that C interprets r in the way that B understands r or intends r to be interpreted. This leads us into matters regarding the interpretation of revelation, to which we will return at the end.

*Eighth*, who is the audience (the C) of the revelation? Insofar as agent revelation entails successful communication, the agent intends an audience. When B reveals r, B reveals r to a particular person or persons. B might have as B's intended audience not only the immediate hearer/receiver of the revelation but nonimmediate (future) receivers of the revelation. This introduces the possibility that the revelation may have many meanings: one meaning for the immediate hearer of the revelation and others for future receivers. This may be the case not only for agent revelation, where B intends a diverse set of messages for different audiences, but also for manifestational revelation, where diverse audiences may interpret e differently. It becomes clear that there is no straightforward way of proceeding from the understanding of the revealees to the intent of the revealer or to any normative meaning of the manifestation. No matter how much one attempts to guarantee the revelation (content)—for example, by claims of infallibility or inerrancy—this has little effect in assuring particular interpretations of the revelation. We will return to this discussion also at the end of the paper.

We have clarified what is meant by "revelation" and have noted some of the important issues that arise from this analysis. The philosopher is concerned with what we mean by the terms we use, that is, how we un-

---

10. Whereas Girle, "The Concept of Revelation," 474, says that B has contradicted himself, Mavrodes, "Revelation and the Bible," 100, notes that it is only paradoxical but neither self-contradictory nor necessarily false.

derstand the concepts. Only once this is done can we move on to carefully address the issues and to give and analyze the proffered justifications.

## Taxonomy of Issues

In this attempt to delineate what is meant by revelation, I have hinted at important issues. To make theological progress, we now need to identify and address the most important of these outstanding issues.

### *What Is the Role of Context in Revelation?*

One of the more interesting questions about divine revelation concerns the background beliefs one must have to receive a revelation or, better, to believe that oneself or another has been revealed to. In the context of agent divine revelation, it seems that one must have a prior belief not only that God exists but that God is the kind of being who can reveal his person, desires, or specific information to individuals. If one must have such a prior belief, then divine revelation would not be the proper basis for coming to believe in God; to hold that God used a specific communication to reveal God's existence would presuppose that one already believed that God existed. For example, when Saul set out to persecute the Christians in Damascus, he did not doubt the existence of God or even that Jesus had existed. What he doubted was the significance of Jesus. Thus Saul's question "Who are you, Lord?" requests identification of the voice (Acts 9:4–5). This may be one reason Richard Swinburne begins his discussion of revelation per se by marshaling background presuppositions. He believes that we have evidence that makes it likely that an all-powerful and good God exists who not only could intervene in history but could and would reveal things to us.[11] Background beliefs about the existence of a God of a certain sort are a foundational piece on which Swinburne builds.

But suppose we consider manifestational revelation; must one believe that events and so forth have the property of being possibly revelatory? Without having a prior belief that God exists, could someone believe that a sunset reveals God's existence? Richard Rolle writes, "I was sitting in a certain chapel, and while I was taking pleasure in the delight of some prayer or meditation, I suddenly felt within me an unwonted and pleasant fire. When I had for long doubted whence it came, I learned by experience that it came from the Creator and not from the creature,

---

11. Richard Swinburne, *Revelation* (Oxford: Oxford University Press, 1992), 69–70.

since I found it ever more pleasing and full of heat."[12] Since Rolle was in prayer, it seems that he already had a prior concept of God and God's existence.

But consider the case of the current SETI program—the Search for Extraterrestrial Intelligence. The program looks for a mathematically sophisticated sequence that the appeal to chance is unlikely to explain. The presence of such a sequence, it is claimed, would provide evidence of intelligent extraterrestrial life. The investigators in such a program do not presume that intelligent life exists elsewhere in the universe; nor do they presume that its intelligence would be displayed in mathematically sophisticated ways. What they presume is that such life is possible (not actual) and that possibly it is mathematically sophisticated, so that the discovery of mathematical sequences would help confirm the existence of such life. That is, the SETI program need not presuppose that such beings exist, only that it is possible that they exist and would attempt to communicate with other intelligent beings. The discovery of such sequences would be evidence for alien existence and their ability to communicate.

We might say the same thing about divine revelation. Believing that there can be revelation presupposes that there *can* be a God who is capable of revealing himself. Affirming that such and such is a reasonable candidate for a revelation would help confirm that a God of this sort exists. Of course, this leaves us with the task of identifying a revelation (in the same way that the SETI investigators are faced with the task of showing that the sequence of numbers they receive is not random but the product of intelligence). In this light, the question about control beliefs becomes not whether the existence of a God of a revealing sort is presumed but what characteristics of a presumed revelation would indicate that God really does exist and has revealed himself. For Rolle to understand that the event revealed God rather than some other being, he would have, at the very least, some fairly well formed idea of what God would be like were he to exist and to reveal himself in this fashion.

The more critical issue relates to the question posed earlier in this chapter: what is the nature of the natural signs in manifestational revelation? When the psalmist says that the heavens declare God's glory (Ps. 19:1), he makes the heavens a sign of God's existence and glory. But how are the heavens a natural sign (to use Wolterstorff's terminology) of God? One might approach this instance of general revelation on the emotional level, suggesting that the very awesomeness of the heavens and the power manifested in them make them a natural sign of

12. Richard Rolle, "I Sleep and My Heart Wakes," in *Varieties of Mystic Experience*, ed. Elmer O'Brien (New York: Holt, Rinehart & Winston, 1964), 161.

a truly wise and powerful being. On the intellectual level, the universe has been frequently interpreted as a natural sign because of its teleological structure. The careful, detailed ordering of the means to the ends is taken as a sign of God's existence. But many in our post-Darwinian age have countered both of these contentions. The very vastness of the universe and the seemingly random rise of conscious beings eliminate any natural-sign connection between the universe and God. Further, the means-ends ordering is sometimes manifest but also at times absent and, when present, can be best accounted for not as revelatory of God's existence but as the result of random mutations naturally selected in a constantly changing environment.

The question of context, then, becomes particularly poignant when manifestational or general revelation is in view. If the theologian wants to speak about general revelation, whether it be in nature or history, attention must be paid to the way in which the manifestation is a (natural) sign of what is revealed and of the revealer. What is there about natural events that leads persons to see the universe as a revelation or handiwork of God? What is there about historical events—the preservation of Israel, the Allies' victory in World War II, and so on—that is revelatory of God and God's providence? And how is this translated into meaningful propositions about God?

If this analysis of manifestational revelation holds true in that it presupposes the possibility but not the actuality of God and if, as argued in the first section, manifestational propositions usually can be translated into agent propositions, might the same hold for agent revelation? That is, could not one say that agent revelation does not presuppose the existence of God but only need presuppose that a God of a certain sort is possible? If God exists and has a certain nature, this is the kind of revelation that we would expect. In this case, should such a revelation occur, it would help confirm the existence of such a being. In short, neither agent nor manifestational revelation presupposes that God exists in a way that would prejudge the revelation. Rather, they presuppose that God of a certain sort is possible, and should apparent communication or events of a certain sort (content) occur, this would provide additional reasons for thinking that God is actual as well. In short, revelation can be the ground for knowledge about the divine as well as about other things revealed.

### Is Revelation Necessary?

If revelation works within a certain context of prior beliefs (what Wolterstorff calls control beliefs) about what is possible, the question arises whether revelation is necessary in any sense for religious faith. In his treatment of revelation, Swinburne indicates that divine revelation is a priori probable, given the existence of God and certain beliefs about what God desires. But he does not contend that revelation is necessary. At the same time, humans need information about moral truths, about how to apply these moral truths, about the process of atonement for sins, and about the afterlife. The issue is whether we can discover this by ourselves or whether "we need help from above, in order to understand the deepest reality."[13] For Swinburne, it is good but not necessary for God to supply this through revelation.

The answer to the question at hand depends on the phrase "Necessary for what?" If one answers that it is necessary for salvation, then the attempt to answer this question links revelation with a host of other doctrines. For one, it connects with views regarding the nature and extent of the effect of the fall on humans. Did the fall so affect our mental capacities that we are incapable of discovering the human predicament on our own, or are the effects on our understanding and knowledge only partial, so that revelation is not necessary but only a welcome aid? It also connects with views regarding the nature of the human predicament. If the predicament involves God (e.g., separation from God), revelation might be necessary to comprehend the nature of the predicament, its extent, and the way to resolve it. Without some guidance from God on these matters, we are involved in intellectual bootstrapping. In short, divine revelation should tell us things that we cannot discover for ourselves. Hence, the question of the necessity of revelation for salvation cannot be answered apart from a consideration of other doctrines related to salvation, the limits of human knowing, and divine purposes.

The question becomes more difficult when one asks whether revelation is necessary to discern and apply moral truths. Can we, by reason, discover how we are to live? Typical utilitarian or Kantian deontological ethical theories have no need of revelation. By experience and reason, we can figure out what ends are intrinsically desirable and whether they are beneficial to the greatest number of persons concerned. Kant proposes that by use of mere reason we can construct from maxims universal principles that guide our actions. On the other hand, some theists advocate a divine-command theory of ethics, according to which ethical principles are rooted in God's commands. And these commands are expressions either of God's will or, more likely, his nature and character.[14] One might acquire these ethical insights in several ways. They might be held to be innate, coming to us through our conscience. Others in the natural-

---

13. Swinburne, *Revelation*, 74.

14. Philip Quinn, *Divine Commands and Moral Requirements* (Oxford: Oxford University Press, 1978); Robert Adams, *The Virtue of Faith* (Oxford: Oxford University Press, 1987), chs. 7 and 9.

law tradition of ethics hold that ethical norms are derivable by reason from the study of natural laws or human nature. Yet others hold that divine commands are accessible by revelation. Only if we are restricted to deriving knowledge of moral truths in the last way would revelation be necessary rather than a mere aid to knowing moral truths. But even here revelation may be taken broadly to include general revelation and hence needs the use of human reason to discern the content of the moral truths, a position advocated by Paul in Romans 1.

### Is Revelation Ongoing?

One of the more difficult questions the theologian faces is whether divine revelation can be ongoing or whether it came to an end during the apostolic period. Some suggest that revelation ended with the death of the last apostle.[15] After Christ and the apostles, the church collected the records of the revelation, canonized them, and through the centuries interpreted this revelation. The Bible is a record of God's revelation to the prophets and to the apostles through the life and teachings of Jesus.

Swinburne's argument for the finality of divine revelation is twofold. "If the church had become the vehicle of new revelation, then there would no longer be an 'original revelation' whose meaning and consequences Church members could tease out by argument and experience and interpret for the benefit of other cultures, and many of the advantages alleged for a revelation (God reveals to us that he wants us to do supererogatory acts to make us supremely worthy for the life of heaven, to enable us to blunt arguments against the existence of God, and to provide information on what the atonement is and how it is provided) would not be available."[16]

For Swinburne, the original revelation encompasses the teaching of God to the Israelites and the teachings of Jesus Christ. Swinburne's unification of the two teachings stems from his treatment of the Bible as a whole, as one record of revelation. But this holistic treatment hides the fact that even in this original revelation, revelation was progressive in that the revelation of the teachings of Jesus in the New Testament both teases out themes present in the Old Testament and contains new revelations. The new revelation in Jesus Christ does not negate the teaching(s) of God to the Israelites: "I have come not to abolish but to fulfill" (Matt. 5:17). But this affirmation does not prohibit Jesus's bringing a new revelation: "You have heard that it was said to those of ancient times. . . . But I say to you . . ." (Matt. 5:21). Indeed, Swinburne himself notes that "Jesus

15. Swinburne, *Revelation*, 102.
16. Ibid., 119.

himself taught and the apostles taught that some of that [Old Testament] teaching had been misunderstood and some was of only temporary and limited application."[17]

The advantages Swinburne specifies likewise provide an inadequate basis to rule out new revelation beyond the apostles. Just as the biblical revelation was progressive, so might the new revelation, for the needs and context have changed. For example, since the issues and cultures twenty centuries after Christ are quite different, one might expect a new word from the Lord regarding how to act in this new context. Although the new word will not necessarily conflict with the old word, it still can be considered a new revelation.

One might advance theological arguments for restricting revelation to the pre-apostolic and apostolic eras, that with Jesus we have the full and final revelation of God—"Whoever has seen me has seen the Father" (John 14:9). But if God is infinite and transcendent, one would think that new revelations of who God is would be in order, since past revelations would be unable to fully capture the being of God. It would seem reasonable that God continually wants to reveal himself throughout the centuries rather than restrict his conversation to a relatively brief interval in human history. Although Swinburne says that God continues to speak through the interpretations of the church, the very fallibility of the church and the existence of multiple cultures suggest the need for continued divine revelation.[18] If God does not speak to me or my contemporaries, why should I think that he spoke in the past to others? Why should Moses and Solomon, Isaiah and Micah, Paul and the apostles be so privileged?

The role of the Holy Spirit is ambiguous here. If one develops a robust doctrine of the Holy Spirit, where the Spirit guides believers into all truth (John 16:13), one might see this guidance as revelatory. It is not that the work of the Holy Spirit necessarily is revelatory; not all acts of guidance are revelatory. If I give you a map of how to find the Pick-Them-Yourself Blueberry Farm, for example, it might be said that I have revealed the location of the farm to you. On the other hand, I might go along with you to the farm, and at every turn you might ask if you made the correct turn (based on a sketch you received on the farm's annual flyer), and I might assure you that you have or have not done so. Here I guide you according to a prior revelation of the location of the farm without myself doing the revealing. So one might interpret the ongoing work of the Holy Spirit in this second sense, as a guide using

17. Ibid., 101–2.
18. Peter Byrne, "A Defense of Christian Revelation," *Religious Studies* 29 (1993): 388–92.

the truths already revealed (rather than making new revelations)—if not in content, at least in application.[19] At the same time, however, a robust pneumatology certainly would allow for the ongoing work of the Holy Spirit to be revelatory.

If revelation is ongoing past the first century, the question arises: is what is revealed subsequent to the first century new information not contained in the Scriptures, or is it the application of the earlier revelation to individual lives? Allowing new revelations opens the door to all those who have, through the centuries, claimed additional revelations and on the basis of those claims created Christian or quasi-Christian sects (Christian Science, Mormonism, Unificationism). If the revelation of new truths continues, one needs to explore the claims of those who believe they have received additional revelations. We might invoke a "consistency with the original revelation" test to sort acceptable revelations from the unacceptable. But if Swinburne is correct that some of the original revelations had a temporary status (e.g., we are no longer under the Mosaic law), even this criterion might not be entirely helpful.

Taking the position that additional revelations do not provide new information but rather assist in the application of earlier-revealed truth to life sets the original texts as standards of what is revealed, and then seeks to use these texts to judge revelation claims in the cultural context of the day. The meaning of these original texts might be hidden, or it might not be clear how these texts are to be applied to our lives. Thus, continuing revelation is at least necessary to know how to apply or live out the truths recorded in the Bible as a record of divine revelation.

In effect, we have no definitive arguments to resolve the question. The infinity of God, the ongoing march of theology and culture, the need for personal guidance in human affairs, and significant numbers of reports of divine encounters or religious experience argue for the legitimacy of ongoing revelation. The finality of the revelation of God in Christ, the worry about the rise of sects rooted in new revelations, and the role of the Holy Spirit as a guide suggest the closure of revelation. Perhaps one way of reconciling these disparate positions is to suggest that revelation, as the conveying of information in a way that would be authoritative for the church as a whole, is no longer an option, but revelation of God and his purposes and direction in individual lives is ongoing. The medium for such might be the canon, but it might also be a personal word from or experience of God or even a manifestational revelation.

19. Mavrodes, "Revelation and the Bible," 408–9.

## How Can We Identify a Genuine Revelation?

Although we have spoken about revelation, it might be more appropriate to speak about revelation claims. This raises the question of how we can show that a revelation claim is truly a revelation. Philosophical discussion of this question often begins with John Locke, who held that faith is "the assent to any proposition, not made out by the deductions of reason, but upon the credit of the proposed, as coming from God, in some extraordinary way of communication," namely, revelation.[20] His sine qua non is that revelation cannot contradict our knowledge or reason. For Locke, reason is the foundation of all knowledge, and if revelation is allowed to contradict reason, all knowledge is overthrown. But what positive evidence must accompany the revelation claim? One cannot require that revelation be provable by reason; otherwise revelation would be unnecessary. Locke suggests that revelation often, though not necessarily, is accompanied by outward signs (miracles) that attest not to the truth of the revelation (that is guaranteed by God) but to the person conveying the revelation. Where there are no signs, we are left with conformity to reason and Scripture. Locke's justification, then, is given not only in terms of the rational content of the revelation but also in terms of its circumstances. One is more justified in accepting a purported revelation if one can see that its content is reasonable and that it is accompanied by some external mark.

Unfortunately, Locke's criteria are not very helpful. The first presupposes that the divine mysteries are not contrary to reason. This may be the case; many Christians argue for the reasonableness of Christianity. But others contend mysteries such as the incarnation and the Trinity are not comprehensible by reason. More troublesome, however, are Locke's positive criteria. That a revelation is accompanied by an outward sign may indeed be helpful in cases of what Locke refers to as original revelation (i.e., signs to the person to whom God is speaking). But they are not helpful in cases of traditional revelation, where other persons are attempting to accredit the revealee. Unless the outward sign is still visible to the accreditors, they are as dependent upon the revealee's report of the miraculous sign as upon their account of the alleged revelation. To use Locke's examples, we have no more evidence that Moses saw an unconsumed burning bush or that Gideon saw his dry fleece than that God spoke to them.[21] The outward sign is at best an aid to the original revealee, though not to be disparaged for that. Further, Locke's appeal to Scripture as an "unerring rule" or criterion is patently question begging. If one is searching for criteria to accredit any revelation, one

20. John Locke, *An Essay Concerning Human Understanding* 4.23.2.
21. Mavrodes, "Revelation and the Bible," 407.

cannot appeal to unaccredited revelation to sanction other revelation. Scripture, much of which comes without an outward sign, would have to be accredited first. Locke is guilty of the same circularity of which he accuses the enthusiasts.

Wolterstorff gravitates to what he terms a historical answer to our question.[22] He argues that a good ground for the plausibility that the Bible is an instrument of divine revelation is the apostolic grounding of the New Testament.[23] "[The apostles] had been commissioned by God through Jesus to be witnesses to Jesus. . . . Thus there emerged an apostolic teaching about Jesus and his significance which had the status in the church of being normative."[24] In effect, the apostles were commissioned to speak on behalf of Jesus and thereby on behalf of God. It is the apostolic teaching, or the teaching of those associated with the apostles, that the church eventually canonized. The teachings of Jesus are historically connected with the acceptance of the Bible as the record of revelation by the church.

This reliance on the commissioning of the transmitters of the tradition faces several difficulties. First, we learn about the commissioning from the very documents that we are asked to accept as records of the revelation. And we accept the records as authoritative because they are the records of that revelation. This argument parallels what we will speak about in the next section as the hermeneutical circle. Second, this kind of transmission criterion might be acceptable to those in the Christian tradition who accept Jesus as the revelation of God, but it would not be all that convincing of a response to the question that Wolterstorff introduces at the end of his discussion: "Is there good reason . . . for preferring, over all its competitors, the interpretative practice which operates on [the assumption that the Christian Bible is in fact a medium of divine discourse]?"[25] Perhaps this question is unanswerable, given Wolterstorff's contention that revelation is contextual; perhaps we have no overall context from which we can determine which revelation claim, as compared with its competitors, is to be preferred. But it seems that this question deserves some answer, given that, for example, Christians,

22. Wolterstorff, *Divine Discourse*, 206–8.

23. Wolterstorff carefully distinguishes between divine discourse and revelation, contending that not all divine discourse is revelatory. Although the distinction he makes is helpful, it is probably too sharp to carry the weight put upon it. See Paul Helm, "Speaking and Revealing," *Religious Studies* 37/3 (2001): 249–58; Phillip Quinn, "Can God Speak? Does God Speak?" *Religious Studies* 37/3 (2001): 259–69. Since our interest is in revelation, which in agent revelation is a mode of divine discourse, we will treat what Wolterstorff says about divine discourse as applying to divine revelation.

24. Wolterstorff, *Divine Discourse*, 292.

25. Ibid., 281.

whether they are exclusivists or inclusivists, recommend the narrative of atonement contained in the Bible.

Another way to go about answering our question is to develop a modified Lockean proposal to identify certain characteristics or traits that one would expect a divine revelation to manifest. What immediately strikes one is that the features often required of propositional revelation differ from those of manifestational revelation. With manifestational revelation, Wolterstorff contends that a natural sign must accord with the revelation. Oftentimes this natural sign is taken to be something like order, magnitude, or beauty. But why cannot chaos be a sign of divine general revelation? Or why not smallness rather than grandeur? If, as Christians hold, God created the entire universe, then we have no reason to focus on one set of features rather than another. The universe contains the small as well as the grandiose, the ugly as well as the beautiful, disorder and dysfunction as well as order and the functional, suffering and decay as well as happiness and life. In short, a clear connection between the sign and the revealer, though the heart of much natural theology, is not so obvious.

When we turn to agent revelation, the task initially seems easier. One would expect a propositional revelation to contain only true propositions and be about what is morally upright. Wolterstorff writes that it is appropriate to believe that God said something if it contains no contradictions, encourages purity of life and sound doctrine, contains no falsehoods, and relates to God's purposes dealing with faith and morals. Swinburne suggests that the revelation would contain details of what God is like, the atonement that is necessary to set things right, and information about the afterlife to encourage our pursuit of the good and character formation.[26]

Swinburne admits that this internal test and the Lockean miracle test, combined with the presupposed considerations that it is probable that God exists and reasonable to expect that God would incarnate himself and reveal himself to us, do not yield certainty. But he thinks this is a virtue rather than a detriment. The fact that we have to act on mere probability strengthens our resolve, for if the revelation and its attending miracles were too evident, we would be unable to make a rational choice not to choose the path to heaven. Working out our own moral views and helping others find the way is an advantage, something that would not be necessary were revelation easily recognizable to all. When revelation is not too easily discernible, people "can manifest their commitment to the goals which it offers by pursuing them when it is not certain that those goals are there to be had."[27]

26. Swinburne, *Revelation*, 85.
27. Ibid., 75.

Swinburne's argument not only presumes that our beliefs lie entirely within our rational control, a view much in dispute these days, but fails to account for the paradox that the One who partially hides the revelation—God—is the very One who stands as judge over whether heaven is to be awarded in any individual case.[28] God would have to be in a position to say, "Even if I had made revelation plainer, this person would not have accepted it." Ascribing such counterfactual knowledge of human free acts to God is dubious. Indeed, why has God made his revelation so obvious to some (witness Abram and Samuel in the Old Testament and Peter and Paul in the New Testament) and not to all?

Despite its promise, however, appealing to internal criteria remains problematic. The truth condition is often qualified. Swinburne, for example, notes that there is scope in scriptural revelation for some error and so for some correction of error.[29] To accommodate this, he qualifies the truth condition by distinguishing between the cultural presuppositions in which the message is cast (which may contain false statements) and the message of the revelation and between the literal and metaphorical interpretations. Although for Swinburne not just anything goes—the church has the function of controlling, expanding on, and interpreting what is given in Scripture, as the church fathers did when they metaphorically interpreted literally false statements—yet such an approach jeopardizes the appeal to truth as an internal test criterion.

Moreover, whether these anticipated internal features of informing us how to live moral lives and attain spiritual well-being are unique to the Christian scriptures or to revelation at all raises questions about whether God has made revelations to other cultures, what they are like, and how they comport with Christian claims to revelation. Questions about identifying revelation lead to further discussion about religious diversity.

### How Should We Interpret Revelation?

This brings us to our final issue. Revelation requires interpretation. This applies to both propositional and nonpropositional revelation. As we noted above, with the exception of what might be termed mystical revelation, what is revealed can be put in propositional form. This is not to say that the propositions fully capture the revelation, but insofar as the communication contains or aims to convey information, propositions are involved. And even where the intent is not to convey propositions but to convey emotions such as conviction and anger, the revealee has

28. Byrne, "A Defense," 385.
29. Swinburne, *Revelation*, 212.

to interpret the significance of what is revealed, including—in manifestational revelation—in what way and to what degree the revelation (content) is the sign of a revelation.

That said, let us focus more directly on the propositional aspect of revelation. Since the goal of interpretation is to produce some kind of understanding, it seems that at the very least we want an understanding of what the author (in divine revelation, God and the human author) intended to convey through the text.[30] Interpreters subsequent to the original revealee (audience) might also be interested in how the original audience understood the revelation. This is important not only for the historian who seeks to understand how the original audience or revealee understood the text but also for those who come afterward and attempt to understand the revelation, since one place to begin to understand the revelation is to understand how the original revealee understood it. We are under no obligation to understand the revelation in the same way that the original revealee understood the revelation, for the original revealee might have misunderstood it. But at the very least, what we can discern about this original interpretation provides a ground or basis for subsequent interpretations. If revelations have multiple audiences, including both the historically contemporaneous and future audiences, then the interpreter has to consider the possibility that the revelations legitimately may be interpreted in several ways as the audience changes.

The difficulty with interpretation in terms of authorial intent is the ascertainment of that intent in any non-question-begging way. The problem arises from what is termed the hermeneutical circle. "We can know authorial intentions only through the meaning of texts, but we can know the meaning of texts only through authorial intentions. If one holds that the meaning of a text is determined by the author's intentions, then knowledge of those intentions becomes indispensable for understanding the meaning of the text. But how are we to know those intentions? For intentionalists, the only source is the text itself."[31] The authorial-intention view "remains a mere formal desideratum without content," for we have no instructions how to grasp what the author intends. We cannot use the text alone without reference to the author, but we know the author through the text.[32]

Because of the hermeneutical circle (along with other reasons), philosophers have abandoned meaning interpretation. Instead, Gracia

---

30. God and the human author might have different intended meanings. For a helpful discussion of double agency and deputized discourse, see Wolterstorff, *Divine Discourse*, ch. 3.

31. Gracia, *How Can We Know?* 67.

32. Ibid., 69.

opts for what he terms relational interpretation. Meaning interpretations aim to understand the meaning of the text, either "as what the
historical author understood or intended . . . or what a particular
audience understood, . . . or as independent of what the historical
author or audience understood," whereas relational interpretations
aim to understand the text "in relation to factors brought into the
interpretive process by the interpreter. . . . Relational interpretations
differ from meaning ones in that their function is to produce an understanding of a text in terms of, or in relation to, factors other than
those considered in a meaning interpretation."[33] He argues that theological interpretations, which are relational interpretations rooted in
the theological traditions from which the interpretations arise, are "the
only interpretation that makes sense for texts regarded as [divinely]
revealed."[34] Since "revealed texts by themselves offer no guidance as
to how they are to be interpreted," the theological tradition provides
the guidance for determining what constitutes revelation and for the
very interpretation of the text.[35]

   Unfortunately, the relational interpretation itself falls prey to the
hermeneutical circle. The task of theology is to develop a consistent,
coherent, experientially adequate account based on revelation, experience, and believers' understanding of the world. But that very revelation,
experience, and understanding have to be interpreted in light of theology,
indeed, a particular theology. Appeals to sources of divine truth other
than revealed Scriptures, such as mystical experience or authoritative
religious figures, to escape the circularity fail, for these other sources
must themselves be interpreted from within a particular theological
context.

   Gracia elsewhere suggests a solution to the hermeneutical circle that
might be applicable to divine revelation.

   In the case of texts to whose authors we have no access, we cannot expect
   behavior to reveal their meaning, and so the subject seeking certainty
   concerning their meaning must make up for that lack. She can do that
   in two ways: First by posing questions based on what she thinks she has
   understood of the text and, second, by anticipating the responses that the
   text should provide to those questions. The familiar exegetical claim that a
   text interprets itself is the key on this matter. . . . Anticipating and finding
   those answers is confirmation that we either have understood the text or at
   least are on the right track toward understanding it. Lack of confirmation

33. Ibid., 38, 41–42.
34. Ibid., 121.
35. Ibid., 144.

of this sort does not entail misunderstanding or lack of understanding, it entails only lack of confirmation.[36]

This provides a fruitful alternative to the postmoderns who would abandon authorial intention altogether.

## CONCLUSION

We have delineated the structure of revelation and sketched out some of the issues, noting the problems and evaluating some proffered solutions. Revelation lies at the core of Christian theological understanding. By employing philosophical tools, theologians can progress in developing a clearer understanding about, analysis of, and evaluation of arguments regarding revelation. Ultimately, though, revelation should help us encounter the divine Revealer, who wills to bring us to a better understanding of himself, ourselves, and our relation to him.

36. Jorge J. E. Gracia, *A Theory of Textuality: The Logic and Epistemology* (Albany: State University of New York Press, 1995), 203. For additional discussion of discerning authorial intent, see Wolterstorff, *Divine Discourse*, 196–97.

# 5

# BEYOND INERRANCY

*Speech Acts and an Evangelical View of Scripture*

⚘| David Clark |⚘

O NE OF DAVID BEBBINGTON'S OFT cited four marks of
evangelicalism is what he calls biblicism, allegiance to the Bible.[1]
Although evangelicals use various phrases to express this theme, one common way is to speak of the Bible as "inerrant." Those not familiar with
evangelical life may assume that biblical inerrancy is a fundamentalist
doctrine.[2] On the contrary, many people who reject central features of
fundamentalism nevertheless worship in faith communities that define
themselves in part by embracing the doctrine of inerrancy.

Although commitment to the inerrancy of the Bible is widespread
among evangelicals, there are debates about how it is to be understood.
Some theological conservatives assume that inerrancy entails detailed
precision. The feeding of the five thousand, in this view, must have been

---

1. D. W. Bebbington, *Evangelicalism in Modern Britain: A History from the 1730s to
the 1980s* (London: Unwin Hyman, 1989), 2–3.
2. Mark I. Wallace calls it the "Protestant fundamentalist doctrine that the Bible is
the inerrant Word of God" ("Postmodern Biblicism: The Challenge of René Girard for
Contemporary Theology," *Modern Theology* 5 [1989]: 310).

an event in which exactly five thousand were fed—no more, no less. In many cases, this requires those who defend this construal of inerrancy to perform a variety of hermeneutical gymnastics in hopes of showing that the Bible is true precisely. Others draw the opposite conclusion. In view of such gymnastic gyrations required to defend inerrancy, they reject the doctrine outright. But defenders of more sophisticated versions of inerrancy say that both the literalists and their detractors wrongly share a questionable premise, namely, that inerrancy entails precision. Defenders of more nuanced versions of inerrancy will plead for a crucial qualification: inerrancy does not entail anything like absolute clarity or exact precision in biblical expression. They will say that what counts as "true"—the criteria by which a biblical statement is judged inerrant— must be defined by notions of truthfulness that are found not in the contemporary technological culture but in the ancient world.

Still there are troubles. An objection that cuts even more deeply goes like this: Does the concept of inerrancy even ask the right question? Does it point to the features of the Bible that are most theologically important, or does it fail to draw attention to the qualities of the Bible that make it truly transforming and powerful? Perhaps it is unwise for evangelical theologians to spend so much capital defending the Bible as inerrant when this move leaves them holding a bag that is emptied of spiritual power. Perhaps they should set aside inerrancy as so much unnecessary baggage. For Christian believers who live in communities defined in part by their allegiance to inerrancy as a way of expressing their biblicism, these are important issues.[3]

## THE POINT OF INERRANCY

The heart of a commitment to biblical inerrancy is this: God by the Holy Spirit inspired the words of Scripture. Since God speaks truly, Scripture is true. This common inference leads evangelical communities to their commitment to the doctrine of inerrancy.

But inerrancy becomes associated with a cluster of unrelated but nettlesome ideas. For example, what are the criteria for deciding whether a statement is true? As mentioned above, fundamentalists equate truth with exactness. They assume a statement is counted as true if and only

3. To be more explicit, many evangelical churches and institutions are shaped by doctrinal affirmations that include a commitment to inerrancy. This concept is simply part of the heritage of post–World War II evangelicalism in North America. Living in a community that describes its commitment to the Bible's authority by using the word "inerrancy" requires giving an account of the concept. In this situation, one can abandon one's community for another, or one can redeem the concept.

if it is precisely accurate. So they quickly infer that if the Bible is true, it must be true exactly and precisely. Harold Lindsell provides a bizarre case of this reasoning. For Lindsell, inexact biblical descriptions constitute theological problems. Second Chronicles 4:12 describes a molten sea that measured ten cubits in diameter and thirty cubits in circumference. This obviously does not square with the fact that pi is 3.14. So Lindsell feels compelled to resolve the discrepancy. He suggests that the biblical author reported a diameter measured to the outside of the rim and a circumference measured on the inside of the rim.[4] But to many—even many who count themselves theologically conservative—this seems absurd. Obviously, the truth of a "true" statement is judged contextually. Regarding the Bible, it is proper to use the normal standards operative in the ancient era when the text was written. Given the purposes of the story and the kinds of measurements that ancients made, a rough approximation—a 3:1 ratio—is completely true.

Beyond this, issues such as the premodern view of the world reflected in the Bible[5] and discrepancies in detail among parallel accounts[6] challenge fundamentalist accounts of inerrancy. Postmodern sensibilities raise more questions. Some self-described postmodern Christians think of the Bible as true for the believer who applies that truth personally. This theme challenges theologians who express their biblicism primarily through a commitment to inerrancy. Some inerrantists seem to care a great deal about a certain way of theorizing about Scripture, but they seem somewhat less concerned about the fact that many Christians do not actually read the Bible very much. Postmodern evangelicals see this as counterproductive. Far better to drop the theological debate over inerrancy and start reading the Bible and living its teachings. Given this, are there better ways to articulate the centrality of the Bible that will ring true to these new generations of evangelical believers?

What questions about inerrancy arise within contemporary thinking about the Bible? First, does the Bible, seen as inerrant, function as an epistemic foundation for evangelical theology? The demise of foundationalism is widely trumpeted. Sadly, in their haste to bury the body, some who are playing taps do not make the effort to tease out the various forms of foundationalism. Obviously, classical foundationalism is dead, but there are other less extreme forms of foundationalism that avoid the problems of classical foundationalism yet still maintain the central

4. Harold Lindsell, *Battle for the Bible* (Grand Rapids: Zondervan, 1976), 165–66.
5. See mentions of Leviathan in Job 41:18–27; Ps. 74:14; and Isa. 27:1, and descriptions of Rahab in Job 9:13; 26:12–13; Ps. 89:9–10; and Isa. 51:9.
6. See Matt. 28:5; Mark 16:5; Luke 24:4; and John 20:12 and ask how many and what sort of messengers appeared at the tomb. Or see Matt. 10:9–10; Mark 6:8–9; and Luke 9:3 and inquire what objects the disciples took on their mission trips.

intuition behind foundationalism: some beliefs serve a foundational role in belief systems (basic beliefs), and other beliefs (derived beliefs) are built on, or inferred from, basic beliefs. Indeed, "modest foundationalism," to the surprise of many, is doing quite well in philosophical circles these days. Nevertheless, given widespread suspicion of the entire idea of "foundational beliefs," is it wrongheaded to conceptualize the Bible as a foundation of theology—to hold that evangelical convictions are in some way grounded in the Bible?

Second, what is the most important kind of utterance in the Bible? Some conservative theologians tended to value literal, descriptive propositions as the most significant, noteworthy, or important aspects of Scripture. This coheres with the traditional philosophical prejudice in favor of clear, literal statements. Philosophers, says William Lycan, "like language to be literal."[7] Like the philosophers Lycan had in mind, mid-twentieth-century evangelicalism preferred statements that give literal descriptions of objective reality. Carl Henry, a giant in the post–World War II evangelical theological renaissance, says of the biblical authors that "regardless of the parables, allegories, emotive phrases and rhetorical questions used by these writers, their literary devices have a logical point which can be propositionally formulated and is objectively true or false."[8] Does a commitment to inerrancy require treating the nondidactic genre of Scripture as ornamental excess? Is it wise to strip away nonliteral features of language in search of rationalistic theology composed of propositions?

Third, does inerrancy entail that the Bible is free of human subjectivity and historical determination? In the desire to preserve evangelical theology against the experiential-expressivist theologies of liberalism,[9] the theological parents of today's evangelicals argued (too rigorously, perhaps) that the Bible is completely objective. But postmoderns "share in the now-common assumption that there is no ahistorical, nonlinguistic, neutral, 'objective' Truth that allows us to escape from the web of words to which all of our inquiries are inextricably bound: we are all dwellers and detainees within the house of language."[10] Is it possible to articulate inerrancy without becoming implicated in naïve versions of objectivism?

Fourth, is it sufficient to understand the message of the Bible cognitively? Scripture should form believers in the image of Christ. How

7. William G. Lycan, *Philosophy of Language* (New York: Routledge, 2000), 209.
8. Carl F. H. Henry, *God, Revelation, and Authority*, 6 vols. (Waco: Word, 1976), 3:453.
9. This is George Lindbeck's phrase in *The Nature of Doctrine* (Philadelphia: Westminster, 1984).
10. Wallace, "Postmodern Biblicism," 310.

does it do so? The model of spiritual formation that evangelical theologians typically assumed in the past goes like this: learn biblical truth cognitively and apply it to life by obeying biblical commands. But if anything seems clear, it is that an overly cognitive approach to faith can leave significant moral soft spots untouched. Because knowing the truth is not the same as doing the truth, the emphasis on inerrancy, by itself, is spiritually incomplete. What is required is an understanding of Scripture that holds to the truthfulness of Scripture and emphasizes the spiritual dimension.

## The Core Insights of Speech Act Theory

In view of these questions, it seems that evangelical theologians have yet to articulate effectively, for the current situation, the core insights of a commitment to the truth of the Bible. This failure may have contributed to what seems like a divide among evangelical theologians. Some want to preserve essential evangelical insights in the forms of expression typical of the previous generation (but they cannot—or see no need to—disentangle themselves from their modernist sensibilities). Others insist on changing the modernist forms of evangelical theology in order to stay relevant (but they risk losing hardcore evangelical commitments). Evangelical theology struggles with a baby-and-bathwater problem. Some seem to cling to the bathwater; others seem willing to toss the baby.

The purpose of this essay is to show how philosophical theology offers a resource to broaden out a widely held evangelical doctrine and to preserve the core insight it was intended to express. If successful, the approach defended here will make it possible both to adopt a properly constructive postmodern attitude (instead of earlier evangelical modernism) and also to sustain the core insight that a commitment to inerrancy was intended to preserve. Speech act theory offers helpful resources for conceptualizing the common evangelical way of expressing its biblicism. By using insights of speech act theory, evangelicals can both redeem the idea of inerrancy and also gain important explanatory advantages.

Speech act theory, associated with J. L. Austin[11] and John Searle,[12] flows from the ordinary-language wing of analytic philosophy. Evangeli-

11. J. L. Austin, *How to Do Things with Words*, ed. J. O. Urmson and Marina Sbisà, 2nd ed. (Cambridge: Harvard University Press, 1975).
12. John Searle and Daniel Vanderveken, *Foundations of Illocutionary Logic* (Cambridge: Cambridge University Press, 1985).

cal theologians such as Kevin Vanhoozer[13] and Nancey Murphy[14] and Christian philosophers such as William Alston[15] and Richard Swinburne[16] use speech act theory to understand religious language. A full account of speech act theory is impossible here, but it is important to lay out a couple of key points. The central insight is this: the paradigmatic function of language is not to *say* things, but to *do* things. Saying things is only one of the functions of language, and those who *say* things also intend to *do* something with their language.

Language is typically uttered (or written) in the form of sentences. Not all sentences express descriptive content about reality, but those that purport to do so are called statements. Embedded in a statement—set into the total linguistic act of uttering a statement—is its descriptive content. This descriptive content, abstracted from the total utterance, is a proposition. A statement and a proposition are not the same thing. A single proposition can find itself embedded in different statements. For example, a single proposition can be expressed in natural statements found in two different languages. "It is hot" and "Atsui desu" contain the same proposition in English and Japanese respectively. Further, a single statement can embed two different propositions. "John hit a home run" could mean that John was playing baseball, hit a home run (literally), and his team won. Or it could mean that John was making a sales presentation, he hit a home run (metaphorically), and the customers placed a huge order.[17]

Language can rightly do other things than say things about the world. That is, both descriptive and nondescriptive utterances are acceptable and important. Neither descriptive nor nondescriptive language is defective. For example, language expresses feelings. Such utterances do not actually describe the world in any way. Yet they communicate. "Wow!" breathes the tourist as he sees the Grand Canyon for the first time right at sunset. This utterance is expressive, not descriptive, yet it is perfectly in order as it stands. Regarding expressive language, Carl Henry would feel an impulse to find buried in the utterance a rational point that could

---

13. See Kevin Vanhoozer, "From Speech Acts to Scripture Acts: The Covenant of Discourse and the Discourse of Covenant," in *After Pentecost: Language and Biblical Interpretation*, ed. Craig Bartholomew, Colin Greene, and Karl Möller, Scripture and Hermeneutics Series 2 (Grand Rapids: Zondervan, 2001), 1–49.

14. Nancey Murphy, "Textual Relativism, Philosophy of Language, and the Baptist Vision," in *Theology without Foundations*, ed. Stanley Hauerwas, Nancey Murphy, and Mark Nation (Nashville: Abingdon, 1994), 245–70.

15. William Alston, *Illocutionary Acts and Sentence Meaning* (Ithaca, NY: Cornell University Press, 2000).

16. Richard Swinburne, *Revelation: From Metaphor to Analogy* (Oxford: Clarendon, 1992), 18, 37–38, 55.

17. That statements embed propositions is not uncontroversial, but this point cannot be defended here.

be expressed propositionally and evaluated for truth value. Now it is true that, as someone listens to the tourist say, "Wow," he or she could *infer* a descriptive utterance that embeds a proposition: "The tourist is feeling excitement as he watches the sunset!" But that is something *inferred from* the expressive. It is not the *meaning of* the expressive. It is possible to make an inference from an expressive, and the inference could take the form of a proposition. But making that inference is like concluding that Jill is nervous from the fact that she is sweating. "Jill is sweating" is a proposition, but it is not the *meaning of* her sweating. It is something someone *infers from* her sweating. So, in a speech act account, the fact that language *does* things is a more basic, more comprehensive fact about language than that it *says* things. Saying things about the world is one thing language does, but not the only thing it does—and not necessarily the most important thing it does.

From a speech act point of view, every utterance communicates holistically. An individual communicative act includes a system of dimensions, all of which communicate. Thus, a descriptive linguistic act in a natural language generally includes other dimensions—something more than the propositional or descriptive content. In statements, this something more could be as important as, or even more important than, the proposition itself. In nonstatements, this something more is all there is, for utterances that are nonstatements need not embed propositions at all.

According to one version of speech act theory, different kinds of sentences can accomplish five different things: (1) *Statements* tell people what is the case. (2) *Commands* try to get people to do certain things. (3) *Promises* commit the speaker to doing certain things. (4) *Exclamations* express feelings or attitudes. (5) *Performatives* create new realities.[18] Only the first of these has a descriptive function, but all five are legitimate linguistic acts.

How could an utterance that does not correspond to anything still succeed as a linguistic act? Utterances can accomplish what their speakers intend without offering descriptions. For instance, Tim and Jose are American sports fans at the summer Olympic Games. They are watching the decathlon and are ecstatic that Smith, an American, is doing very well. Smith runs an outstanding four hundred meters. As a rabid American fan, Tim yells, "Yeah, Smith!" The purpose of his exclamation is to express his feelings. It makes no sense to ask whether "Yeah, Smith!" is true. Tim is conveying his joy. Now if Jose's mind is wandering, Tim's exclamation might enable him to infer that things went well

18. John Searle, *Mind, Language, and Society: Philosophy in the Real World* (New York: Basic Books, 1998), 146–52. See also Frederick Ferré, *Language, Logic, and God* (New York: Harper & Row, 1969), 58–61.

for Smith. Still, it is not Tim's intention to tell Jose how things are. He is emoting, expressing how he feels. So is "Yeah, Smith!" true? No. Does it communicate? Of course. Children could understand it. Further, the assertion "Smith is leading the decathlon" is true. So is "Tim is excited about Smith's lead." The latter two sentences tell what is the case (and they may or may not do other things). But Tim would never intend the perfectly legitimate natural utterance "Yeah, Smith!" to do the same thing as "I am excited about Smith's race." "Yeah, Smith!" expresses Tim's feelings. That is all Tim intends it to do. In this way, some nondescriptive utterances succeed.

Applying these briefly stated claims to a doctrine of Scripture, some perfectly acceptable biblical speech acts are legitimate even though they have no descriptive force. Utterances that lack descriptive content do not possess truth value as such. The purpose of such utterances is not to correspond to the world. So it makes no sense to denote them as either true (in that they correspond successfully) or false (in that they do not). That is, these utterances are neither errant (false) nor inerrant (true), and the evangelical theologian who is obsessed with inerrancy will ask the wrong questions of these utterances. But the fact that these biblical sentences are neither errant nor inerrant is neither here nor there. They are still important and meaningful linguistic acts.

Speech act theory makes it possible to drive a middle road between modernism and deconstructive postmodernism. On the one hand, modernist empiricism and positivism (like many philosophical movements before them) erred in making description the key function, the only important task, of language. And so these movements class as substandard any utterances that do not describe the world in an empirically verifiable way. It is ironic that some of the ways evangelicals conceptualize inerrancy emit a positivist odor, for these evangelical accounts tend to value literal, objective, descriptive propositions most. Contrary to positivism, nondescriptive language accomplishes important tasks. Even Republicans can agree there is nothing *linguistically* wrong with utterances that express joy over a Democratic victory (even if they think they are politically unfortunate).

On the other hand, certain forms of postmodern nonrealism err in disparaging descriptive language. Nonrealism says that religious language commands, expresses, performs, and promises, but does not describe: "The word 'God' marks the point at which the religious man has come up against the final limit of what he can say about the object of his concern."[19] But just as it is a mistake to denigrate nondescriptive

19. Paul M. van Buren, *Edges of Language: An Essay in the Logic of a Religion* (New York: Macmillan, 1972), 135.

spiritual utterances, so it is wrong to claim that theological language never functions properly when it describes the world. The legitimacy of descriptive theological claims (understood in a critical realist manner) and the appropriateness of assigning truth values to theological statements are in part what a commitment to inerrancy is intended to protect. Paul van Buren's claim—that "God" identifies the point at which no more can be said about the ultimate—is not what evangelical people mean by "God."

Both limiting religious language to description and rejecting all meaningful religious description are caught in an either-or vortex: language is either entirely descriptive or not at all descriptive. This either-or leaves theology with only the noncognitive crumbs from the rich empiricist's table. But a speech act approach moves evangelical theology past this unnecessary vortex. In this approach to biblical language, Scripture does many things well. And describing—including predicating concepts of God—is one of the things it does. Expressing spiritual sentiments, evoking worship experiences, and commanding God-honoring behavior are among the other things Scripture does well.

If language is supposed to *do* something, what counts as success? J. L. Austin delineated three technical terms. First, a "locutionary act" is the use of an utterance with a particular sense and reference. Second, every act of communication also has "illocutionary force." This is the effect the speaker hopes to accomplish in uttering the sentence. Not every utterance has descriptive content, but each one has illocutionary force. A speaker is always trying to do *something*.[20] Third, acts of communication also have "perlocutionary force." Perlocutionary force is whatever the utterer actually communicates. So, if Susan, the supervisor, says to James, the assistant, "File these documents," the illocutionary force is Susan's expressing her desire that James actually move the documents into the right file folders. Susan is not really communicating information; she is not describing how things are. She is communicating her will; she is trying to influence James's actions. The perlocutionary force obtains if James understands what his supervisor is attempting to get him to do—if there is an uptake on the assistant's part. (Whether James actually finishes the filing job is another thing. Unfortunately for Susan,

20. Evangelical theology is typically committed to an interpretative philosophy in which the purpose of hermeneutics is to discern, to the degree possible, the meaning an author of Scripture sought to communicate. This author-centered approach to interpretation is not widely admired in mainstream academic theology. Speech act theory gives a way to think meaningfully about an author's intention as a locus of the meaning of language. The idea of authorial intent in hermeneutics may be unpacked in terms of illocutionary force. The phrase "author's intent," then, denotes what a speaker or writer hopes to accomplish through the communication act. See Vanhoozer, "From Speech Acts to Scripture Acts," 18.

she could succeed quite effectively in getting her point across, and James might still decide not to file.)[21]


## THE PAYOFF FOR A DOCTRINE OF SCRIPTURE

Speech act theory can help reshape the evangelical commitment to inerrancy. First, every speech act includes purposive overtones. The descriptive content of an utterance, abstracted as a proposition, is only one of the several dimensions of a statement. In addition, statements can possess persuasive purpose. Suppose Pastor Juan speaks to Billy, a teenager locked in self-hatred. Using a voice choked with emotion, Juan says, "But Billy, God really loves you!" Given his tone of voice and other nonverbal cues, it is obvious the pastor hopes to connect at a spiritual and emotional level. Juan's illocutionary intention is for Billy to feel something, be touched by something—or by Someone. The ordinary-language utterance, full of emotion, does much more than say, "God loves you," in such a way that Billy could pass a theology quiz. In the total linguistic act, Juan does say something that is descriptively true. But he also expresses his own strong feelings. He hopes his honest expression will evoke similar feelings in Billy. Through this connection, Juan hopes he can persuade Billy to adopt certain beliefs, experience a corresponding set of emotions, and act in a particular way. Juan's language is multidimensional. And all of these dimensions, not just the descriptive or propositional dimension, are important.

The same is true of the language of Scripture. The Bible is a vehicle not only for intellectual expression but also for emotional and spiritual connection. The words of Scripture not only inform the mind but also elicit spiritual response. The words of the Bible create proper feelings that lead a reader to God. The psalms, for instance, are not merely informative. They express deep feelings and invite readers to enter emotionally and spiritually into these feelings. God inspired the psalms with the intention that they would elicit certain beliefs, passions, commitments, attitudes, experiences, and actions. The psalms contain many linguistic features to evoke these responses. So the Bible goes beyond propositional truth to achieve the purposes of spiritual transformation. Readers do not just contact ideas about God through the Bible; they *connect with God* through the Bible. And so some of Scripture's dimensions are descriptive. Inerrancy is a way of expressing the conviction that these descriptions are true. But some of the Bible's dimensions go beyond description. Here inerrancy is not germane. Thus, evangelicals who want to express more

21. Austin, *How to Do Things with Words*, 94–132.

fully the purposes of God's acts of revelation through inspiring the Bible will need to go beyond inerrancy.

Second, nondescriptive language communicates meaningfully. Positivism and empiricism equated meaning with cognitive content and empirical verifiability. But against positivism, authors intend that the utterances they make will obviously mean something even when these are not subject to verification. Commands are meaningful. If Bob tells his mechanic, "Please rotate the tires on my truck," this is meaningful. How else could the mechanic know that Bob is asking him to rotate the tires rather than clean up his garage (which might not be a bad idea, by the way)? "Please rotate the tires on my truck" is not empirically verifiable. The question "Did Christ die for all persons?" is not verifiable. It asserts nothing. But it communicates meaningfully; it somehow functions properly. If it did not, how could someone give the meaningful answer "Yes, Christ died for all"? Limiting the meaningfulness of language to descriptive sentences or, worse, to empirical statements is a truncated view of language.

This creates space for the doxological language of Scripture. The purpose of worship is to direct praise and honor to God. Worship is like a lover saying to his beloved, "I love you." This is expressive, not descriptive—but not any less meaningful for that. It is like shouting, "Great race!" to ten-year-old Keiko, who just finished last in the hundred-yard dash at the Special Olympics. The purpose of shouting, "Great race!" is not to give a journalist's account of the race. In the history of humankind, thousands of ten-year-old girls have run faster than Keiko. The purpose, clearly, is to support and encourage Keiko. The language of Scripture can play this kind of role. When descriptive force is in view, the question of inerrancy—the basic truthfulness—of an assertion is important. But when something other than descriptive force is in view, focusing on inerrancy is odd. Again, evangelical theology must go beyond inerrancy.

Third, however, the illocutionary force and the perlocutionary force of commands, promises, exclamations, and performatives must connect in complex ways to true statements. The illocutionary force of these nondescriptive utterances depends on contextual realities described by true propositions and understood by believers as part of background knowledge. For this reason, even though evangelical theology should go beyond inerrancy in describing a doctrine of Scripture, it cannot abandon a commitment to the truthfulness of the Bible without ceasing to be evangelical. Some biblical language is nondescriptive. Asking whether that language is inerrant is truly odd. Ignoring or demeaning that language because it is not descriptive and does not point to "objective" truth is worse. It would lead to missing part of God's purposes in Scripture.

But not all biblical language is nondescriptive. This is exceedingly important. The nondescriptive functions of language are, in very complex ways, completely dependent on background realities. Propositions that describe these background realities speak about the metaphysical context in which the nondescriptive utterances occur. Nondescriptive utterances are parasitic on this metaphysical context. Without these background realities, described accurately by true propositions, the nondescriptive utterances lose their force. This is why evangelical theology must retain, as a core feature of its doctrine of Scripture, a commitment to the truthfulness of the Bible.

Consider an example of the parasitic nature of nondescriptive language. The Immigration and Naturalization Service holds ceremonies to naturalize new U.S. citizens. On one such occasion, someone utters a performative: "I pronounce you citizens of the United States of America." This obviously is not descriptive, but it does have illocutionary force. The official intends to accomplish something through the words. But using these words to make people successfully into new U.S. citizens, as the official intends, requires that dozens of background propositions truly describe actual contextual realities. The utterance would fail to confer U.S. citizenship on anyone if, for example, the following proposition were true: "The official is nervous about his first naturalization ceremony later today, and he is practicing before a mirror." It would take an encyclopedia to give a full account of all the possible relationships between all the descriptive and nondescriptive utterances in the Bible. But clearly, in many cases, nondescriptive sentences are necessarily connected in relevant, contextual ways to realities described by true propositions. Only when they are connected in this way can the nondescriptive utterances actually achieve what their utterers intend.

Sometimes one locution can serve several illocutionary purposes when the background realities differ. Consider "I love you." Sometimes it is descriptive. A lover may have doubts. "Do you love me?" he will ask. "I do love you," she will answer. (And he will listen to things like tone of voice—a dimension of the total utterance—to judge her sincerity.) But "I love you" could function as an example in a philosophy lecture. A professor says, "As an example of expressive language, consider the sentence 'I love you.'" "I love you" could be the words of a movie actress in a romantic comedy to an actor who is actually married to another woman. Or it could be a lover's expression of her commitments and feelings: "I love you."

In the last case, when the sentence "I love you" is an expressive, certain background propositions must be true for the expression to succeed. These propositions would describe two actual people, actually in love, actually talking with each other. Conversely, if these descriptive

statements were false, the sentence "I love you" would not express love
to a lover.

Worship works this way. Consider a religion where Tash[22] is God. If
Jesus is indeed the Lord but Tash is not the true God, could the doxological cry of the Tashian still succeed? The illocutionary forces of "Praise
be to Tash" and "Praise the Lord Jesus" are parallel. But the results—the
perlocutionary forces—could not be. For although the respective believers
both cry out their words of praise, intending to ascribe glory to Tash or
Jesus respectively, an actual ascription of glory is only achieved in case
either Tash or Jesus actually exists. If the doting mother says, "Great
race, Keiko," when no race just happened and no such person as Keiko
exists, her praise misfires. People would stare, thinking she launched a
linguistic dud. If a believer says in all seriousness, "Praise be to Tash,"
and the proposition "Tash exists" is false, the praise misfires. The effect
the believer intended to accomplish in his worship—namely, the ascription of honor to an actual divine being—fails to obtain. So the success of
nondescriptive speech acts is not directly a matter of their being errant
or inerrant. But this success does crucially depend on the nondescriptive speech acts in question being rightly related to certain contextual
background facts where the issue of truth is crucial.

Fourth, a speech act approach shows how the language of Scripture
(as well as the utterances found in worship, preaching, spiritual formation, and moral instruction) is sapiential, or wisdom-producing. Biblical
language is intended to do something—to evoke wisdom in the hearer.
To encourage a flagging student, a theology professor quotes Scripture:
"So whether you eat or drink or whatever you do, do it all for the glory
of God" (1 Cor. 10:31 NIV). This is not an inerrant statement, for it is
not a statement at all. But saying it amounts to one small strategy for
building virtue in that student. Yet obviously it requires the truth of
such statements as "God exists," "God's glory is the ultimate good," and
"Human deeds can glorify God."

Evangelical faith communities are experiencing a revival of interest in
spiritual formation. Evangelical believers are reading spiritual authors
such as Richard Foster and Henri Nouwen even though they come from
other Christian traditions. A generation ago, a well-known evangelical theologian, J. I. Packer, wrote a spiritual-formation book entitled
*Knowing God*.[23] Two decades later, a pastor named Henry Blackaby
wrote a book entitled *Experiencing God*,[24] and Blackaby has outsold
Packer by a wide margin. A prominent writer in this field is University

22. From C. S. Lewis, *The Last Battle* (New York: Macmillan, 1955).
23. J. I. Packer, *Knowing God* (Downers Grove, IL: InterVarsity, 1973).
24. Henry Blackaby with Claude King, *Experiencing God: Knowing and Doing the Will
of God* (Nashville: Lifeway, 1993).

of Southern California philosopher Dallas Willard, who has written a series of books that speak to the formation of the spiritual self. A recent example is *Renovation of the Heart*.[25] This explosion of interest among evangelicals in spiritual formation suggests that an overly rationalistic theological tradition does not speak adequately to the human heart. If Scripture only informs the mind and does not also inflame the heart, evangelical churches will not experience the purpose for which God inspired Scripture.

At the same time, the transformational success of nondescriptive utterances designed to shape believers' hearts depends on the background realities described in the Bible. So, although evangelicals rightly seek the transformational aspects of Scripture, they should not accept a theology that opts for alethic nonrealism regarding Scripture. The Bible is not realistic fiction. The teachings and expressions of theology are not humanly constructed linguistic worlds that shape human lives *as though* these worlds truly referenced a real world. The biblical authors' intentions—both the human authors' and the divine author's intentions—in communicating the words of Scripture are not only to fill believers' minds with Christian ideas but also to ignite personal faith and form spiritual community. Biblical passages would fail to elicit commitments of faith leading to eternal life unless certain background realities do exist and the propositions describing those realities are true. There is a real God. There is a real Son of God who became incarnate. And people are invited by the Spirit to exercise true faith in the real incarnate Son. If these things were not so, evangelicals believe, Christian theology would not have the kind of salutary spiritual impact on human lives God purposed.

The informational and the transformational functions of Scripture reinforce each other. Reading the Bible is the occasion for transformation as the spiritual power of the Triune God flows into the lives of individual people, spiritual communities, and whole cultures. Scripture as information opens a window to the reality of the Triune God, who acts transformationally. Mere information without spiritual transformation is dead. How many times through church history has dead orthodoxy reared its head? Theology as information describes the life and power of the Triune God, whose energy fuels any genuine spiritual transformation. And radical transformation without true information is rudderless. How often has fervent piety fueled heresy? Not only are the *informational* assertions that describe truly the nature of God the Father, the work of Christ, and the presence of the Spirit proper and good; so also are the *formational* utterances that ignite passionate worship, spiritual growth,

25. Dallas Willard, *Renovation of the Heart: Putting on the Character of Christ* (Colorado Springs: NavPress, 2002).

inner healing, godly community, and sacrificial service. These create the venue within which the disciplines of Christian living and the direction of biblical wisdom shape personal faith, life together, and faithful service. They lead believers to the goal God intends: true community with God, with fellow Christians, and with all God's creation, beginning now and for eternity.

## AN EVANGELICAL/POSTLIBERAL CONVERSATION

In light of all this, a brief interchange between Carl Henry and Hans Frei proves illuminating. Postliberal thought, exemplified by Hans Frei and expressed also in George Lindbeck's *Nature of Doctrine*, includes among other things a call for a return to the thought world of the Bible. Inspired by Karl Barth, postliberals move beyond liberal theologies. In his classic work, *The Eclipse of Biblical Narrative*, Frei argues that "a realistic or history-like (though not necessarily historical) element is a feature . . . of many of the biblical narratives that went into the making of Christian belief."[26]

The postliberal movement was responding to liberal higher critical methods that tend to direct attention not to the text of Scripture itself but to something else. Some of those who practice critical methods may locate the key to unlocking biblical meaning in the oral or written traditions that lay behind the text. Others investigate the historical events that lay behind the Bible. Those with such liberal instincts sought meaning, in other words, not by going directly to the Bible itself but by seeking something more primitive than the Bible.

If a variety of sources or events that are more primitive than the Bible are the key to biblical interpretation, then the Bible as a whole certainly does not come from a single perspective. Individual books in the Bible present themes that other books challenge; even sections of a single scriptural book can present contrasting ideas. A prominent example is the Documentary Hypothesis regarding the pentateuchal sources. This theory famously asserts that Genesis 1 and 2 present two stories of creation. The two stories come from different sources, do not agree in detail, and were simply placed side by side in the text by an editor. With attention focused on the oral and written sources that the biblical authors used to stitch together what is now known as the Bible, and with the claim that these varied sources challenged and even contradicted

26. Hans Frei, *The Eclipse of Biblical Narrative* (New Haven: Yale University Press, 1974), 10.

128    REVELATION AND SCRIPTURE

each other, liberals typically did not see any overarching unity in a single biblical perspective.

Against this backdrop, postliberal thinkers, in the spirit of Barth, point out that the narrative of the Bible is in fact realistic. The narrative form of Scripture actually constitutes the meaning of the Bible and should be the focus of scholarly attention. This narrative form does not merely illustrate meaning. Indeed, rightly reading the Bible does not require reinterpreting the parts that fail to square up with contemporary sensibilities. Whereas liberals' instincts lead them to revise the parts of the Scripture that seem irrelevant to current concerns, postliberal sensibilities direct contemporary believers to revise the parts of their own experience that do not cohere with a biblical worldview. Postliberalism encourages contemporary readers to understand their experience of the world in the categories Scripture offers, for this biblical world is the only true world. Readers should not seek to cram the biblical narrative into contemporary thought forms as if the world constructed by contemporary society were the real world.

Given a similar dissatisfaction with liberal theology, some evangelicals today purposefully seek out the benefits of dialogue with postliberal thinkers.[27] But although postliberalism seems, from an evangelical point of view, a movement in the right direction, it is also the case that the post–World War II generation of evangelical thinkers defined evangelical theology in opposition to Barth. From an evangelical perspective, the movement to see the Gospels, for example, as realistic narrative should be taken as a real improvement over liberalism. The call to interpret life in terms of the worldview of the canon of Scripture should also be considered noteworthy. Yet when Frei says that the Gospels are to be read as realistic narrative, Henry quickly jumps on the fact that Frei remains ambiguous about whether the Gospels are *true* narrative. In other words, Henry wants to know whether the Gospels are history or history-like. Certainly, placing their contemporary experiences into the thought world of the Bible is a strategy evangelicals will embrace. But is that thought world a fictive thought world, or is it true to the real world itself?

As the theological giant of the post–World War II generation of evangelical leaders, Henry was dominantly concerned with the objective truth of the biblical text. Mid-twentieth-century evangelicals such as Henry rebuffed liberal tendencies to divide the Bible against itself. But in an essay on postliberal narrative theology in which he argues for a unity in the biblical narrative, Henry comes back to the same general

27. See Timothy Phillips and Dennis Okholm, *The Nature of Confession: Evangelicals and Postliberals in Conversation* (Downers Grove, IL: InterVarsity, 1996).

issue. Although he implies that postliberalism has made some positive points, he still lands heavily on the question of realistic fiction. Narrative theology, he argues, is not clear enough about whether the Bible refers to the real world, and it does not sufficiently emphasize historical actuality. In his words, narrative theology implies that "historical actuality should be considered unnecessary to the interpretation of any narrative literature." He worries that narrative theology's "flight from history to the perspectival . . . enjoins no universal truth-claims."[28] Henry expresses the sorts of concern that those familiar with evangelical theological circles of a generation ago will recognize.

In a response published alongside Henry's essay, Hans Frei offers an unsystematic but interesting response. His approach to Scripture clearly stands against a liberal theological trajectory. Yet he also pushes back against Henry's rationalism.

> Of course I believe in the "historical reality" of Christ's death and resurrection, if those are the categories which we employ. . . . If I am asked to use the language of factuality, then I would say, yes, in those terms, I have to speak of an empty tomb. In those terms I have to speak of the literal resurrection. But I think those terms are not privileged, theory neutral, trans-cultural, an ingredient in the structure of the human mind and of reality always and everywhere for me, as I think they are for Dr. Henry.[29]

The exchange highlights Henry's desire for a guarantee that biblical historical assertions are descriptively true. It reveals Frei's concern that Henry expressed his concern in modernist categories. Frei wants to ensure that Christians use the Bible as a source that shapes the community of faith. Henry wants narrative theology to commit itself unambiguously to the objectivity of biblical history. Did Jesus really die and rise again in history?

This dialogue illuminates the concerns of this evangelical generation as well as its dialogue partners. It seems, however, that with proper qualification, the emphases of both theological trajectories can be retained. For evangelicals, the learning gained from an interchange with narrativism should include appreciation for the spiritual-formation function of Scripture. To the degree that evangelical inerrantists are fixated on views of language that privilege objective, literal, propositional truth as most important, they focus on something other than the rich spiritual purposes of God in Scripture. The haste to defend objective truth can

28. Carl F. H. Henry, "Narrative Theology: An Evangelical Appraisal," *Trinity Journal* 8 (1987): 12–13, 19.
29. Hans Frei, "Response to 'Narrative Theology: An Evangelical Appraisal,'" *Trinity Journal* 8 (1987): 23–24.

lead to oversights. As a corrective, a speech act approach could allow evangelicals to have their linguistic cake and eat it too. One can emphasize the practical effects—the functional impact—of nondescriptive biblical utterances. This is what postliberalism wants to stress. At the same time, functional impact—the perlocutionary force—only obtains when a nondescriptive utterance is in a proper relation to background facts described through true statements. This is what traditional evangelicals want to protect, since, from their perspective, postliberal sensibilities are too skittish about objective truth. A speech act approach to biblicism will enable evangelicals to affirm both the truth of Scripture—the central reason to affirm inerrancy—and also its shaping of community and character.

How would this work out in the use of Scripture by the evangelical church? To see what difference this makes, consider a concrete example, Psalm 104:24, 30 (NIV):

> How many are your works, O LORD!
> In wisdom you made them all;
> the earth is full of your creatures.
> . . . . . . . . . . . . . . . . . . . . .
> When you send your Spirit,
> they are created,
> and you renew the face of the earth.

In the past, evangelical theologians have focused on the idea that Psalm 104 speaks of God as Creator. So in typical evangelical theological textbooks, passages such as Psalm 104:24, 30 are listed as proof texts of the doctrine of creation. This is just what one would expect if one took Henry's claim as a directive on how to do good biblical interpretation: "Regardless of the parables, allegories, emotive phrases and rhetorical questions used by these writers, their literary devices have a logical point which can be propositionally formulated and is objectively true or false."[30] But when the textbooks make this inference, they overlook the fact that God saw fit to inspire this verse in the form of doxological poetry. It seems obviously the case, as narrative theology would emphasize, that Psalm 104 does not appear in Scripture as a proof text for the doctrine of creation. Rather it is expressive language that gives voice to the believer's faith and evokes from the community of believers appropriate experiences of worship. Of course, as evangelical theology emphasizes and a speech act account explains, the doxology of praise for God the Creator misfires unless God is indeed Creator. Still, the church

30. Henry, *God, Revelation, and Authority*, 3:453.

should read Psalm 104 as doxology, not as a theological proposition somehow misshapen into poetry.


## CONCLUSION

Evangelicals who live in faith communities that express their biblicism by using a well-qualified concept of biblical inerrancy will defend the Bible as true. (And the criteria of truth are the canons of truth operative in the eras when Scripture was written.) If the Bible is merely realistic fiction, evangelical theology is wrongheaded. Although evangelicals consider the objective truthfulness of the Bible—the word "inerrancy" expresses this—as theologically essential, it is not adequate. Evangelicals routinely say that the church needs a truthful message from God about God's own character, passions, and purposes. Although this is all to the good, a wise stance is to insist on inerrancy *plus*. Evangelicals should allow Scripture to wash over a person's soul. The Bible should cleanse and transform, bring healing and inspiration, evoke feelings and passions, promote commitments and virtues, and shape distinctively Christian hopes and loves. The words of Scripture should form the blueprint for Christian community by providing a vision of life together—including a vision for the practices that shape that life and the values that guide it. A single-minded focus on objective truth directs attention away from these formational functions of Scripture. This is tragic because these spiritual functions are, in the end, *the whole point of the Scripture*. If someone finds objective truth but does not experience passion for God, forgiveness through Christ, and healing by the Spirit, he or she is like the man who has secured a marriage license but has no bride.

Evangelicals today will profit by rethinking the issues and perspectives that have dominated the theological concerns of the post–World War II evangelical community. Application of speech act theory to a doctrine of Scripture is a case where philosophical clarity helps shape formulations of historical beliefs in ways that not only capture the insights and truths that are obviously central to evangelical faith but also exemplify fresh ways to understand them. The baby is the idea that the Bible is true; the bathwater is the claim that theology should reduce all biblical language to contentful propositions. Appropriating the philosophical insights of speech act theory allows evangelicals to keep the baby and lose the bathwater. And this will help evangelical theology capture the hearts and minds of new generations of Christian pastors and teachers.

P A R T  3

# DOCTRINE
# OF GOD

# 6

# PANTHEISTS IN SPITE OF THEMSELVES

*God and Infinity in Contemporary Theology*

❋| William Lane Craig |❋

## INTRODUCTION

Christian theology has traditionally affirmed that God is infinite. But some contemporary theologians seem to think that this affirmation stands in tension with the Christian belief in the reality of a finite world distinct from God. These theologians exhibit an unsettling tendency toward monism—the view that all reality is one, namely, God—and hence toward pantheism. Although they may shrink from this conclusion and try to provide ways to avoid it, these escape routes may strike us as less than convincing, so that their rejection of pantheism represents merely a failure on their part to carry out their views to their logical conclusions.

## THE MONISTIC ARGUMENT

Although the roots of this tendency may be traced back to German idealism, its contemporary progenitor is Wolfhart Pannenberg, whose

135

theology is deeply influenced by Hegel's metaphysics. Here, for example, is how the problematic comes to expression in Pannenberg:

> In the concept of infinity freedom from limitation is not the primary point. Strictly, the infinite is not that which is without end but that which stands opposed to the finite, to what is defined by something else.[126] . . . The basic point in the concept of the Infinite is the antithesis to the finite as such. Hence the concept of the Infinite could become a description of the divine reality in distinction from everything finite. . . .[1]

Pannenberg's footnote numbered 126 in the above quotation reads as follows:

> Cf. Schleiermacher, *Christian Faith*, I, ¶56.2; and Hegel, *Science of Logic*, I, ¶1, ch. 2c, whose first simple definition is that the Infinite is the "negation of the finite." To be finite is to be in distinction from something and to be defined by the distinction. The relation of something to something else is an immanent definition of the something itself. From this fact Hegel derives his famous thesis that the Infinite is truly infinite only when it is not thought of merely as the opposite of the finite, for otherwise it would be seen as something in relation to something else and therefore as itself finite.[2]

Now, prima facie this definition of the concept of the infinite does not seem to make sense. Pannenberg appears to say that the basic concept of the infinite is *that which stands opposed to the finite*, where the finite is understood as *what is defined by something else*. So on this account, the infinite is defined relationally with respect to the finite, in terms of the relation "stands opposed to." But then it follows that, since the infinite is defined by something else, the infinite is finite, which is a contradiction.

Similarly, in the attendant footnote, we are told that the finite is *that which is in distinction from something and is defined by the distinction*. Now, as the "negation of the finite," the infinite must lack at least one of these properties of the finite; that is, either the infinite is not distinct from anything or the infinite is not defined by the distinction. But we have just seen that the infinite *is* defined by its distinction from the finite. The infinite is the opposite of the finite. It follows that the infinite must not possess the first property of the finite: being in distinction from

1. Wolfhart Pannenberg, *Systematic Theology*, trans. Geoffrey W. Bromiley, 3 vols. (Grand Rapids: Eerdmans, 1991), 1:397.
2. Bromiley's translation of Pannenberg here is rather free. In the German it is apparent that the sentence footnoted by 126 is a direct quotation from Schleiermacher.

something. Therefore, the infinite and the finite cannot really be distinct; rather the infinite must be finite, which is a contradiction.

I suspect that the problem here arises because Pannenberg endorses the idea that because the *concept* of the infinite is relationally defined, the infinite *itself* is determined in its being. He appears to conflate a word or concept's being *defined* relationally in terms of something else with that word's referent's being *determined* by something else (note that in German the same word *bestimmen* means "define" or "determine"). He thinks that if a word is relationally defined, then its referent is determined by something else. So if the concept of the infinite is defined as the negation of the finite, it follows that the infinite is determined in its being by the finite, which implies that it is finite. This reasoning is confused, since a word's being relationally defined or even a thing's standing in relation to something else is quite different from a thing's being determined by something else.

In any case, from the conclusion that anything standing in relation to something else is determined in its being and therefore finite, Hegel is said to develop his famous thesis that the true infinite is not to be thought of as merely the opposite of the finite, lest it be seen as itself something over against something else and therefore as finite. As Pannenberg notes, in Hegel's thinking, if the infinite were merely the opposite of the finite, it would stand in relation to something else and therefore be finite.[3] Hegel sought to solve this perceived problem by distinguishing between the spurious infinite and the true infinite: "The infinite as thus posited over against the finite, in a relation wherein they are as qualitatively distinct others, is to be called the *spurious infinite*."[4] What Hegel called the "true infinite" he identified as the process of becoming, which includes both the spurious infinite and the finite as moments.[5] This is the ultimate reality. Because the finite and the infinite are ultimately One, there is no real opposition or distinction between them.

Pannenberg appears to endorse such reasoning:

> The Infinite that is merely a negation of the finite is not yet truly seen as the Infinite (as Hegel showed), for it is defined by delimitation from something else, i.e., the finite. Viewed in this way the Infinite is something in

3. "This contradiction occurs as a direct result of the circumstance that the finite remains as a determinate being opposed to the infinite, so that there are two determinatenesses; *there are* two worlds, one infinite and one finite, and in their relationship the infinite is only the *limit* of the finite and is thus only a determinate infinite, an *infinite which is itself finite*" (Georg Wilhelm Friedrich Hegel, *Science of Logic*, trans. A. V. Miller [London: Allen & Unwin, 1969], par. 278).

4. Ibid., par. 277.

5. Ibid., par. 300.

distinction from something else, and it is thus finite. The Infinite is truly infinite only when it transcends its own antithesis to the finite.[6]

Here Pannenberg seems to repeat the Hegelian argument and endorse Hegel's escape from the looming contradiction.

The argument as Pannenberg explains it seems to be something like the following:

(P1)  The finite is that which is defined by its distinction from something else.

(P2)  The infinite is defined as that which is not finite.

(P3)  Therefore, the infinite is defined by its distinction from something else.

(P4)  Therefore, the infinite is finite.

Since P4 is a logical contradiction, either P1 or P2 must be false. Pannenberg, following Hegel, seems to reject P2 in favor of something like this:

(P2′)  The infinite is that which includes the finite.

No contradiction follows from P1 and P2′, since the infinite is not defined in terms of its distinction from something else. Indeed, given P2′, there just is nothing apart from the infinite. Such an infinite is, in Hegel's view, truly infinite.

Since the concept of the infinite can be used as a description of divine reality, Pannenberg does not shy away from expressing his theological understanding of the God-world relation in the Hegelian language of absolute idealism.[7] There is thus a strong tendency toward monism in Pannenberg's understanding of God as truly infinite.

Certain followers of Pannenberg seem to have also ventured in the direction of monism. Here, for example, is how the argument from infinity appears in Philip Clayton:

> It turns out to be impossible to conceive of God as fully infinite if he is limited by something outside of himself. The infinite may without contradiction include within itself things that are by nature finite, but it may not stand *outside of* the finite. For if something finite exists, and if the

6. Pannenberg, *Systematic Theology*, 1:400.

7. See esp. ibid., 1:443–44, where Pannenberg affirms that God is the Absolute, the all, not one who is one among others. At the same time, he insists that such a doctrine is not pantheistic.

infinite is "excluded" by the finite, then it is not truly infinite or without limit. To put it differently, there is simply no place for finite things to "be" outside of that which is *absolutely unlimited*. Hence, an infinite God must encompass the finite world that he has created, making it in some sense "within" himself. This is the conclusion that we call panentheism.[8]

Though obviously inspired by Pannenberg, Clayton's argument takes as its point of departure what Pannenberg denied: that freedom from limitation is the primary meaning of the concept of infinity.[9] To be truly infinite is to be absolutely unlimited. Clayton elsewhere explains,

> Being limited or bounded (*begrenzt*) intuitively implies the idea of some-thing that is *un*bounded or infinite. To think a something is to think at the same time the border that makes it this something rather than another. Beginning with finite things, our mind stretches toward the indefinite, whether it is indefinite in number, size, or quality. But to (try to) think the totality of things that are bordered leads to the idea of something that is beyond all borders, which Hegel calls the "truly infinite."[10]

This explanation helps us to understand why Clayton thinks that if the infinite exists "outside" the finite, then it is not truly infinite. For if the infinite is distinct from the finite, then there is a "border that makes

8. Philip Clayton, *God and Contemporary Science* (Grand Rapids: Eerdmans, 1997), 99. Cf. his endorsement of the argument in Philip Clayton, "Panentheism in Metaphysical and Scientific Perspective," in *In Whom We Live and Move and Have Our Being*, ed. Philip Clayton and Arthur Peacocke (Grand Rapids: Eerdmans, 2004), 81.

9. Elsewhere Clayton distinguishes between what he calls the *intuition* of the infinite and the *concept* of the infinite. He thinks that the primitive intuition of the infinite is the idea of "something without limits" or "the unlimited." He claims that this intuitive idea is underdeterminative for the concept of the infinite; indeed, one should really speak of a plurality of concepts, since the intuitive idea of the infinite can be variously conceptualized. He thinks that "each [concept] demands separate evaluation as one moves from one's starting intuitions to constructing metaphysical systems based on them" (Philip Clayton, *The Problem of God in Modern Thought* [Grand Rapids: Eerdmans, 2000], 119; see 118–20). It is odd, then, that in the quotation cited in the text he says it is "impos-sible to conceive of God as fully infinite if he is limited by something outside of himself." Since different conceptions of the infinite are possible, this assertion seems plainly false. Clayton's argument is based, rather, on his intuitive idea of the infinite, an intuition that reflection might reveal to be incoherent and therefore untenable as a concept of the in-finite. It may turn out that what is impossible is to conceive of God as "truly infinite" as that expression is (mis)understood by Hegel and his *Anhänger*. Indeed, Clayton seems to admit this (pp. 152–53; but cf. 168).

10. Clayton, *Problem of God*, 125. Cf. Hegel's statement: "The infinite *is*; in this imme-diacy it is at the same time the *negation* of an other, of the finite. As thus in the form of simple being and at the same time as the *non-being* of an *other*, it has fallen back into the category of *something* as a determinate being in general—more precisely, into the category of something with a limit" (Hegel, *Science of Logic*, par. 275; cf. par. 278).

it this something rather than another." There will be something that
the infinite is not, and thus in this sense a limit to it. In this peculiar
sense, even a metaphysically necessary, self-existent being is limited in
its existence by the presence of some metaphysically contingent, causally dependent being because it is *this* and not *that*. It follows that a
truly infinite being must have no borders to its existence: nothing other
than it can exist. Thus we are brought to the same conclusion toward
which Pannenberg gravitated: there is nothing distinct from God. God
is everything there is, which is pantheism.[11]

Clayton's argument, then, is not infected by the confusion between
"define" and "determine" that besets Pannenberg's version. Rather
it appeals to the idea that the infinite must be absolutely unlimited.
Clayton's reasoning can be formulated in terms of a conditional proof
as follows:

(C1)   God is infinite.

(C2)   If something is infinite, it is absolutely unlimited.

(C3)   If something is absolutely unlimited, it has no bounds.

(C4)   If something is distinct from another thing, then that other
       thing bounds it.

(C5)   If something is bounded by another thing, then it has bounds.

(C6)   God is distinct from the world. (premise for conditional
       proof)

(C7)   Therefore the world bounds God. (C4, C6)

(C8)   Therefore God has bounds. (C5, C7)

(C9)   Therefore God is not absolutely unlimited. (C3, C8)

(C10)  Therefore God is not infinite. (C2, C9)

(C11)  Therefore, if God is distinct from the world, God is not infinite.
       (C6–C10, conditional proof)

(C12)  Therefore God is not distinct from the world. (C1, C11)

This argument can be generalized to show that God is not distinct from
anything else.

Even a few evangelical theologians seem to have been mesmerized by
this sort of reasoning. For example, in explaining Pannenberg's doctrine
of God, LeRon Shults opines,

---

11. An alternative reading of Clayton's argument would be that if the finite is not part
of the infinite, then there is a border that makes it this something rather than another.
This interpretation of the argument leads to the conclusion not that the world is identical
with God but that the world is part of God.

It is important to stress the importance of the "true infinite" concept. Here we have a distinction that transcends yet embraces the distinction between God and the world. This special distinction has been emphasized by many theologians over the centuries, but recently it has been radically thematized. Robert Sokolowski describes it in this way: "(God plus the world) is not greater than God alone." . . . If the world and God together were "more" than God alone, then we have something "greater" than God, namely, God and the world.[12]

This is not, in fact, Pannenberg's argument, although it is one rooted in the tradition of absolute idealism.[13] Shults's argument presupposes the Anselmian notion of God as the greatest conceivable being and claims that if God and the world are distinct entities, then there is some entity greater than God, which is impossible. Shults elsewhere expands on the assumption that God and the world together constitute some greater reality:

Often we imagine "all that is" as divided into two generic kinds: divine and non-divine. This way of construing the distinction between Creator and creation succeeds in protecting against pantheism, but it easily leads us into the opposite problem: conceptualizing the relation between Infinity and finitude (or between Eternity and time) in terms of a simple dualism in which God and the world are two parts of a broader whole. . . . If one conceptualizes the God-world relation in terms of two kinds of being (infinite and finite) that together compose "All," then this All replaces God as the Absolute. Both God and world become parts of the "Whole." . . . This way of speaking is not consistent with the idea of God as the unlimited and unconditioned, but marks "God" off as that part of the Whole that is limited (and so conditioned) by the finite.[14]

In this last remark we see how Shults's argument links up with Clayton's (and in fact Shults at this point footnotes Clayton's argument cited above). In Shults's view, if God were an entity distinct from the world, then God would be just a part of a greater reality comprising God and the world and thus be limited by the world. Thus, one is led once again

12. F. LeRon Shults, *The Postfoundationalist Task of Theology* (Grand Rapids: Eerdmans, 1999), 100–101.
13. Cf. Hegel's reflection that if we think of the infinite and the finite as existing without connection, then "the infinite, in that case, is *one of the two;* but as only one of the two it is itself finite, it is not the whole but only one side; it has its limit in what stands over against it; it is thus the finite *infinite.* There are present only two *finites*" (Hegel, *Science of Logic*, par. 288).
14. F. LeRon Shults and Steven J. Sandage, *Faces of Forgiveness* (Grand Rapids: Baker, 2003), 161–64.

to deny that God and the world are distinct entities and, hence, to pan-theistic monism.

We may formulate Shults's reasoning as follows:

(S1) God is the greatest conceivable being.

(S2) If God were an entity distinct from the world, then God and the world would be parts of a greater whole.

(S3) If God and the world were parts of a greater whole, then there would be something greater than God.

(S4) If there were something greater than God, then God would not be the greatest conceivable being.

(S5) Therefore there is nothing greater than God. (S1, S4)

(S6) Therefore God and the world are not parts of a greater whole. (S3, S5)

(S7) Therefore God is not an entity distinct from the world. (S2, S6)

Thus God, as the greatest conceivable being, a truly infinite being, must encompass all there is.

## ESCAPE FROM MONISM

None of these three Christian theologians wants to be a pantheist, and so each tries to escape or reinterpret Hegelian monism so as to maintain Christian orthodoxy. Pannenberg is clearly neither a panthe-ist nor a monist. Rather he reconstrues the antithesis of the infinite to the finite in such a way that they are reconcilable even as their distinct-ness is preserved. Simplifying, we may say that Pannenberg construes the antithesis between God and the universe as an almost literal sort of opposition, which is then overcome by some sort of relationship of God to the world that achieves reconciliation. In this reconciliation, the distinctness of the *relata* is not dissolved. Pannenberg is fond of the word *aufgehoben* to characterize the opposition between God and the universe. The connotation is that the distinction at issue is not annulled but taken up to a higher level where the opposition is overcome even as the distinction is preserved. To give our own illustration, in marriage the antithesis of two persons is *aufgehoben* as husband and wife come together in a deep unity even as their distinctness as persons is preserved. In the same way, the opposition between infinite and finite, God and the world, is *aufgehoben* in that God is intimately related to the world in various ways even as the ontological distinctness between God and the world is preserved.

To see this worked out systematically, one should turn to Pannenberg's exposition "The Infinity of God," a brief summary of which is given here.[15] Pannenberg expounds divine infinity in terms of God's attributes of holiness, eternity, omnipotence, and omnipresence. He takes the idea of holiness to be so closely linked to divine infinity that it is needed for its elucidation, and eternity, omnipotence, and omnipresence may be seen as "concrete manifestations" of God's infinity.

Pannenberg takes the basic point in the concept of the infinite to be the antithesis to the finite as such. The emphasis here is on the notion of the infinite as standing opposed to the finite. "In this regard," says Pannenberg, "the concept of the Infinite links up especially with that of the holiness of God, for the basic meaning of holiness is separateness from everything profane."[16] God's holiness threatens the profane world because of divine judgment; yet this same holiness goes beyond judgment to bring salvation. Pannenberg sees this motif of reconciliation overcoming opposition as the key to understanding divine infinity:

Thus the holiness of God both opposes the profane world and embraces it, bringing it into fellowship with the holy God. We see here a structural affinity between what the Bible says about the holiness of God and the concept of the true Infinite. The Infinite that is merely a negation of the finite is not yet truly seen as the Infinite (as Hegel showed), for it is defined by delimitation from something else, i.e., the finite. Viewed in this way the infinite is something in distinction from something else, and it is thus finite. The Infinite is truly infinite only when it transcends its own antithesis to the finite. In this sense the holiness of God is truly infinite, for it is opposed to the profane, yet it also enters the profane world, penetrates it, and makes it holy. In the renewed world that is the target of eschatological hope the difference between God and creature will remain, but that between the holy and the profane will be totally abolished (Zech. 14.20–21).[17]

What we see here is that when Pannenberg speaks of the infinite's transcending its own antithesis to the finite, he is speaking in purely relational

15. Pannenberg, *Systematic Theology*, vol. 1, part 6. The notion of infinity plays a prominent role throughout his *Systematic Theology*. Read in isolation, some passages might be misleading. For example, when Pannenberg says that "finite objects are conditioned by their being carved out of the infinite and defined by it" (1:140; cf. 1:165, 353, 356), this sounds monistic; but in fact Pannenberg is talking about our vague, preconceptual awareness of the infinite, which is then differentiated by rational reflection (see 1:114).
16. Ibid., 1:397–98.
17. Ibid., 1:399–400.

terms. The ontological difference between God and creatures is not abolished, but God and creatures come to be related in a special way.

Pannenberg thus thinks that the problem posed by Hegel's monistic argument is met by emphasizing the relationality of God and the universe, which overcomes their opposition while preserving their distinctness.

> The abstract concept of the true Infinite . . . contains a paradox. . . . It tells us that we have to think of the Infinite as negation, as the opposite of the finite, but also that it comprehends this antithesis in itself. But the abstract concept of the true Infinite does not show us how we can do this. The thought of the holiness of God and the understanding of the essence of God as Spirit bring us closer to a resolving of the contradiction. They express the fact that the transcendent God himself is characterized by a vital movement which causes him to invade what is different from himself and to give it a share in his own life. The biblical view of the divine Spirit in his creative and life-giving work also contains the thought that God gives existence to the finite as that which is different from himself, so that his holiness does not mean the abolition of the distinction between the finite and the infinite.[18]

Pannenberg sees the reconciliation of God and the world as the way in which the antithesis between finite and infinite can be overcome while the difference or distinction between them is preserved.

Pannenberg's handling of eternity, omnipotence, and omnipresence is similar to his analysis of holiness. In each case, the antithesis to finite existence is overcome by postulating some relation between God and creatures that preserves the ontological distinction between them.[19] So when Pannenberg comes to discuss the unity of God and says, "The thought of the true Infinite means that the distinction between one thing and another cannot be applied unrestrictedly to God as the true Infinite,"[20] the force of the word "unrestrictedly" is that although God is distinct from other things, God must also stand in relation to them. When Pannenberg says that God "transcends the difference between one and all" and is "the One that also embraces all,"[21] he is speaking loosely of the various relationships in which God as concretely infinite stands to his creatures, affirmatively embracing them just as a husband embraces his wife.

God's unity is thus not a matter of ontological unity with the world but God's being united to the world in relationship.[22] Here the infinite's

18. Ibid., 1:400.
19. Ibid., 1:445–46.
20. Ibid., 1:443.
21. Ibid., 1:443–44.
22. Ibid., 1:446.

transcending the antithesis to distinct entities is accomplished by love, which bridges the gulf between God and the world. The overcoming of the perceived antithesis between the infinite God and the finite world is thus achieved not by blurring the distinction between them but by seeing them as existing in a loving relationship. Pannenberg sums up:

> The same holds good finally for an understanding of the basic statement of God's infinity. The thought of the true Infinite, which demands that we do not think of the infinite and the finite as a mere antithesis but also think of the unity that transcends the antithesis, poses first a mere challenge, an intellectual task which seems at first glance to involve a paradox. In the abstractly logical form of the question there appears to be no way of showing how we can combine the unity of the infinite and the finite in a single thought without expunging the difference between them. . . . Divine love in its trinitarian concreteness . . . embraces the tension of the infinite and the finite without setting aside their distinction. It is the unity of God with his creature which is grounded in the fact that the divine love eternally affirms the creature in its distinctiveness and thus sets aside its *separation* from God but not its *difference* from Him.[23]

This last phrase encapsulates Pannenberg's solution to the problem of the infinite and finite: God's love overcomes the world's estrangement from him while affirming its ontological distinctness.

Pannenberg, then, eschews both pantheism and monism. But very little reflection is needed to realize that Pannenberg has greatly underestimated the force of the Hegelian argument. His affirmations of God's being related to the world while remaining distinct from it display Pannenberg's orthodoxy (despite his use of rather unorthodox language), but they do nothing to refute the argument for monism. Pannenberg, it will be recalled, seeks to avoid the contradiction that the infinite is finite by rejecting P2 ("The infinite is defined as that which is not finite") in favor of P2' ("The infinite is that which includes the finite"). But P2' appears to be monistic. In order to avoid monism, Pannenberg interprets words such as "includes" (e.g., "embraces," "transcends the antithesis to," "removes the antithesis between") to have the force "is positively related to." The perceived antithesis of God to the world is a sort of antagonism that is removed by God's being related to the world in affirming ways. But if this is all that is meant by God's (or the truly infinite's) inclusion of the world (or the finite), then P2' is impotent to resolve the original contradiction. For Pannenberg is still thinking of God or the infinite as something that is distinct from the world or the finite. So what he means by P2' may be more accurately expressed thus:

23. Ibid. (my emphasis).

(P2″)  The (truly) infinite is that which is distinct from the finite but
       positively related to it.

But in this case the infinite is still being defined in terms of its distinction from something else and therefore, according to premise P1 of
his argument, is still finite. (In one sense, this whole line of reasoning
is sloppy and confused, since, as we have said, *words* or *concepts* are
defined, not *things*, but to the extent that we accept for the sake of argument the original premises, it remains the case that the infinite is "defined" by its distinction from the finite.)[24] One cannot avoid the infinite's
being relationally defined if one merely piles on more relations, such
as *being temporally related to, being present to*, in line with the concrete
ways in which God is supposed to be truly infinite. If we let R stand for
any of the special relations in which the infinite God is said to stand to
the finite world, then, in Pannenberg's view, God is infinite $=_{def.}$ God R
the world. But then God's infinity is defined in terms of something else,
that to which God stands in the relation R. So it follows from P1 of the
argument that God is finite. Therefore Pannenberg has not avoided the
contradiction that impelled Hegel to a monistic understanding of P2′
in terms of ontological inclusion.

It is difficult to understand how Pannenberg could have thought that
by positing additional, positive relations of God to the world, he had
thereby overcome Hegel's contradiction. It seems that he took the antithesis involved to be an almost literal sort of opposition or antagonism
that could then be overcome by positing some positive relations. But
the antithesis here is of a conceptual and ontological sort: the infinite is
defined as the not-finite, and so an infinite being is one that is distinct
from every finite being. Postulating further relations between them has
no effect on this fundamental antithesis.

---

24. Perhaps we could formulate the argument more accurately as follows: For any
being $x$,
  (1) $x$ is finite $=_{def.} x$ is distinct from something else.
  (2) $x$ is infinite $=_{def.} x$ is not finite.
  (3) God is infinite.
  (4) Therefore, God is not finite.
  (5) Therefore, God is not distinct from anything else.
  Pannenberg would avoid the conclusion by replacing statement 2 with:
  (2′) $x$ is infinite $=_{def.} x$ is not finite, but $x$ is positively related to the finite.
  But (2′) does nothing to avert the problem. For from statements 2′ and 3 it follows
that:
  (6) God is not finite, but God is positively related to the finite.
  From which it follows logically (by simplification) that:
  (4) Therefore, God is not finite.
  And the conclusion then follows as before.

Clayton also tries to avoid pantheism. He proposes that we adopt panentheism instead as a way of affirming God's true infinity. Such nomenclature is misleading, however, for panentheism is typically taken to be the view that the world is partially constitutive of the divine being, that is, the world is a proper part of God. But Clayton, despite some incautious statements that "we are 'composed' out of him who is Being itself,"[25] explicitly affirms that the world is ontologically distinct from God, having been created *ex nihilo* at a point in the finite past and subsequently conserved in being by God.[26] What, then, does Clayton mean when he calls his view panentheistic? He means that the universe is literally located in God.[27] At first blush, this is reminiscent of Newton's view of divine immensity and absolute space. According to Newton, infinite space is the physical by-product of God's omnipresence, and objects moving through space are actually moving through God, who is present throughout space.

But how can any such Newtonian view be compatible with Clayton's affirmations of *creatio ex nihilo* and his recognition that standard big bang cosmogony supposes an absolute origin not just of matter and energy but of physical space and time themselves at the initial cosmological singularity? Clayton's answer is that the divine space "transcends and encompasses physical space."[28] By this assertion, Clayton seems to mean that God exists in an embedding hyperspace in which our four-dimensional space-time manifold exists. Moreover, Clayton affirms repeatedly that God literally existed temporally before the big bang singularity, at which physical time began.[29] So there must be an embedding dimension of hypertime as well. Clayton's view, then, is that God exists in a hyper-space-time in which our four-dimensional universe is located, a view very close to the thesis of God's "extra-dimensionality" popularized by the Christian apologist Hugh Ross. God is thus ontologically distinct from the world although the world exists in God.

Such a novel view of God's relation to the world is, however, once again simply irrelevant to the Hegelian argument for monism as Clayton formulated it. Recall that according to premise C2 of Clayton's argument, anything that is infinite is absolutely unlimited. In premise C3, being absolutely unlimited is explicated in terms of having no bounds. Clayton explains very radically the notion of having bounds: even to *think* of something is to think at the same time the border that makes it this

25. Clayton, *God and Contemporary Science*, 47.
26. Ibid., 20–21, 157–58, 260–62.
27. Ibid., 87–90.
28. Ibid., 89; cf. 90.
29. Ibid., 95, 157–58, 190.

something rather than another.[30] Even bare identity conditions for an entity thus constitute bounds for that entity. So premise C4 tells us that if anything is distinct from another thing, that other thing bounds it, and premise C5 asserts the obvious, that if something is bounded by another thing, then it has bounds. Now since Clayton emphatically affirms that God and the world are not identical but are ontologically distinct, it follows immediately that God is not infinite, since God is bounded by the world. Even if the world exists in God, the world remains as distinct from God as a bacterium in the stomach of a cow is distinct from that cow. Just as the cow is not a bacterium and so has a boundary to its existence set by that bacterium (and vice versa as well), so God is not the world and thus has a boundary to his existence. It follows, then, that God is not absolutely unlimited (God is not the world) and therefore, according to the argument, is finite.

Again, it is bewildering that Clayton could have thought that by embedding the universe spatiotemporally in God, he had done anything to remove the boundaries to God's existence. He seems to have been misled by his own naive language of the impossibility of the infinite's existing "outside of" the finite. He proposes to solve the problem by embedding the world "within" God.[31] This solution fails to appreciate that the exteriority with which one is grappling is not spatial but ontological. Any being that is distinct from another is bounded by that other on this analysis, regardless of where they happen to be spatiotemporally located. So even if God has the world inside him, God is bounded by the world in that he and the world are two different things. Being thus limited, God, in Clayton's proposal, remains finite.

Finally, LeRon Shults tries to avoid monism by emphasizing God's relationality:

> After the (re)turn to relationality, the metaphysics of substance that forced the choice between pantheism (one substance) and dualism (two substances) was severely challenged. If the divine nature is truly Infinite, so that God embraces while transcending the distinction between infinite and finite, then finite creaturely sharing in this nature does not have to mean that the finite becomes (substantially) infinite, nor that the finite is a constitutive "part" of the infinite, nor that God's nature is one (infinite) substance defined over against other (finite) substances.[32]

30. Clayton, *Problem of God*, 125.
31. Ironically, according to Clayton's view, the infinite God still exists outside the world even though the world does not exist outside God. So the infinite remains "outside of" the finite on his view.
32. Shults and Sandage, *Faces of Forgiveness*, 166.

Despite his opening sentence, Shults does not, it seems, really mean to abandon a metaphysics of substance in favor of pure relationality. Such a recourse would appear absurd, since relations obtain between substances. Moreover, Shults goes on to speak approvingly of God's having a nature and later of things existing in relation to God. In any case, premise S1 of Shults's argument, that God is the greatest conceivable being, itself affirms that God is a substance, a being, so that if this is denied, one cannot reach the conclusion (S7), which, on this interpretation, Shults means to affirm, namely, that God is not an entity. So Shults does not mean to assert that there literally are no things. He errs in thinking that Christian theism affirms dualism, for in this context that would be to assert that there are only two substances, two things, in existence. Christian theism is committed to a plurality of substances. Moreover, Christian theism affirms that those substances, including God, stand in a wide variety of relations. So what does Shults mean by the (re)turn to relationality? He explains:

> I suggest a terminological distinction between existing, participating, and sharing in the divine nature. Romans 11.36 tells us that *all things* are from, through, and to God. This means that to be creaturely is to *exist* in their dynamic movement in relation to God. . . . Human persons *participate* in a way that is qualitatively different than the experience of other creatures; self-conscious creatures experience a personal knowing, acting, and being as *becoming*. . . . I normally reserve the term *sharing* for the intensification of the religious relation to God, which Christians experience as the indwelling and transforming presence of the Spirit.[33]

This exposition is altogether innocuous and unremarkable. But it is also impotent to turn back the force of the monistic argument endorsed by Shults. According to premise S2 of that argument, if God were a distinct entity from the world, then God and the world would be parts of a greater whole. Shults could avoid this conclusion by holding that there is no such entity, no such substance, as God. But this would be to affirm that there is no God, which Shults does not seem to want to do. Rather he wants to say that creatures, though distinct from God, share in the divine nature. But this sharing relation is then explicated in terms of an intensification of one's religious relation to God in Christian experience. As we saw with Pannenberg, the positing of such a relation does absolutely nothing to defeat any of the premises of the argument for monism that Shults endorsed. In Shults's view, God's nature may not be one substance "over against" other substances in the sense of antagonism or opposition, but it certainly is in the sense of ontological

33. Ibid., 167.

distinctness. So long as God is an entity (which Shults seems to affirm), it follows from Shults's argument that God cannot be distinct from but related to the world, as Shults wants to affirm, for then there would be something greater than God, namely, the entity comprising God and the world. So the world and God must be the same entity, which is to affirm pantheism.

In sum, these three Christian theologians have not been able to frame successful defeaters for the monistic and pantheistic conclusions of the Hegelian-style arguments they have endorsed. So long as they continue to endorse the premises of these arguments, they will be stuck with pantheism in spite of themselves.

## FAILURE OF THE MONISTIC ARGUMENT

Fortunately, the Hegelian-style arguments offered by our three theologians are not at all compelling. In the first place, the premises of these arguments presuppose a concept of the infinite that is deeply flawed and even incoherent. About fifty years after Hegel's death, revolutionary developments in the concept of the infinite were taking place in mathematics, spearheaded by his compatriot Georg Cantor. Cantor also claimed, on behalf of his concept of the infinite, that it was the "true infinite," in contrast to the "improper infinite," which had prevailed up until that time.[34] Cantor's positive conception of the infinite soon swept through mathematics and lies at the foundations of modern set theory (which many mathematicians believe to be foundational for all of mathematics) and transfinite arithmetic.

Cantor differentiated between a potential infinite and an actual infinite. Up until his time, the concept of infinity was purely a limit concept. Infinity serves as the ideal terminus of unceasing processes that ever more closely approach but never arrive at infinity. For example, the number of segments into which some distance could be divided exceeds any natural number; as the dividing goes on, the number of segments approaches infinity. Aristotle had maintained that the infinite thus exists merely potentially but never actually. By contrast, Cantor enunciated the concept of a quantity that is actually infinite. In Cantor's analysis, a collection is actually infinite if and only if it has a proper part that has the same number of elements or members as the whole collection.[35] A proper part of a collection is a

---

34. Georg Cantor, *Contributions to the Founding of the Theory of Transfinite Numbers*, trans. and intro. Philip E. B. Jourdain (New York: Dover, 1915).

35. This definition of the infinite originated with Richard Dedekind, and so a collection exemplifying this property is often said to be Dedekind infinite. See Richard Dedekind, *Was sind und was sollen die Zahlen?* (Braunschweig: Friedrich Vieweg, 1888).

part that is not coextensive with the whole collection; that is, there are members of the whole collection that are not members of the part. Two collections have the same number of members if and only if their members can be paired in a one-to-one correspondence. So, for example, in this analysis, the natural number series 0, 1, 2, 3, . . . is actually infinite, having a proper part (e.g., the odd numbers) that is numerically equivalent to the whole series.

$$0, \quad 1, \quad 2, \quad 3, \ldots$$
$$\updownarrow \quad \updownarrow \quad \updownarrow \quad \updownarrow$$
$$1, \quad 3, \quad 5, \quad 7, \ldots$$

On the other hand, a collection is finite if and only if the number of members of the collection is some natural number n.

Cantor's definitions completely subvert the Hegelian argument. For it is not true, as Pannenberg's version of Hegel's argument affirms, that "the infinite is defined as that which is not finite" (P2). Cantor gave positive content to the concept of the infinite; it was not defined merely as the negation of the finite. Even apart from Cantor's analysis, the ineptness of P2 should have been evident anyway. The "not-finite" is no more synonymous with "infinite" than the "not-black" is synonymous with "white." The not-finite encompasses not only the actual infinite but also the potential infinite. For example, the size of a geometrically closed but ever-expanding universe is potentially infinite and so cannot be equated with any finite number or any actually infinite number. Thus, the definition offered in P2 is clearly defective.

Neither, in Cantor's account, is it true, as Pannenberg suggests, that "the infinite is that which includes the finite" (P2'). P2', as Pannenberg understands it, is by Cantor's definitions clearly false, for one can have infinite collections that have no members in common. So, for example, the negative number 2 is not included in the natural number series despite the fact that this series is infinite.

Cantor's definitions also make it clear that Clayton's premise C2 ("If something is infinite, it is absolutely unlimited") is false. The collection of natural numbers has a lower bound 0 but is nonetheless infinite. The series of fractions between 1 and 2 has both an upper and lower bound, namely, $\frac{2}{1}$ and $\frac{1}{1}$, but is, notwithstanding, infinite. Thus, given Cantor's definitions, the crucial premises in the monistic arguments are false.

Of course, Pannenberg and Clayton will respond that the true infinite is not a mathematical but a metaphysical concept. Pannenberg differentiates between Hegel's "qualitative definition" of the infinite and the "quantitative mathematical definition."[36] He sees the former as more basic than the latter, for

> freedom from limitation is a consequence of negation of the finite, and this freedom can have the form of unlimited progress in a finite series. The infinite series—including the indefinite sequence of finite magnitudes in space and time—actualizes the antithesis of the infinite and the finite only in a one-sided way, namely, by an unrestricted addition of finite steps.[37]

This explanation makes it evident that Pannenberg is still thinking of the mathematical infinite in pre-Cantorian terms, as a merely potential infinite. As we have seen, the concept of the actual infinite has nothing to do with the absence of limits. This is the case even if, historically speaking, the idea of the actual infinite evolved out of reflection on the potential infinite and freedom from limits. The definition of the concept of actual infinity makes no reference to absence of limits and so is independent of that notion.

Now suppose we do distinguish between the mathematical (or quantitative) and the metaphysical (or qualitative) infinite (as, in fact, I think we should).[38] Two questions then present themselves. First, why think that the metaphysical infinite is privileged over the mathematical infinite as the concept of the "true infinite"? Why not think that the true infinite is the mathematical concept and the qualitative idea just an analogical notion? Indeed, given the rigor and fecundity of Cantor's analysis in contrast to the imprecise, subjective, and poorly understood metaphysical concept, do we not have good grounds for elevating the mathematical concept to the status of the true infinite? At least there is no reason to make it play second fiddle to its metaphysical cousin.

Theologians might plausibly reply that they are not privileging the metaphysical over the mathematical infinite so much as maintaining that mathematical or quantitative concepts are simply not at issue here, since one's concern is with God's infinity and divine infinity is not a quantitative notion, having nothing to do with collections of definite and discrete members.

This reply seems quite correct. But then we come to the second question occasioned by the distinction between the mathematical and metaphysical infinite, namely, why think that the Hegelian concept of the metaphysical infinite is correct? Why think that Hegel has correctly understood the notion of the metaphysically infinite? Here we come to

36. Pannenberg, *Systematic Theology*, 1:397.
37. Ibid.
38. On this distinction, see the fine treatment by A. W. Moore, *The Infinite* (London: Routledge, 1990).

the heart of the issue, which is most clearly expressed in Clayton's C2: "If something is (metaphysically) infinite, it is absolutely unlimited." Why think that C2 is true? The intuition behind C2 consistently seems to be that if something has any limits at all, then it is finite. Moreover, limits are understood here very loosely, so that even the existence of another entity constitutes a limit to a thing's existence. Although he denies that freedom from limitation is the primary concept of the infinite, such an understanding seems to be presupposed by Pannenberg's (P1): "The finite is that which is defined by its distinction from something else." If something is distinct from something else, then that other thing constitutes a limit to its existence, revealing it to be finite. Similarly, one will recall, Shults thinks that conceiving of God and the world as substantially distinct is inconsistent with speaking of God as unlimited but marks God off as that part of the whole which is limited by the finite.

So in this view, if it were the case that only God and the moon existed as distinct entities, then even if God is necessary, self-existent, omnipotent, omniscient, eternal, omnipresent, and so on, with the rest of his superlative attributes, God is nonetheless finite because he is not the moon. This is because the moon is a boundary to God's existence and so limits God to being *this* thing but not *that* thing.

This understanding of "limit" has peculiar consequences. For, perversely, had God in this case not created the moon, then only God would exist and thus nothing would limit God's existence, so that God would be infinite! In this case, God would be all there is. But if God exercises his omnipotence and creates the moon *ex nihilo*, then he is not all there is. Even though God has undergone no intrinsic change whatsoever in his attributes, God is now a finite rather than an infinite being simply in virtue of the moon's existence.

The above thought experiment suggests that our neo-Hegelians have confused "infinite" with "all." If God and the moon exist, then God is not all there is, but it does not follow that God is not infinite. God is intrinsically the same with respect to his attributes whether the moon exists or not. So, if we take Clayton's C2 to mean this:

(C2′) If something is (metaphysically) infinite, it is all there is,

then this premise is plausibly false. The infinite need not be absolutely unlimited in this sense.

Here we connect with Shults's argument, which makes no explicit appeal to the metaphysical infinite but also conflates "infinite" with "all." We may agree with Shults that if God and the world were parts of a greater whole, there would be something greater than God. But why accept his premise S2, "If God were an entity distinct from the world, then God and the world would be parts of a greater whole"? This premise assumes a philosophical analysis of parthood that most philosophers would find incredible. Shults seems to think that for any two entities, their mereological sum constitutes a thing of which they are parts. But this seems fantastic. Do my left hand and the lamp on Jim Beilby's desk constitute an object of which they are parts? The answer seems obvious: no. Ironically, Shults turns out to be a more radical substance metaphysician than those he criticizes, for he reifies such arbitrary sums into bona fide substances. He must take these sums to be real substances; otherwise his claim that God would no longer be the greatest conceivable being would be unjustified. So if Shults is to defend S2, he needs to give some powerful argument for thinking that arbitrary mereological sums constitute objects, or else show why in God's special case the mereological sum of, for instance, God and the moon is an object of which God is a part. We all agree that if God and the moon exist, then God is not all there is; but it does not follow that there exists therefore some object of which God is a part.

To return, then, to Clayton's C2, not only is there no good reason to accept C2 as true; we have, moreover, good reason to reject it. For the concept of an absolutely unlimited being is incoherent. According to Clayton, a border or limit is that which makes a thing *this* thing rather than another. But this entails that even if God existed alone, in utter solitude, so that he was all there is, God would still be a limited being. For God would still have specific properties that make God what he is rather than something else. God would still have limits to his being in that he is not, for instance, a mouse or the moon. Indeed, if God's attributes are essential to him, then God is necessarily limited in his existence to what he is. Hence, for a being to be absolutely unlimited, there cannot be any predicates at all that are applicable to it.

But then incoherence immediately follows. For if nothing can be truly predicated of some being, then the predicate "being absolutely unlimited" cannot be truly predicated of that being. But then statement C2, "If something is (metaphysically) infinite, it is absolutely unlimited," is false or truth-valueless, which contradicts the hypothesis. To put the same point another way: if a being is absolutely unlimited, then it is *not* limited. Hence, there is a boundary to its existence; there is something it is not: it is not a limited being. An absolutely unlimited being *cannot* have any predicates—which is to posit a limit to its being.[39]

39. Cf. the critique of Avaita Vendanta Hinduism by Robin Collins, "Eastern Religions," in *Reason for the Hope Within,* ed. Michael J. Murray (Grand Rapids: Eerdmans, 1999), 188–92. The monism implied by Hegel's argument is not one according to which the world is a part of God, in the way that one's hand is a part of one's body. For the whole and the part are in such an account still distinct; the body is not a hand. Hence, Hegel's

Therefore we have compelling reasons to reject Clayton's C2, for the notion of an absolutely unlimited being, in the curious sense in which "limit" is being employed, is self-referentially incoherent. Hence, the understanding of the metaphysically infinite presupposed by our neo-Hegelian theologians must be rejected.

So what, then, do we mean when we affirm with Clayton that "God is infinite" (C1)? Here Pannenberg's insight that God's infinity has concrete manifestations provides the key. There really is no separate divine attribute denoted by "infinity." Rather "infinity" serves as an umbrella term for capturing all the properties that serve to make God the greatest conceivable being. In saying that God is infinite, we mean that God is necessary, self-existent, omnipotent, omniscient, holy, eternal, omnipresent, and so forth. Were we to abstract these properties from the concept of God, there would not remain some further, undefined property *infinity*. Rather God's infinity is constituted precisely by these great-making properties. All of these properties have been given careful definitions by Christian philosophers in the analytic tradition, definitions that do not surreptitiously reintroduce the concept of infinity; but unfortunately the Christian theologians whom we have discussed in this essay evince little familiarity with this literature.[40] This is greatly to be regretted, for these discussions in analytic philosophy of religion could have helped them to steer clear of the conceptual *Sackgasse* into which their reliance on Hegelian idealism has led them.

## Conclusion

In conclusion, then, the idea that God is metaphysically infinite should not incline us toward monism. Neither should we think that the fact that a real world exists and God is not all there is implies that God is finite. If there were a tension between God's infinity and the reality of the world, the mere postulation of relations of God to the world while preserving

---

own solution to the contradiction between the infinite and finite was inadequate, for so long as the distinction between God and the world is preserved in their higher unity, they still limit each other. As Collins points out, views that deny the reality of distinctions between beings amount not to pantheism but to illusionism. The Absolute is the only reality and the world of objects distinct from it is illusory (*maya*). Thus, what our neo-Hegelian Christian theologians are driving toward is a monism akin to that of Taoism, Mahayana Buddhism, and Vendanta Hinduism, on which see Stuart C. Hackett, *Oriental Philosophy: A Westerner's Guide to Eastern Thought* (Madison: University of Wisconsin Press, 1979). Cf. Alvin Plantinga's critique of John Hick's notion of the ineffable Real in Alvin Plantinga, *Warranted Christian Belief* (New York: Oxford University Press, 2000), 49–55.

40. For discussion and literature, see William Lane Craig, ed., *Philosophy of Religion: A Reader and Guide* (New Brunswick, NJ: Rutgers University Press, 2002), part 3, "The Coherence of Theism."

their ontological distinctness would avail for nothing. Nothing short of
monistic illusionism would avert the contradiction. But there is no reason
to think that God's metaphysical infinity entails being absolutely unlimited
in this radical sense. Indeed, such a notion is self-referentially incoherent.
Rather God's metaphysical infinity should be understood in terms of God's
superlative attributes, which make him a maximally great being.

# 7

# DIVINE SIMPLICITY

*The Good, the Bad, and the Ugly*

⸾ Jay Wesley Richards ⸾

## INTRODUCTION

Not only is the doctrine of divine simplicity widely rejected by contemporary Christian theologians; it now seems to be virtually unknown
among ordinary Christians. In contrast, the doctrine has been both
prominent and widely accepted in the classical Christian tradition. As a
result, Christian philosophers and theologians who seek continuity with
the tradition should hesitate before dismissing the doctrine. Admittedly,
in some of its forms the doctrine has serious problems. Nevertheless, I
think much of its underlying motivation, and a good bit of its traditional
content, can still be defended.

So, what does it mean to say that God is simple? Philosopher Barry
Miller takes the doctrine to mean the following: "In God there is no
composition of any kind whatever."[1] Notice that this is not quite a de-

---

1. Barry Miller, *A Most Unlikely God: A Philosophical Inquiry* (Notre Dame, IN: University of Notre Dame Press, 1996), 11.

scription of a divine perfection, such as omniscience or omnipotence. It is, rather, a "formal feature" of divinity, or so it has been understood traditionally.[2] Catholic philosopher David Burrell says that this means that simplicity "defines the manner in which such properties might be attributed to God."[3]

Although the doctrine of divine simplicity is a common theme in the Christian tradition, Thomas Aquinas was the first to treat it with systematic rigor. Indeed, in his *Summa theologica,* he treats the doctrine before all the divine attributes or perfections, since he believes it should qualify how we attribute all other things to God. Because God is simple, Thomas argues that we cannot predicate properties to God and creatures univocally but only analogically.[4] So he begins with the simplicity of God's being and, in its light, develops his understanding of the divine attributes instead of beginning with God's properties or perfections and then considering how one might predicate them of God.[5]

In speaking of simplicity, then, we are not merely reflecting on one of several divine attributes; we are considering how the classical theist understands God's essence and considering the propriety of attributing things to God in general. Perhaps we should think of the doctrine, then, as a regulative principle that states something like this: however we attribute properties and an essence to God, we should do so in a way that does not require or imply that he is *composed* of them.

In the last century, many theologians criticized the doctrine of divine simplicity as a piece of unjustifiable philosophical speculation, derived not from Scripture or salvation history but from the concept of God as the Absolute or the One of the ancient philosopher Parmenides. There is some truth in their charge, but it is an overstatement. For, as we will see, central aspects of the doctrine follow from commitment to God's perfection and aseity, both ideas that Christians should affirm (as I have argued

2. As is eternity according to David Burrell, "Distinguishing God from the World," in *Language, Meaning, and God,* ed. Brian Davies (London: Geoffrey Chapman, 1987), 75; *Aquinas: God and Action* (Notre Dame, IN: University of Notre Dame Press, 1979), 14–17. Burrell even goes so far as to say that "God's simpleness and God's eternity are part of what assures us we are talking about divinity" ("Distinguishing God," 77).

3. David Burrell, *Knowing the Unknowable God* (Notre Dame, IN: University of Notre Dame Press, 1986), 46.

4. See, e.g., his argument in Thomas Aquinas, *Summa theologica* Ia, q. 15, art. 5, and *Compendium theologiae* 27. See discussion of the role of simplicity in Thomas's doctrine of analogical predication in Christopher Hughes, *On a Complex Theory of a Simple God: An Investigation in Aquinas' Philosophical Theology* (Ithaca, NY: Cornell University Press, 1989), 57–59.

5. Hughes, *On a Complex Theory,* 58.

elsewhere).[6] For this reason, we should try to oblige as much of the doctrine as is compatible with other basic Christian commitments.

What are the traditional motivations for defending divine simplicity? Many see it as arising from the idea that God's existence is self-explanatory, that God is an absolutely perfect being of pure actuality.[7] Similarly, Alvin Plantinga attributes it to a "sovereignty-aseity intuition" held by most traditional theists.[8] This intuition inspires theologians to preserve (in theological formulations) God's "uncreatedness, self-sufficiency and independence of everything else" as well as "his control over all things and the dependence of all else on his creative and sustaining activity."[9] David Burrell asserts that divine simplicity or "simpleness" (along with eternity) "assures God's distinction from 'all things'" and provides "the ground for asserting the gratuity of creation."[10] There is no explicit defense of this doctrine in Scripture, but Scripture does say that God is love (1 John 4:8). Although the claim that God is love does not entail simplicity, some versions of divine simplicity entail the claim that God is love. Despite direct biblical affirmations, however, we might see divine simplicity as a philosophical extension of the biblical concept of God's holiness, by which the biblical authors distinguish God from God's creation.

When Thomas Aquinas takes up the topic early in his *Summa theologica* as part of his natural theology, he first treats it as a conclusion of the *via negativa*. Immediately following his discussion of the existence of God, he says,

> When the existence of a thing has been ascertained there remains the further question of the manner of its existence, in order that we may know its essence. Now, because we cannot know what God is, but rather what He is not, we have no means for considering how God is, but rather how He is not. . . . Now it can be shown how God is not, by denying of Him whatever is opposed to the idea of Him—viz., composition, motion, and the like.[11]

So, for Thomas—in this passage at least—simplicity is a product of negative theology.

6. Jay Richards, *The Untamed God: A Philosophical Exploration of Divine Perfection, Immutability, and Simplicity* (Downers Grove, IL: InterVarsity, 2003).

7. Eleonore Stump and Norman Kretzmann, "Absolute Simplicity," *Faith and Philosophy* 2/4 (October 1985): 353.

8. Alvin Plantinga, *Does God Have a Nature?* (Milwaukee: Marquette University Press, 1980), 28.

9. Ibid., 1–2.

10. Burrell, "Distinguishing God," 78. Burrell also claims more strongly that this distinction is "the central issue" with respect to divine simpleness.

11. Aquinas, *Summa theologica* Ia, q. 3.

But why does Thomas feel the need to engage in such denials as required by the *via negativa*? And why should the Christian distinguish God from the world, as Burrell advises? Presumably, among other reasons, we should do so because of the radical and asymmetrical dependency relation between God and the world. The world is utterly dependent on God for its continued existence and essence whereas God has no analogous ontological need for the world. God has no cause outside himself and does not depend on anything outside himself—he enjoys perfect *aseity*. In contrast, creation's essential cause is found in God. Preserving this asymmetry in how we speak of God suggests some elements of the doctrine of divine simplicity, even if it does not require or justify every version of the doctrine.

Of course, there are other forms of the doctrine of simplicity besides the claim that God is not made of parts. For instance, some have claimed, in the name of simplicity, that God is "identical with" his essence and that all of God's properties are really identical with his essence and with each other. So the question is whether commitment to God's aseity requires us to affirm these things. To answer, we need to tease out the various senses of the doctrine of divine simplicity.

## THE SENSES OF SIMPLICITY

Regarding simplicity, we may consider whether God is simple in all respects, in some respects, or in no respects. Any purported defense of simplicity will conclude that God is simple in at least some respects, so we will ignore the last option. Now, obviously God is not simple in just *any* sense. One meaning of "simple," after all, is "unintelligent." So we should specify in what sense we mean that God is simple. It should then become clear that there are several crucial senses in which Christians should say that God is simple and a few senses in which we should deny it.

Among the senses of simplicity that appear in Christian theology are the following:

(1) All divine properties are possessed by the same self-identical God.
(2) God is not composite, in the sense of being made up of elements or properties more fundamental than God is. God has no external cause(s), such as Platonic forms.
(3) God's essence is "identical with" his act of existing. (Or perhaps: God's existence is not extrinsic to his essence.)
(4) All God's essential properties are coextensive.

(5) All God's perfections are identical.
(6) All God's properties are coextensive.
(7) God's essential properties and essence are (strictly) identical with God himself.
(8) All God's properties are (strictly) identical with God himself.

Sense 1 is the easiest to accommodate; sense 8 is the most difficult. In fact, of these eight possibilities, we can defend plausible renderings of senses 1, 2, 3, 4, and perhaps 5. But it should become clear that the Christian must deny senses 6, 7, and 8.[12] Interestingly, there seems to be an asymmetrical entailment relation between these claims going from 8 to 1. So, for instance, sense 8 entails sense 7, but 7 does not entail 8, and so on. If this is correct, then sense 8 is clearly the strongest form of simplicity and sense 1 is the weakest. We should not mistake the strongest version of the doctrine, however, with the most traditional. It may be that the strongest versions of the doctrine have resulted from misinterpreting certain traditional claims. Indeed, I suspect that sense 2 is the primary burden of the traditional doctrine, rightly interpreted.

The most perplexing senses in this list are 7 and 8. Strictly speaking, if either were true, it would be incorrect to say that God has properties or even that he has an essence. Rather, these would be identical with God and a fortiori identical with each other (unless, obscurely, one denies classical identity). So, to say God is simple in senses 7 and 8 may be to deny that God has properties or an essence.[13]

Some affirm God's simplicity because of the conviction stated in sense 1, that the divine attributes or perfections all refer to one and the same God. In this form, simplicity is more or less synonymous with God's unity and expresses the monotheistic conviction common to Judaism, Christianity, and Islam.[14] So, obviously any monotheist would affirm sense 1. Philosopher Richard Swinburne claims that so long as we affirm divine unity, we need not be shackled with the more difficult aspects of the doctrine.[15] Commitment to God's unity, however, is not the only traditional motivation for defending divine simplicity.

Sense 2 is closely linked to the notion of divine aseity, transcendence, and sovereignty. If God were dependent on universals such as being or goodness or knowledge as Platonic forms or causal powers, so that God were somehow composed of these things, then God would not be

12. At least according to certain contemporary interpretations. But see the conclusion to Richards, *The Untamed God*, for an important qualification.
13. As Brian Davies notes in "The Doctrine of Divine Simplicity," in *Language, Meaning, and God*, 58–59.
14. Burrell, *Knowing the Unknowable God*, 50.
15. Richard Swinburne, *The Christian God* (Oxford: Clarendon, 1994), 160–63.

self-existent. Presumably, God would depend on the things of which he was composed. Moreover, if God were composed of (metaphysical) parts, one could construe those parts as God's formal causes for his being what he is,[16] an idea that surely contradicts the claim that God exists *a se*. Further, anything made of parts could seemingly come apart. So in the sense of "noncomposite,"[17] simplicity seems well founded. This sense may come closest to preserving the basic motivation behind various classical defenses of the divine simplicity. For this reason, we will postpone treating sense 2 until we have analyzed senses 3–8. (If I am correct, then it would have been better for Christian theology if the doctrine had been called divine noncomposition rather than divine simplicity. But it is too late now.)

The central questions for evaluating senses 3–8 are these: To what degree does the claim that God is noncomposite require the various *identity theses* (3–8)? Can we reject or qualify some or all of senses 3–8 while maintaining that God is noncomposite in the relevant sense?

Sense 3 is particularly tricky because its meaning shifts from the medieval to the modern philosophical context. If we are not careful, we could perceive disagreements where none really exist. In the *Summa theologica* Thomas says both that God is the "same as" his essence and that essence and existence are the "same in" God.[18] This sounds baffling to a modern essentialist, who might respond, How could God, who is the actual living God on whom all things depend, be identical with a set of facts or truths such as an essence, which is just a set of essential properties?[19] This is a reasonable question, assuming the modern essentialist definition of properties and essences. This is not, however, Thomas's conception. As Nicholas Wolterstorff notes, we (or at least those of us who engage in essentialist discourse) now speak of an entity as *having* an essence, as essentially exemplifying it. Wolterstorff calls this view "relation ontology," in which an essence as such is an abstraction or, as I would understand it, a way of describing the set of fundamental facts or truths about an entity's existence in the world. One who understands "essence" in this way would not be inclined to identify God with God's essence. God is not simply a set of facts or truths.

But Thomas and other medievals thought of an essence of a thing as a *"what-it-is-as-such."* That is, for them, an "entity does not *have* a certain [essence] in the way that it has a certain property. It *is* a certain [essence]." When they spoke of an entity as "having" a nature or es-

16. Ibid., 40. See Aquinas, *Summa theologica* Ia, q. 3, art. 7.
17. Or perhaps "essentially noncomposite."
18. Aquinas, *Summa theologica* Ia, q. 3, art. 3–4.
19. This is akin to Plantinga's objection in *Does God Have a Nature?*, 57.

sence, they meant it as "having as one of its constituents" rather than as exemplifying it.[20]

In addition, Thomas denies that God "has" an essence, in the sense that God is one instance of some more general essence of divinity. For Thomas and Aristotle, individuals such as Socrates and Plato "have" the same—human—essence. That is, one of their constituents is the essence "human." How, then, are they individuated? They are individuated by the matter that uniquely constitutes them as individuals as well as by their various accidents, not by their abstract individual essences or haecceities as a modern essentialist conceives them. This is not the case for an immaterial entity, since such an entity is not composed of matter. Moreover, it cannot be the case for God, since this would require that God be a composite of matter and form, which Thomas wisely denies.[21] It would also imply that God merely instantiates a generic "kind essence" of divinity. So for God (as for other immaterial entities), it would be natural for Thomas to say that God "is identical with" God's own essence. When he speaks in this way, he is not really asserting an identity relation between God and God's essence in the Leibnizian sense of the indiscernibility of identicals, even if his words sometimes suggest this. So Thomas's claim is understandable, given his philosophical context, although modern essentialists will want to state things a little differently to avoid the impression that we are identifying God with an abstraction.

But what about the claim that essence and existence are the same in God? Is this an identity claim, meaning that there is simply nothing to God other than that God exists? Could we translate this assertion into the formula God's essence = God's existence? Is God "just a lump or bit of existence"?[22] If I were to say that God's essence equals God's existence, I would mean this:

For any property P of God's essence, *God's essence* has P if and only if *God's existence* has P.

From this I could infer that since God's essence is exemplified in all possible worlds, God is exemplified in all possible worlds. And this certainly sounds strange. What I would want to say is not that God is exemplified in all possible worlds but that God exists in all possible worlds. But once again we may be led astray by Thomas's way of speaking.

---

20. Nicholas Wolterstorff, "Divine Simplicity," in *Our Knowledge of God: Essays on Natural and Philosophical Theology*, ed. Kelly James Clark (Boston: Kluwer, 1992), 140–41.

21. Aquinas, *Summa theologica* Ia, q. 3, art. 2.

22. Wolterstorff, "Divine Simplicity," 144.

Perhaps we should join Nicholas Wolterstorff in preferring Thomas's formulation in *Summa contra gentiles* 1.22: God's "essence or quiddity is not something other than his being." That is, "God's existence is not something distinct from God's [essence]."[23] Better, God's existence is not extrinsic to, or separable from, God's essence. Thomas's point seems to be that unlike finite creatures, God necessarily exists. Unlike the rest of us, the "whatness" of God includes his existing, even if we cannot deduce this to produce a self-evidently valid ontological argument for God's existence. Such a claim seems unproblematic.

In this interpretation, it is clear why some contemporary Thomists regard the fundamental burden of the doctrine of simplicity to be the identity of God's essence with God's act of existing. This interpretation has two senses. The first sense, as David Burrell puts it, is that the existence of anything presupposes the notion of its essence as *that which is*, and so the existence of a substance or essence cannot be accidental to the entity.[24] A fortiori, existence cannot be accidental to God. So in defending the claim that essence and existence are the same in God, Thomas quotes Hilary, who says, "*In God existence is not an accidental quality, but subsisting truth. Therefore what subsists in God is His existence.*"[25] As Wolterstorff explains it, whereas, for Thomas, only *potentiality for existing* belongs to every nondivine essence; *existing* itself belongs to the divine. Again, rather than a real disagreement, we have a translation problem.

This understanding of sense 3 alone is so modest, however, that according to it every substance or essence, and not just God, is simple when translated into the contemporary essentialist idiom. For this reason, it probably does not fully capture the doctrine of simplicity. For in essentialist terms—fleshed out with possible-worlds semantics—everything that exists exists essentially because nothing can exist in any possible world in which it does not exist. Existence is for every entity either an essential property or, if Kant is correct, a necessary condition for having any essential properties.

In essentialist jargon, what distinguishes God absolutely from created things in this regard is that God exists *necessarily*. So here we have a second understanding according to which God's existence is identical with God's essence (to put it in Thomas's terms): since God necessarily exists, it is one of God's essential properties that he necessarily exist. In contrast, in the case of any finite creature, for instance, Socrates, we can distinguish his essence as human from his contingent existence. Socrates'

23. Ibid.
24. Burrell, "Distinguishing God," 84.
25. Aquinas, *Summa theologica* Ia, q. 3, art. 4.

existence is essential *to him*, but his existence as such is contingent. Moreover, there could have been humans—that is, human nature or essence could have been instantiated—even if Socrates had never existed. In God's case, there is no such distinction. There is no possible world in which God's essence could be instantiated but God not exist, since there is no world in which God does not exist. God's essence is necessarily instantiated (or exemplified). His essence and existence are coextensive. We cannot get the daylight between God's essence and existence as we can with finite creatures. This fact certainly marks a profound "distinction" between God and the created world.[26] So the Christian can certainly maintain that God is simple in the sense that his existence is not an accidental quality.

Sense 4, the claim that all God's essential properties are coextensive, is another easily defensible sense of simplicity. This is one of two theses in William E. Mann's defense of simplicity, and it seems to account for much in the views of Thomas and other classical theists.[27] Mann maintains that one can preserve simplicity by defending the following theses:

(A) All the divine attributes are necessarily coextensive. According to this thesis, it would be impossible for any being to instantiate the attribute "being omniscient," for instant, without also instantiating the attribute "being omnipotent" and vice versa.

(B) Necessarily coextensive attributes are necessarily identical.[28]

Now, thesis A is clearly unproblematic so long as "attributes" refers only to God's essential properties. For, assuming God exists necessarily— that is, in every possible world—then God has all his essential properties in all possible worlds. There is no world in which God has one but not the others. Therefore they are necessarily coextensive. Of course, this does not establish that, abstractly considered, the properties "being omnipotent" or "being perfectly good" are coextensive. What we can maintain is that *God's* omniscience and perfect goodness, for example, are coextensive. But this is not a problem, since God exists necessarily. So God exemplifies all his essential properties in every possible world. Moreover, there is no omniscience other than God's omniscience. This formulation also

26. As David Burrell puts it in *Knowing the Unknowable God*, 2–4; also Robert Sokolowski, *The God of Faith and Reason*, 2nd ed. (Washington, DC: Catholic University of America Press, 1995).

27. William E. Mann, "Simplicity and Immutability in God," in *The Concept of God*, ed. T. V. Morris (New York: Oxford University Press, 1987), 256; "Divine Simplicity," *Religious Studies* 18 (1982): 451–71. This is also how Hartshorne takes simplicity; and so he can argue that God is simple in essence but not in actuality.

28. Mann, "Simplicity and Immutability," 256.

reinforces a commitment to divine unity, since God's essential properties could not come apart or cease to be divine properties.

Mann's inference from A to B, however, requires a doubtful premise, namely, that properties—at least in the case under consideration—are nothing more than a function from possible worlds to individuals. They are certainly not abstract entities and not even meanings or facts. But this view of properties seems a bit coarse-grained, since it does not capture what most people mean when they refer to properties or attribute them to various entities. I discuss the relationship between identity and coextensiveness of properties below. But whatever can be said on its behalf, it is a contemporary way of understanding properties and is surely not equivalent to the traditional way of viewing properties in either broadly Aristotelian or Neoplatonic terms. Although securing coextensiveness of essential divine properties is necessary for capturing the identity of divine perfections—a goal of Mann's simplicity doctrine—it is not sufficient.

Let us skip sense 5 for a moment and consider sense 6, the claim that all God's properties are coextensive. This sense of simplicity is more problematic. A few distinctions should make this clear. First, note that the distinction between essential and accidental properties entails that such properties are not modally coextensive. An entity has its essential properties in every world in which it exists. Since God exists necessarily, God exemplifies his essential properties in every possible world. Accidental properties, on the other hand, are properties an entity has in some worlds in which it exists but lacks in others. So, if we have good reason to say that God has both essential and accidental properties, then we must deny that God's properties are *not* all coextensive. In this case, we would need to deny that God is simple in sense 6 and, a fortiori, in senses 7 and 8. As we will see, this is a real and not merely hypothetical dilemma.

Thankfully, most traditional defenders of divine simplicity do not unambiguously affirm senses 6, 7, and 8. Denying that God has accidents is common among traditional advocates of divine simplicity, including Thomas Aquinas,[29] Anselm,[30] and Augustine[31] (although their meanings are not synonymous). Superficially, one might suppose that this directly contradicts the claim that God has contingent properties or accidents (in the sense described above). On closer inspection, however, we discover another translation problem, since they are not denying what the modern essentialist would affirm in saying that God has some accidental properties, such as this:

29. Aquinas, *Summa theologica* Ia, q. 3, art. 6, and *Summa contra gentiles* 1.23.
30. Anselm, *Proslogion; Monologion*.
31. Augustine, *The City of God* 11.10.

(C) being the Creator of the actual world.

Thomas at least does not include among accidents such items as C. So he would not bother distinguishing between senses 4 and 5. While it makes sense for the contemporary essentialist to include contingent relations as divine accidents,[32] Thomas would define such relations as either extrinsic "operative" relations or actions of God *ad extra* rather than "entitative" properties of God *in se*.[33] As such, he would not count them among God's properties at all. So the conflict on this point is somewhat indirect. The conflict becomes explicit with certain contemporary defenders of Thomas who argue that God's external relations are for Thomas and other medievals mere Cambridge properties (see below), that is, merely extrinsic properties that really have nothing to do with God. But Thomas did not have the distinction between real and Cambridge properties, so it may be somewhat anachronistic to attribute it to him.[34]

It is crucial, in any case, to understand the traditional motivation for denying that God has accidents. Thomas, Anselm, and others in the Christian tradition who deny that God has accidents do so to forestall the idea that such things as goodness, justice, and wisdom are merely divine *qualities*. To say this would be to imply that God merely participates in his perfections, in the way finite creatures do. For example, when we say that an individual subject such as Plato is wise, we are speaking of a quality Plato happens to have, namely, being wise. At the same time, Plato might not have been wise. There is nothing about Plato as such that entails that he be wise. Wisdom is one of Plato's qualities in the actual world, but he might have been dropped as a baby and rendered quite dull. So Plato has wisdom contingently or accidentally.

Clearly, this is an inadequate way of describing God's relation to wisdom. Such notions as wisdom are, for God, perfections. God does not merely "have," for instance, justice as I might "have" it by habitually acting in a just manner. God is essentially just; God exemplifies justice and his other perfections necessarily.[35] As Thomas puts it, God's perfections are to be attributed to God *per se* rather than merely *de subjecto*.[36]

32. As I argue at length in Richards, *The Untamed God*, ch. 3.

33. Diogenes Allen, *Philosophy for Understanding Theology* (Atlanta: John Knox Press, 1985), 141.

34. For this interpretation, see Miller, *A Most Unlikely God*, 106–12; Stump and Kretzmann, "Absolute Simplicity," 372. To be precise, Thomas considers "Creator" as a "name" of God rather than a mere external relation.

35. F. G. Immink, *Divine Simplicity* (Uitgeversmaat-schappij: J. H. Kok-Kampen, 1987), 92–93.

36. Aquinas, *Summa theologica* Ia, q. 3, art. 6. See also Immink, *Divine Simplicity*, 176.

Otherwise God would not be the greatest possible being, since it would surely be greater to have such perfections in all possible worlds than in only some. So the traditional denial that God has accidents is at least in part an insistence that God's perfections are not accidents as they are in creatures. Even if God has many accidental properties, we have no reason to say that his perfections are among them.

So our treatment of simplicity reduces to two questions: Are all God's essential properties identical? And does God have accidents in another sense—namely, as the result of his free choices? This leads to sense 7, the claim that God's essential properties and essence are identical with God himself. This is the less strict version of the thesis that (all) God's properties are identical with God's essence, with God himself, and with each other. At first glance, one might suppose that if we distinguish God's essence and accidents, we could still defend simplicity of essence in sense 6. That is, presumably one could argue that although God has accidents other than the ones classically denied and although God's contingent properties are certainly not equivalent to God's essential ones, nevertheless, all God's essential properties are equivalent to each other. Since God's essence only includes God's essential properties, one could still argue that God is simple in essence even if in actuality God has sundry contingent properties, since there are many facts about God that would not be facts in every possible world. So God would still be simple in sense 6.

Some of Thomas's arguments and other traditional defenses of the doctrine seem to suggest that God is simple in the sense that all of God's properties are identical to God's essence—and to each other if we assume that any two things identical to a third are equivalent to each other. Interpreting Thomas and other medievals is very difficult on this point, however, since they do not explicitly defend identity in Leibnizian terms, such as with the indiscernibility of identicals. So we should avoid attributing this view to them without qualification. Of course, when strong identity *is* explicitly joined with the denial that God has accidents—as in some contemporary defenses of simplicity—we get sense 7. Let us set aside the claim that God has accidents and consider first the claim that God's *perfections* (a subset of God's essential properties) are identical. Can we uphold this more modest claim?

I am initially inclined against the notion that, for instance, perfect or infinite goodness, knowledge, and power are just the same properties, even in God, whether we understand them as maxima or some kind of infinite limit case. Although the perfections are coextensive in God, this is clearly not synonymous with identity. For instance, trilaterality and triangularity are coextensive properties of triangles, but they are surely different properties. Similarly, all necessary truths are coextensive; that is, they are true in the same set of possible worlds, namely, all of them. Thus the propositions "All red things are colored" and "All bachelors are unmarried" are both true in all possible worlds and so they are coextensive. Nevertheless, these propositions are not identical.

Still, perhaps *God's* perfections are in some sense identical. Mann concedes that although, for instance, being knowledgeable and being powerful are not the same properties, since they have different connotations, nevertheless, in God, who possesses the maxima of these properties (according to Mann), they converge or coalesce.[37] The idea is something like the following. When we speak of different perfections, such as omniscience or omnipotence, we connote different things, and so the assertions have different meanings. Nevertheless, perhaps all of these different meanings have the same denotation; that is, perhaps they refer to some single capacity in God. This does not seem implausible. After all, the perfections do seem to relate to each other, and in fact, perhaps being omnipotent entails being omniscient, perhaps being perfectly loving entails being perfectly just, and so forth. If Mann is correct, then sense 5 is another sense of simplicity that the Christian can accept.

In another recent argument, Barry Miller defines the divine perfections not as maxima (limits *simpliciter*) but as limit cases, which—owing to their infinity—are identical in God, who is pure subsistent existence.[38] Since the concept of limit case is such as to prevent much comprehension, I do not know how to evaluate Miller's argument. Even if correct, however, Mann's and Miller's arguments can apply only to God's perfections. But God has other essential properties for which their arguments will not work, namely, the specifically trinitarian attributes, which are a sine qua non for any Christian doctrine of God.

## TRINITY AND SIMPLICITY

Christian theologians have traditionally recognized that some divine attributes concern God's essence generally whereas others concern the three divine persons "individually." In some sense, then, trinitarianism requires that we gingerly distinguish between two classes of attributes. Of course, if trinitarianism is true, then all these attributes are coextensive. Nevertheless, even if we claimed more strongly that the attributes *shared* by the three persons are equivalent in God, the trinitarian claim requires that at least some of the attributes or properties in the second

37. William Mann, "Simplicity," *Religious Studies* 18 (1982): 461.
38. Miller, *A Most Unlikely God*, 7–14. If God's perfections are limit cases rather than intrinsic maxima, then Anselm's claim—that God is *that than which none greater can be conceived*—is a necessary thing to attribute to God, but it is not sufficient.

class, namely, those that distinguish the divine persons, *not* be identical. Therefore the Christian (assuming all Christians are trinitarians) should not affirm simplicity in the sense of equivalence or identity of all essential divine properties. It should not be surprising, incidentally, that recent defenses of strong divine simplicity lack any consideration of the problems the doctrine of the Trinity raises for the notion.[39]

The most basic trinitarian claims are impossible to square with simplicity in senses 7 and 8. Consider, for example, the "person-constituting" relations of paternity, filiation, and spiration.[40] Paternity is the relation the Father has from eternity with the Son and the Spirit. To put it differently, paternity is the property that expresses this relation. Filiation is the Son's eternal relation to the Father, and spiration is the Spirit's eternal relation to the Father (and perhaps the Son). Insofar as these constitute the divine persons uniquely (although they do not exhaust them—the divine persons are not merely relations without remainder) and distinguish them from each other, clearly we cannot identify or equate them or claim they are the same as God's essence.[41] For example, if paternity is equivalent to filiation, then the Father exemplifies filiation, and the Son exemplifies paternity. But if we say this, we have obliterated the very claim by which we secure the distinction between Father and Son.

One could say that there is only one relation between Father and Son. Nevertheless, we must maintain that this relation is asymmetrical. The Father and the Son could not change places. There is some fact about the Father that makes him the Father and not the Son, and some fact about the Son that makes him the Son and not the Father, even if we can refer to these separate facts by means of a single asymmetrical relation. Moreover, the relation of the Father to the Son is not the same as the relation of the Father to the Spirit. Therefore, if one wishes to retain the trinitarian distinctions, one must deny that every essential divine property or relation is strongly equivalent.

The problem here is not with trinitarianism per se but with trinitarianism shackled with strong simplicity. Since trinitarianism is fundamental to the Christian doctrine of God, if there is a conflict between it and strong simplicity, then surely the latter should give way.

39. See ibid.; Immink, *Divine Simplicity*.

40. For discussion, see Catherine Mowry LaCugna, *God for Us* (San Francisco: HarperSanFrancisco, 1991), 179–80 n. 133. Of course, it does not follow that we know much about *how* these properties differ. What is required is at least that we maintain that they do differ somehow.

41. Aquinas argues that these are real relations in God (*Summa theologica* Ia, q. 28, art. 1) and that they are really distinguished from each other (Ia, q. 28, art. 4); but he also says in the same question that relation in God is the same as God's essence (Ia, q. 28, art. 3). This way of speaking certainly contributes to the problem.

This conclusion affects the status of senses 7 and 8. If not even God's essential properties are equivalent to each other, then one common objection to the claim that God has contingent properties no longer stands, and we must consider that claim on its own.

## IF GOD HAS BOTH ESSENTIAL AND CONTINGENT PROPERTIES, IS GOD COMPOSITE?

So the strongest senses of simplicity (6, 7, and 8) seem to contradict key tenets of the Christian doctrine of God. But simplicity in sense 2, that God is not composite, is surely binding on anyone who seeks to affirm God's aseity and sovereignty.[42] Indeed, this seems to be the main burden of the doctrine of divine simplicity despite the complicated ways in which it is often expressed. If God were composed of his properties, then God would be constituted by them. They would be metaphysical parts. At best, God would somehow supervene his properties and essence, making God dependent on them.

In *Summa theologica* Ia, q. 3, Thomas Aquinas mentions eight ways God is not composite. God is not composite by being composed of (i) body and soul, (ii) matter and form, (iii) quiddity, essence, or nature and subject, (iv) essence and existence, (v) genus and difference, (vi) subject and accident, (vii) potentiality and actuality, or (viii) things outside him versus things inside him. But if we claim that God has several properties that are in some sense distinct and if we even distinguish between two fundamental types of properties, essential and accidental, do we imply that God is composite and thereby violate this requirement of simplicity? There are several reasons to suppose this is not the case.

What we want to preserve is the conviction that God is not dependent on properties or on his essence in a way that compromises God's aseity. As Alvin Plantinga says, "There is a difference between thinking of God as *having* properties and thinking of his properties as *constituents* of him."[43] I have argued elsewhere that at the very least, when we speak of an entity as having a property, we are attributing some fact or intending to refer to some truth about that entity.[44] Similarly when we refer to divine properties.

42. Even Charles Hodge, no friend of the doctrine of simplicity in some of its manifestations, sees this aspect of the doctrine as worthy of protection. So he argues, "We must not represent God as a composite being, composed of different elements," Charles Hodge, *Systematic Theology*, vol. 1 (Grand Rapids: Eerdmans, reprinted 1995), 1:369.
43. Plantinga, *Does God Have a Nature?* 55.
44. Richards, *The Untamed God*, 64, 242, 246.

Saying that God has different classes of properties, some essential and some contingent, does not imply that God is composite in senses i–v and viii. So our concern is with senses vi and vii, thus reducing the issue at stake to a single question: Is it appropriate to attribute to God any real multiplicity or diversity with respect to actuality and potentiality and to essence and accidents? Does Thomas's claim that God is "altogether simple" or "absolutely simple"[45] entail that all of God's properties are strictly identical with each other, with God's essence, and with God himself? We have already seen that Christians must deny this strongest form of the doctrine of divine simplicity because they are committed to at least one type of essential, internal, eternal distinction in God, namely, the person-constituting differences of the three eternal divine persons. Speaking of multiplicity or distinction of some sort, however, need not be equivalent to speaking of composition *simpliciter*. Here we must insist on the difference between ontological diversity or multiplicity and composition per se. To say that God exists eternally as three persons, for instance, is not to say that God is "composed" of the three persons like cogs on a wheel or fingers on a hand. Trinitarianism does not imply that the divine persons are a divine triumvirate that made a pact to exist eternally together.

If we allow essential distinctions of the divine persons with respect to their person-constituting properties, we have already admitted that simplicity in its strongest senses (7 and 8) contradicts basic requirements for any Christian concept of God. So the doctrine of simplicity cannot be reinstated to deflect the distinctions between essence and accident and between potential and actual in God. There may be some other reason to reject these distinctions in a doctrine of God, but for the trinitarian, strong simplicity cannot be the weapon of choice.

And in fact, we need these distinctions, not because of requirements extrinsic to the doctrine of God or from penchant for novelty in theology but simply because Christians speak of the gratuity and freedom of God's creating and, a fortiori, of the contingency of creation itself. For instance, if God is free in creating the actual world ($w_a$), then God could have refrained from doing so or could have created a world different from the one God has created. But in such a case, God exists with countless potentialities, that is, unactualized possibilities, which are just those things God could choose to do but does not, and those things precluded because of the choices God does take. So if God could have created a world ($w_d$) different from and incompossible with the world God actually created ($w_a$), then God has a potentiality to create $w_d$ that can never be realized, since it is precluded by God's actually creating $w_a$.

45. Aquinas, *Summa theologica* Ia, q. 3, art. 7.

But these claims may not, despite appearances, quite contradict Thomas. One of his motivations for denying "potency" in God was his belief—following Aristotle—that the movement from potency to act (and from essence to accident) is how individuals who share a common essence are individuated.[46] To have accidents in this sense would be to be one contingent individual who instantiates a generic common or "kind essence." Given his broadly Aristotelian intellectual framework, then, Thomas would have been remiss to ascribe accidental properties to God. The modern essentialist can also deny that God has accidents or "potencies" in this Aristotelian sense.

So the disagreement may be less with Thomas than with the contemporary philosophers, such as James Ross, Barry Miller, and perhaps David Burrell, who take Thomas's claim as denying potentiality or possibility in the more modest modern sense and seek to defend it accordingly. Their interpretations augment Thomas's view in various ways. As mentioned above, their first strategy is to construe all relational properties of God *ad extra* as Cambridge properties, such as "being such that Augustine prays" or "being such that 2 is the only even prime." This argument, however, is clearly unsuccessful for certain relational properties, such as God creating the actual world, and the Word uniting with human nature in Christ.[47] On the face of it, these look like obvious examples of real but contingent properties. In fact, among contemporary defenders of strong simplicity, the very reason for construing such properties as Cambridge properties is a prior commitment to strong simplicity.[48] But God's choosing to create the world itself, or God the Son actually uniting with human nature in Jesus, is clearly not extrinsic in the mere Cambridge sense.

To take the first example, how can God's willing to create be contingent if God's willing is identical with every other one of God's properties? Again, Barry Miller and others who pursue this strategy must argue that although the creation is contingent and God is free in creating it, nevertheless, God has no choice or alternative in the matter. And so Miller contends, "Although choice may entail freedom, freedom entails neither choice nor the possibility of a change of mind." To say otherwise is to attribute a potentiality or ability to God that God might not exercise, which is not possible, since God is Pure Actuality.[49] "*Choice* is alien to

46. So Thomas, in arguing that God does not have accidents, says, "A subject is in some sense made actual by its accidents" (Aquinas, *Summa theologica* Ia, q. 3, art. 6).

47. As with immutability, simplicity is difficult to reconcile with the doctrine of the incarnation, especially the relation between Christ's human and divine natures.

48. Miller, e.g., frequently deduces the lack of potentiality and accidents in God from the proposition that God is utterly simple (*A Most Unlikely God*, 95).

49. Ibid., 166.

God because it entails potentiality, but *willing* is not."[50] He argues that there is no "moment" either temporally or logically in which God could survey a range of options and choose one. Nevertheless, God is free in creating the universe, which is therefore contingent.

Miller goes beyond other advocates of this view—who offer little explanation—by distinguishing between internal and external uses of the modal operator, superficially akin to the distinction between a necessity of the consequent and a necessity of the consequence. (*If a, then necessarily b* is a necessity of the consequent. *Necessarily, if a, then b* is a necessity of the consequence.) For example, he argues that since God is absolutely simple, it is incorrect to say, "Even if God had not created the Universe, he could nevertheless have done so." To preserve divine simplicity, one must say, "Even if God had not created the Universe, it was possible that (God create the universe)." Presumably, the latter imputes no potentiality to God.[51] Similarly, instead of saying that God contingently creates the universe, we should say, "God's creation of the Universe is an object of the divine will in less than every possible world." (Because it holds in less than every possible world, this proposition is a contingent one.)[52] And instead of saying, "God can either create the Universe or not create it," we should say (according to Miller), "It can be that (God create the Universe), or it can be that (God not create the Universe)."[53]

I find this argument not only unpersuasive but utterly perplexing. How could it be that God not create the universe if God had no alternative in so doing? If I were to say that it could be so, part of what I would *mean* would be that God had some alternative, that God could have done otherwise. Miller's distinction here bears little analogy to the clear analytical cut between the necessity of the consequence and necessity of the consequent. The first ascribes necessity to the conditional as a whole—*Necessarily (if a, then b)*. The second ascribes necessity to the consequent within the conditional—*If a, then necessarily b*. In contrast, Miller's claim fails to capture any such nuance. It seems to make God's creative freedom far more obscure than it need be and depends on an ineffable distinction without a difference. Moreover, it fails to accommodate the truth that God could have created a universe different from the one God actually created, which is entailed by the claim that the constituents of the universe and the universe itself are contingent.

Perhaps most important, the primary reason for marshaling such recondite distinctions is to preserve strong divine simplicity at all costs.

50. Ibid., 105.
51. Ibid., 165.
52. Ibid., 167.
53. Ibid., 102. Miller capitalizes "Universe" in these quotes.

Such esoterica surely outstrip the meaning of Christian theological discourse. Admittedly, Miller has an additional, unique motivation: he seeks to defend the cogency of God as Uncaused Cause and pure, *simple*, subsistent existence, or Pure Actuality, because he believes he has proven the existence of such a being in a previous work.[54] This is an understandable and even noble motive. Nevertheless, it is incompatible with any robust doctrine of divine triunity. It is telling that although he defends his view as the proper Christian conception of God both philosophically and theologically, he makes no reference to the complexities the Trinity and incarnation pose for his theory.[55] His commitment to strong divine simplicity determines his options, and he sticks to them consistently.

Baldly asserting freedom without choice is no solution. Thomas, incidentally, does not take this course but rather claims there are different ways the world may have been. Contrary to Miller, he says flatly, "We must simply say that God can do other things than those He has done."[56] This may not comport well with Thomas's additional claim that there is no potentiality in God; but Thomas's conviction that freedom includes choice—at least with respect to divine creation—apparently forces him into an inconsistency at this point. I suspect that the problem is that Thomas's Aristotelian understanding of potentiality simply did not provide him with a conceptual tool adequate to make the distinction he needed to make. Miller resolves the inconsistency by opting for strong simplicity over divine choice.

Miller is not the only one to take this route. For instance, in treating divine simplicity, David Burrell says that God's "freedom need not (and I contend, ought not) primarily to be considered as freedom of choice." He admits this "defies our articulation," but notes,

> The sense in which creation is at once gratuitous yet utterly fitting, according to the axiom that "good diffuses itself," reminds us that divine freedom may be better understood on the model of Zen "resonance" than on that of a western penchant for *decisions*.[57]

For Burrell, then, since God is good, he invariably (if not necessarily) diffuses himself by creating.

Perhaps there is some narrow sense of "freedom" that applies in such a scenario. At best, however, such a freedom would be of the "compatibilist" sort that God has with respect to his essence. This type of "freedom"

54. Barry Miller, *From Existence to God* (London: Routledge, 1992).
55. Miller, *A Most Unlikely God*, 168.
56. Aquinas, *Summa theologica* Ia, q. 25, art. 5–6. See also Hughes, *On a Complex Theory*, 109.
57. Burrell, "Distinguishing," 86.

allows us to say that there is never a time at which God does not affirm his essence, that he never feels constrained by it. God never finds himself shackled with, for example, necessary omniscience. Similarly in Burrell's proposal, God never fails to affirm the existence of creation, which is determined by God's self-diffusing nature. Although there is no sufficient external cause for God's creating, there is also no alternative. At best, this is a diminutive sense of freedom and not the robust type appropriate to divine freedom in creation. It is much more restrictive than Leibniz's view, in which God is under a moral but not logical necessity to create the best world (if God creates at all). Such necessitarianism, when combined with language of "diffusion" and "resonance," is also reminiscent of Neoplatonism and even pantheism, which, for the Christian theist, should suggest that Burrell has made a mistake somewhere.

What exactly is the problem with God exercising choices and making decisions? Quite clearly, the problem is that they are inconsistent with a type of simplicity that denies the distinctions of essence and accident and of actual and potential in God. And so the person enamored by strong simplicity must settle for a truncated definition of divine freedom.

By my lights, neither Miller's nor Burrell's suggestion preserves what most Christians mean when they say that creation is contingent and that God's creating is free. Certainly, God's freedom exceeds our own in incomparable ways, not least because God need not work on a pre-existent substratum as all finite creatures must. Nevertheless, if choice and alternatives must be positively barred from our understanding of God's creation of the world, we should conclude that God is not even as free as we are in many situations.[58] This denial of choice does not imply a supereminent but rather an anemic freedom in God. Claiming that creation is contingent while denying that God had any choice in creating it empties the word "contingent" of all determinate logical and theological sense.

If, as I have argued, the strongest form of simplicity is incompatible with trinitarianism, then why should the Christian accept it in this instance? The better course seems to be to retain the claim that God is free (at least with respect to some things) in the libertarian sense. God could have created a world different from the one God actually did create, or God could have created none at all. And the presence of the actual world, or of any world for that matter, neither increases God's perfection nor

58. Burrell is perhaps correct to note that "it would seem jejune to presume, without further analysis, that God's freedom in creating would be given adequate expression by a mere freedom of choice" (*Knowing the Unknowable God*, 104). Mere freedom of choice may not be sufficient to express divine freedom, but certainly it is necessary. Surely God is at least as free as we are when we exercise freedom (assuming, as I do, that we sometimes exercise libertarian freedom).

assails God's aseity. In choosing to create this actual world, God closes off all alternatives not compatible with this choice. This is because of God's free choice and not from any necessity intrinsic or extrinsic to God. God chooses eternally to create the actual world and, by implication, to be the Creator, Sustainer, and Redeemer of this world. We attribute a type of potentiality to God not because we conceive of God as built up from fundamental parts of potency and act but because God is free. God's essential freedom is the source of God's potentiality and contingency. Therefore Christians should affirm that God is simple in just those senses—and only those senses—appropriate to, and compatible with, God's perfect, free, sovereign, and trinitarian reality.

# 8

# JUSTICE OF GOD

## ⸭| Nicholas Wolterstorff |⸬

## THE NEGLECT OF GOD'S JUSTICE BY PHILOSOPHERS AND THEOLOGIANS

The Christian scriptures speak of God as just, of God as doing justice, of God as loving justice and hating injustice, of God as bringing justice, of God's justice. They speak of Jesus as the just one. In short, in the biblical presentation of God, justice is prominent among the divine attributes. Yet in the contemporary revival of philosophical theology, little attention has been paid to God's justice. The ontological attributes traditionally ascribed to God—simplicity, aseity, eternity, immutability, impassibility—have received extensive and probing attention, with some writers defending the traditional ascriptions and a good many others vigorously opposing them. The personal attributes traditionally ascribed to God—omniscience, omnipotence, omnibenevolence—have also received extensive attention, with, in this case, many more defenders of the traditional ascriptions among present-day philosophical theologians than opponents. The distinct moral attributes have received little attention;

love, as one might expect, has received the most. God's justice has either been overlooked or been judged to be of minor importance.

This neglect by philosophers reflects their theological inheritance. In his discussion of God in the *Summa theologica*, Aquinas takes God's justice and his mercy together and devotes one very brief question to the pair (Ia, q. 21). In his earlier *Summa contra gentiles* 1, none of the 102 chapters devoted to a discussion of God and God's attributes deals with God's justice; God's justice is mentioned only in a list of the moral virtues that God possesses (1.93). In the *Systematic Theology* of the "scholastic" Dutch-American Reformed theologian Louis Berkhof, there is a chapter devoted to the "communicable attributes" of God, a page and a third of which deals with what Berkhof calls the righteousness of God; under this rubric, he makes a few remarks about God's justice. In Karl Barth's vast *Church Dogmatics*, one part of one section of the volume devoted to the doctrine of God deals with the mercy and righteousness of God. (The German, translated or mistranslated as "righteousness," is *Gerechtigkeit*).

Though extremely limited, this survey is not, I think, unrepresentative; I firmly expect that a comprehensive survey would confirm the judgment that God's justice has been a very minor component of how Christian theologians have thought and written about God.

The aim of this essay is to begin to right the imbalance. Most of my time, unfortunately, will have to be spent clearing away the brush and framing the issue. And before we even set about doing this, the legitimacy of the topic has to be defended.[1]

## NYGREN'S REJECTION OF JUSTICE IN FAVOR OF LOVE

An influential strand of thought within Christianity denies that the Christian scriptures attribute justice to God. The Hebrew scriptures attribute justice to God, so this line of thought says, but not the Christian scriptures. The latter tell us that God is a God of love rather than a God of justice.

This position was most powerfully developed by the Swedish Lutheran theologian Anders Nygren in *Agape and Eros* (late 1920s).[2] If my experience is representative, no theologian nowadays is willing to admit that he or she follows Nygren. Yet Nygren's presence haunts a great deal of

1. All the positions taken in what follows are defended more amply than I can defend them here in Nicholas Wolterstorff, *Justice* (tentative title), forthcoming.

2. The work was translated piecemeal into English. A full and revised translation appeared in Anders Nygren, *Agape and Eros*, trans. Philip S. Watson (London: SPCK, 1953).

the theology of the past half century. Or perhaps the situation is rather
that Nygren gave systematic expression to a line of thought that runs
deep in modern Christianity, especially modern Protestant Christianity.
In any case, Nygren's work is remarkable for the relentless brilliance
with which he develops his argument. What many of us regard as re-
ductio ad absurdum implications of his basic thesis are viewed by him
as fundamental truths that most Christians are too weak-kneed and
compromised to embrace.

The legalist, says Nygren, thinks in terms of justice. In reflecting on
his relationships with others and theirs with him, the legalist's primary
consideration is always what people deserve, what they merit, what
is due them. Christianity presents a radical alternative to the justice
mentality of the legalist. God does not treat us according to our merits.
God does not ask what is due us and then act accordingly. God loves
us, loves us gratuitously, loves us not because we have some worth that
requires love—we have no such worth—but because it is God's nature
to love. And if we are truly submissive to God, this same divine love will
flow through us and determine our mode of engagement with our fellow
human beings. We will put behind us all thought of what justice requires
and simply promote the neighbor's well-being. Love has nothing to do
with the calculations of justice.

Nygren sees three "fundamental motifs" locked in a struggle for the
heart and mind of the West: the eros motif, the nomos motif, and the
agape motif, which respectively received their finest and purest expressions in the Platonic tradition, in the Old Testament, and in certain of
Jesus's parables, Paul's teaching about God's love, and Martin Luther.

For Judaism, "love to God is the deepest and most inward expression
of man's relation to God which the Old Testament knows. Even so, fellowship between God and man is based on justice and regulated by the
Law. Nomos is the controlling idea, and love has its place within the legal
framework. Christianity, however, effects a complete revolution" (*Agape
and Eros*, 250). "Agape shatters completely the legal conception of the
relationship between God and man. That is the reason for the conflict
of Jesus with the Pharisees and Paul's campaign against 'the Law.' Agape
is the opposite of 'Nomos,' and therefore a denial of the foundation on
which the entire Jewish scale of values rested" (pp. 200–201).[3]

Jesus "enters into fellowship with those who are not worthy of it."
His doing so is directed, says Nygren, "against every attempt to regulate
fellowship with God by the principle of justice" (86). Those whom Jesus

---

3. Nygren does not conceal the affinities between his line of thought, given its sharp
contrast between the God of the Old Testament and the God of the New Testament, with
the ancient heretic Marcion. See ibid., 252.

opposed in word and deed were "the spokesmen for justice in the relation between God and man" (83). "That Jesus should take lost sinners to
Himself was bound to appear, not only to the Pharisees, but to anyone
brought up and rooted in Jewish legal righteousness, as a violation of
the order established by God Himself and guaranteed by His justice"(83).
For them, it was "a violation, not merely of the human, but above all of
the Divine, order of justice, and therefore of God's majesty" (70). What
we learn from Jesus's words and deeds is that "where spontaneous love
and generosity are found, the order of justice is obsolete and invali-
dated" (90). Agape is justice-blind. This is Nygren's theme, repeated in
countless variations and developed with a single-mindedness wondrous
to behold.

The argument cries out for response at many points. I must confine
myself to just one. There is an incoherence at the very heart of Nygren's
argument. For Nygren, God's forgiveness of the sinner is paradigmatic
of God's love, and God's love, in turn, is both paradigmatic for, and motivating of, our relation to our fellows. Two features of God's forgiveness
stand out for Nygren. As with all forgiveness, God's forgiveness of the
sinner is not a species of doing what justice requires; it is of the very
nature of forgiveness that the recipient does not have a right to it. And
second, God does not forgive the sinner as a means to the end of enhanc-
ing God's own well-being. God's forgiveness is an act of benevolence,
done purely out of the goodness of God's nature.

Forgiveness does indeed have these features. But there is another
feature of forgiveness that Nygren ignores, that he has to ignore on pain
of giving up his dismissal of justice. Or to put it the other way round, if
justice goes, forgiveness goes. To see what this feature is, we must have
in mind the distinction between what I shall call *primary* justice and
*secondary* justice.

The basic idea behind the distinction is that when the demands of
primary justice are violated, new rights are created by the wrongdoing;
the honoring of these rights is then *secondary* justice. The distinction
is related to, but not identical with, the traditional distinction between
commutative and distributive justice, on the one hand, and retributive
justice, on the other. As argued in some detail later, primary justice includes commutative and distributive justice but other types as well; and
although I will not argue the point in this essay, the right to retribution
does not exhaust the rights created by violations of primary justice.

Now, to forgiveness. One cannot dispense forgiveness indiscriminately
hither and yon. I can forgive you only if you have wronged me and only
*for* the wrong you have done me. If you have not deprived me of something to which I had a right, then there is nothing for me to forgive you
for—although I may size up the situation incorrectly and *believe* that I

can forgive you. I cannot forgive you if the life good you failed to accord me was not one to which I had a right or if your imposition of a life evil on me harmed but did not wrong me.

It follows that if we never employ the concepts of primary justice and injustice in our engagements with fellow human beings, we cannot understand ourselves as forgiving them. To understand ourselves as forgiving someone presupposes understanding ourselves as having been wronged by the other; it presupposes understanding ourselves as the victim of a breach of primary justice. The concept of forgiveness has the concept of primary justice as one of its components.

Might we nonetheless forgive someone without understanding ourselves as doing so—in the way, say, that we might kick someone without having the concept of kicking and thus without understanding ourselves as kicking him? More to the point: can we forgive someone without recognizing that this person has treated us unjustly? Surely not. To forgive someone requires not only that the person has wronged us but also that we recognize that this person has done so. Forgiveness can only occur in the moral context of a violation of primary justice and in the conceptual and epistemic context of the agent recognizing that he or she has been wronged.

Take a further step. I hold that to forgive the person who has wronged us is to forego claiming certain of the rights that we now have as a victim. If this is correct, then not only must persons who understand themselves as forgiving employ the concept of primary justice and injustice; they must employ the concept of secondary justice as well. I will not contend that we cannot forgive without understanding ourselves as forgiving; perhaps it is possible to forego claiming our rights to secondary justice in a way that counts as forgiving without understanding ourselves as doing so. But even if this is a possibility, what remains true is that the concept of forgiveness has the concept of secondary justice as one of its components.

In short, although it is true, as Nygren never tires of emphasizing, that forgiveness by its very nature is not a case of doing what justice requires, nonetheless persons who have abolished from their minds all thought of primary justice and injustice can neither understand themselves as forgiving, nor can they in fact forgive. The very action that Nygren takes as exemplary of God's actions and paradigmatic for ours requires the concept of primary justice for its intelligibility. Likewise, it requires the reality of both primary injustice and of rights to retributive justice for its actuality. Where there has been no primary injustice and where there are no rights to secondary justice, forgiveness cannot occur; and without these concepts it cannot be understood. To abolish all consideration of justice is to abolish forgiveness. But divine forgiveness is at the heart of the Christian gospel. To cut God's forgiveness out of the gospel would be to eviscerate it. It follows that to cut justice out, God's and ours, would be to eviscerate it.

## THE ASSUMPTION THAT GOD'S JUSTICE IS RETRIBUTIVE JUSTICE

Many Christians, perhaps most, if they heard the justice of God announced as the topic of a discussion, would expect the discussion to be about God's retributive justice. In their minds, God's justice consists of God's righteous punishment of the wrongdoer. Of course, they would add that God is a God of love. Thus it is that discussions on the relation of God's justice to God's love usually take the form of discussions on the relation of God's *retributive* justice to God's love.

Chapter 9 of Anselm's *Proslogion* is an illustration of the point. If Anselm were asked point-blank whether God's retributive justice constitutes the whole of God's justice, he would emphatically deny that it does. Yet the topic of God's justice is introduced in the *Proslogion* under the rubric "How the all-just and supremely just One spares the wicked and justly has mercy on the wicked." The topic, in short, is the relation of God's love to God's retributive justice. Anselm approaches the issue from the end opposite to that of how it is usually approached. Instead of asking how the exercise of retributive justice is compatible with God's love, Anselm asks how foregoing retribution out of love for the sinner is compatible with God's justice. How can a just God "spare the sinner"?

> How do you spare the wicked if You are all-just and supremely just? For how does the all-just and supremely just One do something that is unjust? Or what kind of justice is it to give everlasting life to him who merits eternal death? How then, O good God, good to the good and to the wicked, how do You save the wicked if this is not just and You do not do anything which is not just? Or, since Your goodness is beyond comprehension, is this hid in the inaccessible light in which You dwell?[4]

There is a world of difference between Anselm and Nygren. Nygren refuses to ascribe justice to God; Anselm never hesitates doing so. But this difference should not be allowed to obscure from view some fundamental similarities. For both Anselm and Nygren, God's loving forgiveness of the wrongdoer is the context for the discussion of God's justice. Nygren sees God's loving forgiveness of the wrongdoer as incompatible

4. Translation by M. J. Charlesworth, in Brian Davies and G. R. Evans, *Anselm of Canterbury: The Major Works* (Oxford: Oxford University Press, 1998).

with the ascription of justice to God; to forgive is to forego the exercise of retributive justice. So he repudiates the ascription of justice to God. Anselm takes for granted that God is not only forgiving but also just and sets himself the theological challenge of explaining how a just God can forgive a sinner. Thus both of them set their reflections on God's justice in the context of breakdowns in primary justice and God's response to these breakdowns. Both have retributive justice in mind when they attribute or refuse to attribute justice to God. And both see love and justice as in tension with each other. In Nygren's view, the tension amounts to incompatibility.

## LOVE PITTED AGAINST JUSTICE IN NIEBUHR

Whether God should be thought of as just seems not to have been of much interest to the twentieth-century American theologian Reinhold Niebuhr; in this respect he is distinctly different from Nygren and Anselm. But the underlying premises of his well-known thoughts on love and justice are exactly the same as theirs. When Niebuhr thinks about justice, it is breakdowns that he has in mind—specifically, situations of conflict. Justice becomes relevant when conflicts arise. And as with Nygren and Anselm, love and justice are pitted against each other.

A serene optimism concerning the effects of agapic love in our world pervades Nygren's discussion. Here, by contrast, is Niebuhr's estimation of the effects of agape:

> The divine love can have a counterpart in history only in a life which ends tragically, because it refuses to participate in the claims and counterclaims of historical existence. It portrays a love "which seeketh not its own." But a love which seeketh not its own is not able to maintain itself in historical society. Not only may it fall victim to excessive forms of the self-assertion of others; but even the most perfectly balanced system of justice in history is a balance of competing wills and interests, and must therefore worst anyone who does not participate in the balance.[5]

From the time of the publication of his early book *An Interpretation of Christian Ethics*,[6] Niebuhr never tired of insisting that in our world of conflicting claims, we often find ourselves in situations where pure agape aids and abets injustice. This, for Niebuhr, was history's greatest

5. Reinhold Niebuhr, *The Nature and Destiny of Man: a Christian Interpretation*, 2 vols. in 1 (New York: Charles Scribner's Sons, 1949), 2:72.
6. Reinhold Niebuhr, *An Interpretation of Christian Ethics* (New York: Harper & Brothers, 1935).

irony, that agape should abet injustice. Yet often the only alternative to imposing "evils" on one party in cases of conflict is to stand by and let injustice rule. It is pure "idealism" to think otherwise. In such situations, we must choose justice and forego agape. "The ordinary affairs of the community, the structures of politics and economics, must be governed by the spirit of justice," not by the spirit of agape.[7] Moral life in this world requires the "realism" of recognizing that justice, not agape, is ordinarily the best we can do.

Yet we are not to put agape out of mind. We are to lament the fact that justice and not agape is often best, we are to long for that "impossible possibility"[8] of "frictionless harmony"[9] where agape can be practiced without abetting injustice, and we are to stand ever alert for openings in our present world where we can act agapically without acting unjustly and where justice itself can be tempered with a mercy that does not yield injustice.[10]

What Niebuhr has done, in effect, is divide Nygren's line of thought into two parts, one part about love and justice in God's life, the other part about love and justice in our lives. Niebuhr has no substantial disagreements with Nygren about love and justice in God's life: God as revealed in Jesus Christ is justice-blind agape. For us, justice-blind agape is an eschatological hope but not a "realistic" option. To think that one can practice agape in situations of conflict without making matters worse is naïve and irresponsible "idealism."

## BASIC IN GOD'S JUSTICE IS PRIMARY JUSTICE, NOT RETRIBUTIVE

I submit that understanding God's justice requires that we break with the habit, so deeply ingrained in the Christian tradition, of focusing our attention on claiming and foregoing the rights one has in situations of secondary justice—the habit, in other words, of focusing our attention on breakdowns and threatened breakdowns in primary justice. Secondary justice presupposes primary justice; it is parasitic on primary justice.

7. Reinhold Niebuhr, *Love and Justice: Selections from the Shorter Writings of Reinhold Niebuhr*, ed. D. B. Robertson (Philadelphia: Westminster, 1957), 25.

8. The phrase comes from "The Relevance of an Impossible Ethical Ideal," ch. 4 in Niebuhr, *An Interpretation of Christian Ethics*.

9. The phrase is found in Niebuhr, *Nature and Destiny*, 2:78.

10. Niebuhr, ibid., 2:81–85, offers a systematic discussion of the role that agape can play, as a sort of regulative ideal, in the practice of justice. He never allows his readers to lose sight of his conviction, however, that a straightforward attempt to put agape into practice results in either injustice or one's own death or both.

To understand justice and, in particular, God's justice, one has to begin with primary justice. Beginning there also enables us to reframe the question on the relation of love to justice. Love is not in tension with justice; love practices justice.

## JUSTICE IN THE NEW TESTAMENT

The person who reads the Bible exclusively in English will justifiably view with suspicion many of the things I have said—for example, that the Christian scriptures speak of Jesus as the just one. Where do they speak of Jesus this way? The answer is that Luke reports Peter and Stephen as calling Jesus the just one. In one of his speeches to a crowd in Jerusalem, after Jesus's death, resurrection, and ascension, Peter reproaches them for having rejected the holy and just one (Acts 3:14); and in the speech Stephen gives at his martyrdom, he accuses his hearers of killing the just one (Acts 7:52). Very few of our English translations report Peter and Stephen as saying this, however. Almost all of them report Peter and Stephen as calling Jesus the righteous one. The Greek term translated as "righteous" is *dikaios*. Jesus is the *dikaios* one.

We are touching here on a fundamental and complex issue of translation. Words with the *dik-* stem occur hundreds of times in the Greek of the New Testament—in the adjectival form, *dikaios*; the nominative form, *dikaiosynē*; the verb form, *dikaioō*; the negative adjectival form, *adikos*; and so forth. The verb form, *dikaioō*, occurs most prominently in Paul's letter to the Romans and is almost always translated "to justify." In most translations, the other forms of the *dik-* stem are treated inconsistently. Sometimes *dikaios* is translated "just," but usually "righteous"—as in the two passages from Acts that I mentioned. And although *dikaiosynē* on occasion is translated "justice," usually it is translated "righteousness."

The pattern, insofar as there is one, appears to be that if a *dik-* stem word is used when some aspect of secondary justice is clearly in view, then the translators tend to use a grammatical variant on our term "just" to translate; whereas, when secondary justice is not clearly in view, then the translators tend to use a grammatical variant on our word "right" to translate. In short, the traditional way of thinking that I said we must break with if we are to understand God's justice is embedded in English translations of the New Testament.

The New Revised Standard Version is typical of the lot. It is not clear that Peter and Stephen have some aspect of secondary justice in mind when they describe Jesus as the *dikaios* one; so the translators report them as describing Jesus as the *righteous* one. And when Matthew records one of the beatitudes spoken by Jesus as "Blessed are those who hunger and thirst for *dikaiosynē*," it is also not clear that he has secondary justice in mind; so the translators translate the term as "righteousness"—as they do when *dikaiosynē* is used in a later beatitude, "Blessed are those who are persecuted for *dikaiosynē* sake" (Matt. 5:6, 10).

Near the beginning of his letter to the Romans (1:16–17), Paul announces the topic of his letter this way: "The gospel . . . is the power of God for salvation to everyone who has faith, to the Jew first and also to the Greek. For in it the *dikaiosynē* of God is revealed through faith for faith; as it is written, 'The one who is *dikaios* will live by faith.'" It is not evident from the immediate context that Paul has secondary justice in mind here; so the translators translate *dikaiosynē* as "righteousness" and *dikaios* as "righteous."[11] On the other hand, Paul clearly has secondary justice in mind when he asks rhetorically, in Romans 3:5, "But if our *adikia* serves to confirm the *dikaiosynē* of God, what should we say? That God is *adikos* to inflict wrath on us?" So the NRSV translators translate the passage as follows: "But if our injustice serves to confirm the justice of God, what should we say? That God is unjust to inflict wrath on us?"

Here I cannot possibly treat this translation issue with the care and detail that it deserves. But the fact that those who are learned in the Greek of New Testament times sometimes translate the *dik-* stem words with variants on our term "justice" and sometimes with variants on our term "righteousness" indicates to me that the Greek term was ambiguous as between our "justice" and our "righteousness." Accordingly, context has to determine our translation. And when context does not resolve the issue one way or the other, it is best to use similarly ambiguous English terms—such as "the right thing" and "doing the right thing."

Allowing context to determine the translation is obviously a different principle from the quasi-Nygren principle at work in our translations. And not only are the principles different; every now and then they yield conflicting results. The passage from the first chapter of Romans, in which Paul announces the topic of his letter, can be used to make the point.

His topic, says Paul, is the *dikaiosynē* of God—translated by the NRSV and almost all other English translations as the "righteousness" of God. Paul then proceeds to discuss for roughly the first ten chapters of the letter the evenhandedness of God, the fairness of God, in God's treat-

11. In the next verse, 1:18, Paul says that "the wrath of God is revealed from heaven against all ungodliness and wickedness." Here the NRSV translates *adikia* as "wickedness," although, as we will see, it translates the same term in 3:5 as "injustice." Once again, the pattern appears to be that if secondary justice is clearly in view, then the *dik-* stem words are translated with grammatical variants on our "justice" whereas, if secondary justice is not clearly in view, then they are translated in some other way—usually with variants on our "righteousness," but sometimes as "godly," sometimes as "innocent," and so forth.

ment of Jews vis-à-vis Gentiles. Of Jews and Gentiles alike God requires obedience if they are to escape the divine wrath. Had circumcision been sufficient for Jews whereas obedience was required of Gentiles, this would have been unfair to the Gentiles; obedience is required of both. Both have failed to live up to God's requirements, however; so God would be within his "rights" were God to "inflict his wrath" on both of them. But there is now a new dispensation: to both Jews and Gentiles salvation is available on the basis of faith. God reckons their faith to them as *dikaiosynē*. Over and over and in several different contexts, Paul returns to the theme: God's fairness, as between Jews and Gentiles. But fairness is justice, not righteousness. The topic of Paul's letter to the church at Rome is the precise topic of this essay: the justice of God. Not the retributive justice of God but the primary justice of God. Paul does speak of the retributive justice of God in Romans, but only within the embracing context of the primary justice of God.

The primary justice of God is also one of Luke's main topics in his Gospel and the Acts of the Apostles. Luke presents his narrative as the continuation of the story told in the Old Testament about God's dealings with God's covenant people, Israel. Luke's own narrative, picking up where the old left off, is about what it was that God was doing in the life, execution, and resurrection of Jesus and the early growth of the church. Luke interprets what God was doing in Jesus from a variety of different angles. One of the most prominent is his presentation of Jesus as the Spirit-appointed servant who proclaims the coming of justice in his own person and deeds.

Shortly after he began teaching and preaching in public, Jesus attended the synagogue in Nazareth on a Sabbath and was invited to read from Scripture and to comment on the reading.

> The scroll of the prophet Isaiah was given to him. He unrolled the scroll and found the place where it was written:
>
> > "The Spirit of the Lord is upon me,
> > because he has anointed me to bring good news to the poor.
> > He has sent me to proclaim release to the captives
> > and recovery of sight to the blind,
> > to let the oppressed go free,
> > to proclaim the year of the Lord's favor."

Jesus then "rolled up the scroll, gave it back to the attendant, and sat down." Everyone's eyes were fixed on him, expecting him to say something. And he said, "Today this scripture has been fulfilled in your hearing" (Luke 4:17–21).

The basic text that Luke reports Jesus reading is Isaiah 61:1–2. But Luke has left some lines out of the passage and introduced a couple of lines from other passages in Isaiah—for example, the line "to let the oppressed go free" from a sentence in Isaiah 58:

> Is not this the fast that I choose:
> to loose the bonds of injustice,
> to undo the thongs of the yoke,
> to let the oppressed go free,
> and to break every yoke? (Isa. 58:6)

The import is unmistakable. Jesus identified himself in the synagogue as God's anointed one whose vocation it is to proclaim good news to the poor, the blind, the captives, the oppressed—that is, whose vocation it is to proclaim the arrival of justice and shalom in his person and deeds.


## WHAT IS PRIMARY JUSTICE?

What is primary justice? An efficient way into the issue is to consider what Aquinas says about justice in *Summa theologica* IIa-IIae, qq. 57–58.[12] Aquinas treats justice, *iustitia*, as one among the virtues. But immediately he takes note of the fact that justice differs from all other virtues in that whether an act is an act of justice is determined entirely by what is done, not by how it is done. "A thing is said to be just, as having the rectitude of justice, when it is the outcome of an act of justice, without regard to the way in which that act is done by the agent; whereas in the other virtues nothing is deemed to be right unless it is done by the agent in a certain way" (q. 57, art. 1, resp.).

What must be the thing done if the act is to be an act of justice? The thing done must be *iustum* or *ius*, that is, the just or the right. This is not helpful if one is looking for an explanation of justice and not merely for a description of its structure. To explain what justice is, Aquinas employs the well-known definition found in the opening section of Justinian's *Digest* and attributed to the Roman jurist Ulpian: justice is a steady and enduring will to render to each his or her right—*suum ius cuique tribuere*.[13]

---

12. I will be using the translation in Thomas Aquinas, *Political Writings*, trans. R. W. Dyson (Cambridge: Cambridge University Press, 2002). A much more extended analysis of Aquinas's treatment of justice is found in Eleonore Stump, *Aquinas* (New York: Routledge, 2003).

13. Aquinas defends this definition in q. 58, art. 1.

A point that Aquinas makes right off in his articulation of the Ulpian idea, and to which he returns several times in the course of his discussion, is that justice is always "towards another"; that is, the right (*ius*) brought about by an act of justice is a social relationship of a certain sort. He quotes Cicero as saying that "the purpose of justice is the association of men with one another, and the maintenance of the life of the community"; and he then adds that "this implies a relationship of men with one another. Therefore justice is concerned only with those things that are towards another" (q. 58, art. 2, sed contra). The word *iustitia* can be used figuratively to speak of the relation to each other of various aspects of a single person, but "justice, properly speaking, requires that there be distinct concrete individuals, and, consequently, it exists only in one man in relation to another" (q. 58, art. 2, resp.).

How must individuals be related to each other for the relationship to be just? Aquinas calls on his Aristotelian heritage to address this question. Justice pertains to the exchange and distribution of goods and evils. In one way or another, it "commensurates" (q. 57, art. 3, resp.) goods and evils with persons. We can say that "the 'right' or 'just' is defined by the commensuration of one person with another" (q. 57, art. 4, resp.).

Specifically, "justice denotes a kind of equality" (q. 57, art. 1, ad 3). "A right or just act is one which is 'adjusted' to someone else according to some kind of equality" (q. 57, art. 2, resp.). In slightly different words: justice consists "in a certain proportion of equality as between the external thing and the external person" (q. 57, art. 10, resp.). Aquinas drops the matter at this point. He does not follow Aristotle in trying to explain what sort of equality an act must bring about to be an act of justice.

Recall that the Ulpian definition says that justice consists in rendering to each his or her right (*ius*) and that the Aristotelian definition says that justice consists in some kind of equality. Aquinas has integrated these two parts of his intellectual inheritance, the Ulpian and the Aristotelian, by taking the Ulpian definition of justice as basic and employing the Aristotelian definition as a way of fleshing out the Ulpian definition. I base my interpretation on Aquinas's treatment of the question "Whether the act of justice is to render to each his own?" (q. 58, art. 11).

The definition that justice is rendering to each his own (what is his) comes from Ambrose. Aquinas wants to defend Ambrose's definition. As usual in the *Summa theologica*, Aquinas leads off his discussion of the question posed by lodging some objections to an affirmative answer. It is the third objection, with Aquinas's subsequent response to it, that is of crucial importance for interpreting his understanding of justice. Since Aquinas cites no authority for the objection, it is presumably one that occurred to Aquinas himself.

The objection Aquinas offers is this: "It pertains to justice not only to distribute things in a suitable fashion, but also to restrain harmful acts such as homicide, adultery and so forth. But to render to each what is his seems to belong solely to the distribution of things. Therefore the act of justice is not sufficiently described when it is said to be the act of rendering to each his own" (q. 58, art. 11, obj. 3).

The objection is acute but stated so compactly that it is easy to miss the point. The Ambrosian formula, rendering to each what is his, pertains to distribution situations; a just distribution requires, as a minimum, that one give people what is theirs. Now, consider murder and adultery; rape and torture would serve Aquinas's point equally well. Each of these is a violation of justice. But it would be a mistake to think of any of them as a case of maldistribution. What is wrong about such acts is not that the agent failed to distribute certain goods in a suitably equal manner among a body of recipients, or that the good that the agent chose, from among the goods available, to "distribute" to a single recipient was not suitably equal to the status of that recipient. Nor is what is wrong about such acts that the agent failed to distribute certain evils in a suitably equal manner among a body of recipients, or that the evil that the agent chose, from among the evils available, to distribute to a single recipient was not suitably equal to the status of that recipient. Maldistribution is not the problem.

Having stated three objections to an affirmative answer to the question posed, Aquinas then proceeds in the *responsio* to offer what is, in effect, an Aristotelian interpretation of the Ambrosian formula: "Justice takes external activity as its field of concern insofar as either the activity itself or something that we use in performing it is made proportionate to some other person to whom we are related by justice. Now each person's 'own' is said to be that which is due him according to equality of proportion. Therefore the proper act of justice is nothing else than to render to each his own." And then he offers his replies to the objections. The one that is important for our purposes, his response to the third objection, goes as follows:

> As the Philosopher says in *Ethics* V, in matters of justice, the word "gain" is used wherever there is an excess of any kind and "loss" wherever there is a deficiency. This is because, first and more commonly, justice is exercised in voluntary exchanges of things such as buying and selling, where those terms are used strictly, and the terms are then transferred to all other cases where questions of justice can arise. And the same applies to the rendering to each of what is his own. (q. 58, art. 11, ad 3)

The reply lacks the customary lucidity of Aquinas's prose. Nonetheless, it is not difficult to see what he is driving at.

Homicide and adultery are examples of injustice; they are "cases where questions of justice can arise." Recall that Aristotle focused on two sorts of situations when crafting his definition of justice: voluntary transactions and distributions. When explaining what constitutes justice in situations of the former sort, he employed the concepts of gain and loss. But one can "transfer" the terms of his description and use it to describe cases of justice and injustice that are not voluntary transactions—as murder is not. When one does this, however, one is not using the terms of the definition "strictly." So too for the Ambrosian formula. When taken strictly, it tells us what constitutes justice in distribution situations. But we can transfer the terms of the formula and use it to describe other kinds of justice and injustice—although, once again, we would then not be speaking strictly.

At no point in his entire discussion does Aquinas cite cases of justice and injustice to which the Ulpian formula does not apply in the strict sense of the terms. So I infer that, for Aquinas, the basic formula for justice is that justice is rendering to each his or her right, his or her *ius*. We can then debate whether it is illuminating to describe murder, adultery, rape, and torture as inequitable distributions or transactions. I feel much less piety for Aristotle on this point than Aquinas did. To use the model of an inequitable transaction (exchange) or distribution for thinking and speaking about such violations of justice obscures rather than illuminates. Be that as it may, what we can take from Aquinas is his basic thought, that justice is rendering to each what is his or her *ius*.

## JUSTICE UNDERSTOOD AS ENJOYING ONE'S RIGHTS

It is not immediately evident how we should understand the term *ius* in the Ulpian formula. An important clue, however, is the fact that Ulpian speaks of his or her *ius*: *suum ius*. *Ius* is something that persons have, something they possess. So, what is it that persons have or possess such that justice consists of rendering it to them? The answer is obvious. *Rights* and *deserts*. A person's *ius* is what that person has a right to or what that person deserves. And justice, then, consists of rendering to each what he or she has a right to or what he or she has a desert to, the result of the rendering being that the person now enjoys what he or she has a right to or undergoes what he or she deserves. To put it in other words: justice consists of rendering to each what is *due* the person, whether as something that person has a right to or as something that person deserves. (In q. 57, art. 4, ad 1, Aquinas takes *what is owed* or *due* a person as the equivalent of that person's *ius*.)

194                                        Doctrine of God

We are now plunged into the much debated issue of what a right is. Let us henceforth focus on rights and set deserts off to the side. Whereas the Latin term *ius* covered both rights and deserts, we have no English term of this sort—other, of course, than the disjunctive term "rights or deserts." In saying what a right is, I will have to state my view without, on this occasion, being able to argue for it.[14]

Rights are normative social relationships of a certain sort, with the limiting case of the relationship being that in which a person has a right against himself or herself. The fundamental structure of a right is always *X having a right against Y to Y's doing (or refraining from doing) Z*. Here are three examples: Paul having a right against Peter to Peter's making food available to him, Paul having a right against Peter to Peter's refraining from interfering with his (Paul's) walking in Central Park, and Paul having a right against Peter to Peter's telling him the truth about so-and-so.

Consider the first of these examples, and suppose that Paul does not merely have this right against Peter but is actually enjoying that to which he has a right. Then the following will be a state in Paul's life:

(1) Paul's enjoying his right against Peter to his having food made available to him by Peter.

And not only is it a state in Paul's life; it is a good in his life. It is a state in his life that contributes positively to his well-being.

The state in Paul's life mentioned in item 1 has another state in Paul's life embedded within it:

(2) Paul's having food made available to him by Peter.

This state in his life is what Paul has a right to. And it too, like the state mentioned in item 1, is a good in his life, something that contributes positively to his well-being. Notice, though, that although it is a state in Paul's life, it is at the same time an action on Peter's part. This is more evident when we employ the active voice: Peter's making food available to Paul.

Let us generalize. Enjoying a right is a state in the life (or history) of the person who enjoys it; and this state is a good in the life (or history) of that person.[15] And when one is enjoying a right, that to which one has the right is also a state in one's life, a state that is likewise a good in

14. Wolterstorff, *Justice*, argues in detail for my analysis.
15. This generalization needs an exception and a qualification in order to be fully true. The exception is that in the case of some socially conferred rights, those who conferred the right thought that it was to a good that they were conferring the right, when in fact it was

one's life. Paul's enjoying his right against Peter to his walking in Central Park without Peter's interfering with him is a good in Paul's life; and that to which he has the right, namely, walking in Central Park without Peter's interfering with him, is also a state in his life that is a life good of his. Lastly, the state in his life to which Paul has a right is at the same time a restraint from action on the part of Peter: Peter's refraining from interfering with Paul's walking in Central Park.

It follows from all this that an account of rights presupposes an account of life goods. And one thing that such accounts will have to take cognizance of is that a person's life goods are of wider scope than his or her rights; not everything that is or would be a good in one's life is something to which one has a right. This is the case even if the good in question has the requisite structure, of being an action or restraint from action on the part of someone. Your giving me that painting hanging in your living room would be a great good in my life, but I don't have a right to it.

What accounts for the fact that to certain life goods one has a right whereas to others one does not? Some life goods will be of the wrong structure for one to have a right to them; this is what accounts for it in those cases. But many of those that are of the correct structure are not ones to which one has a right. So, what is it to have a right to some life good? The answer, as I see it, is that rights are grounded in what respect for the worth of persons requires. If Peter's refraining from making food available to Paul amounts to his treating Paul with disrespect, then Paul has a right to Peter's making food available to him.

## ANSWERING THE OPPONENTS OF JUSTICE AS RIGHTS

One last time we have to contend with an alternative approach. There is abroad in the land today strong antipathy to thinking of justice in terms of rights. The antipathy is focused especially on the claim that there are natural rights. And among theorists, the antipathy is typically grounded in a narrative whose central thesis is that natural rights are an invention either of the Enlightenment or of late medieval Ockhamism. Either way, the idea of natural rights was born, so it is said, of individualistic and egoistic modes of thought and continues to have its home among such modes of thought. Those who embrace the idea of natural rights think that the justice of society is ultimately determined by whether the members of society enjoy the rights that belong to them naturally. But

---

not a good. The qualification is made necessary by so-called third-party rights, as when X has a right to Y keeping his promise to X to act in such-and-such a way toward Z.

there are no natural rights, only socially conferred rights. A society is just when it measures up to objective right order, not when its members are enjoying their "subjective" rights. There is natural objective right; there are no natural subjective rights.[16]

As with all the alternative modes of thought that I have rehearsed, this deserves careful and extended consideration. Here I will have to neglect the proffered narrative and confine myself to offering two systematic arguments for the existence of natural rights.[17]

To be wronged is to be deprived of a life good to which one has a right. Recall our reflections on forgiveness. We can forgive someone only if we have been wronged by that person and we recognize that we have been. Being deprived by someone of some life good to which we do not have a right may well be something that we regret, but it cannot be that for which we forgive. The right for whose violation we forgive someone may, of course, be a socially conferred rather than a natural right. But the wrongs Christ enjoins us to forgive are by no means confined to violations of socially conferred rights. Denying the existence of natural rights is incompatible with the scope of the forgiveness that Christ enjoins.

My second argument for the same conclusion goes as follows. Rights have duties as their correlatives: if X has a right against Y to Y's doing (or refraining from doing) Z, then Y has a duty toward X to do (or refrain from doing) Z. Now a duty of charity, as traditionally understood, is a duty that Y has toward X, to do (or refrain from doing) Z, when X does not have a right against Y to Y's doing (or refraining from doing) Z. So if there are duties of charity, the converse of the principle stated above does not hold; there will be duties toward a person to do something without that person having a right against one to that being done. It follows that the person who holds that there are no natural rights must hold either that there are no natural obligations or that all natural obligations are duties of charity.

A good many thinkers today do hold that there are no natural obligations. But this is not an option open to the Christian. We have obligations toward God, and in the nature of the case, these are not obligations that have been socially conferred by human law or practice. So the Christian who holds that there are no natural rights will have to hold that all natural obligations are obligations of charity. But the obligations that we have toward God are not obligations of charity. God has a right to our obedience—a natural right.

16. One finds this attack against natural rights mounted so often that it seems almost pointless to give references. One readily accessible example is Joan Lockwood O'Donovan, "The Concept of Rights in Christian Moral Discourse," in *A Preserving Grace*, ed. Michael Cromartie (Grand Rapids: Eerdmans, 1997) 143–56.

17. A devastating critique of the narrative is now available in Brian Tierney, *The Idea of Natural Rights* (Atlanta: Scholars Press, 1997).

Consider also what Scripture says about the injustices that we perpetrate on our fellows. It does not confine itself to presenting the oppressors as guilty—though it does present them thus. It presents the widows, the orphans, the aliens, and the impoverished as *wronged*, wronged whether or not there are socially conferred rights of which they have been deprived. Enslavement of the Israelites by Egypt was evidently not in violation of Egyptian law. The Israelites were wronged nevertheless, deprived of their rights. Christian scripture requires not only that we think of justice in terms of rights but also that we acknowledge the existence of natural rights.

## GOD'S JUSTICE

We can now pull things together quickly. Justice is constituted of normative social relationships. Primary justice reigns when the rights of persons to the actions and restraints from action of others are honored. A person is just insofar as he or she honors the rights of others to actions and restraints from action on his or her part. A person enjoys justice insofar as others honor his or her rights to actions and restraints from action on their part. The charge that rights are individualistic makes no sense; rights are inherently social. Likewise the charge that rights are egoistic makes no sense; the very existence of the other places claims upon me. Equally senseless is the insistence one sometimes hears that we should think in terms of obligations rather than rights. If rights go, most obligations go.

To praise God for his justice is to praise God for honoring the rights of his creatures. God does not violate us. God does not treat us with disrespect for our worth. It would be perplexing indeed if God did. For we have the intrinsic worth we do have on account of being created thus by God.

We must not forget or ignore the other side of the picture. God has the right to be honored. We do not honor God as we should. God has the right to be obeyed. We do not obey God as we should. We wrong God, deprive God of what he has a right to. God is victim of our injustice.

This last comment brings into view the relation between the moral and the ontological attributes of God. If God is wronged, then God is not impassible. That will lead some to conclude that God cannot be wronged. But I take divine forgiveness to be at the heart of the Christian gospel. And if God forgives, then God is not only capable of being wronged but has in fact been wronged. To say it one more time: one can forgive someone only if that person has wronged one and only for the wrong he has done one.

PART 4

CREATION

# 9

# EVOLUTION AND DESIGN

## ⋙| Alvin Plantinga |⋘

## IS EVOLUTION INCOMPATIBLE WITH DESIGN?

Our topic is evolution and design. To begin with, we need a brief account of what we propose to mean, for present purposes, by these two terms. As for evolution, we should note that the term covers a multitude—not necessarily a multitude of sins, but a multitude nevertheless. First, there is the claim that the earth is very old, perhaps some 4.5 billion years old: the *ancient-earth thesis*, as we may call it. Second, there is the claim that life has progressed from relatively simple to relatively complex forms of life. In the beginning there was relatively simple unicellular life, perhaps of the sort represented by bacteria and blue-green algae, or perhaps still simpler unknown forms of life. (Although bacteria are simple compared with some other living beings, they are in fact enormously complex creatures.) Then more complex unicellular life, then relatively simple multicellular life such as seagoing worms, coral, and jellyfish, then fish, then amphibia, then reptiles, birds, mammals, and finally, as the culmination of the whole process, human beings: the *progress thesis*, as we humans may like to call it (jellyfish might have a different view as to where the whole process culminates). Third, there is the *common-ancestry thesis*: that life originated at only one place on

202

CREATIONCREATION

earth, all subsequent life being related by descent to those original living creatures—the claim that, as Stephen Gould puts it, there is a "tree of evolutionary descent linking all organisms by ties of genealogy."[1] According to the common-ancestry thesis, we are literally cousins of all living things—horses, oak trees, and even poison ivy—distant cousins, no doubt, but still cousins. (This is much easier to imagine for some of us than for others.)

Fourth, there is the claim that there is a (naturalistic) *explanation* of this development of life from simple to complex forms: the most popular candidate is natural selection operating on random genetic mutation. Since Darwin made a similar proposal, call this thesis *Darwinism*. Finally, there is the claim that life itself developed from nonliving matter without any special creative activity of God but just by virtue of processes described by the ordinary laws of physics and chemistry: call this the *naturalistic-origins thesis*. These five theses are different from each other in important ways. They are also logically independent in pairs, except for the third and fourth theses: the fourth entails the third, in that you cannot sensibly propose a mechanism or an explanation for a process without agreeing that the process has indeed occurred. Suppose we use the term "Evolution" to denote the conjunction of these five theses.

As for design, we need only one distinction. "According to Dr. Sam Ridgway, physiologist with the US Naval Ocean Systems Center in San Diego, seals avoid the bends by not absorbing nitrogen in the first place. 'The lungs of marine mammals,' Dr. Ridgway explains, 'are designed to collapse under pressure exerted on deep dives. Air from the collapsed lungs is forced back into the windpipe, where the nitrogen simply can't be absorbed by the blood.'"[2] And according to Daniel Dennett, "in the end, we want to be able to explain the intelligence of man, or beast, in terms of his design; and this in turn in terms of the natural selection of this design."[3] In this use of the term, organisms have a design or exhibit a design plan: a way in which they work when they are working properly, when there is no dysfunction or malfunction. Of course, this terminology does not commit us to supposing that seals and human beings and other organisms have been literally designed—by God, for example. There is no implication here that organisms are actually artifacts. And in this first sense of "design," there is no incompatibility at all between

1. Stephen Gould, "Evolution as Fact and Theory," in *Hen's Teeth and Horse's Toes* (New York: Norton, 1983).
2. Quoted in Roger L. Gentry, "Seals and Their Kin," *National Geographic* 171/4 (April 1987): 489.
3. Daniel Dennett, *Brainstorms: Philosophical Essays on Mind and Psychology* (Montgomery, VT: Bradford Books, 1978), 12.

evolution, taken as the conjunction of the above theses, and the thesis that human beings and other organisms display design.

But there is a stronger and more interesting sense of "design." In this stronger sense, something exhibits design only if it or some of its parts display design in the weak sense and have also been literally designed by one or more conscious, intelligent, intentional agents. Artifacts, naturally enough, are prime examples: a pencil or Buick or cathedral, for instance. These things have been designed by conscious and intelligent agents with the intention that they work a certain way and fulfill a certain function, broadly conceived. We can also ask whether human beings and other organisms exhibit design of this sort. Christians and other theists claim that these things do in fact exhibit design of this sort; they claim that God, who is maximally conscious, intelligent, intentional, has designed them. All the living creatures the world displays are a result of divine design, and God has designed and created human beings in his own image. I shall use the word "Design" as a name for this view, the view that human beings and other organisms have been intentionally designed by one or more conscious and intelligent agents. And our first question is whether Design is incompatible with Evolution.

Well, some people seem to think so. According to Stephen Gould, "before Darwin, we thought that a benevolent God had created us." After Darwin, however, he says, we realize that "no intervening spirit watches lovingly over the affairs of nature."[4] Gould's sentiments are stated more clearly by the biologist Douglas Futuyma:

> By coupling undirected, purposeless variation to the blind, uncaring process of natural selection Darwin made theological or spiritual explanations of the life processes superfluous. Together with Marx's materialistic theory of history and society and Freud's attribution of human behavior to processes over which we have little control, Darwin's theory of evolution was a crucial plank in the platform of mechanism and materialism—of much of science, in short—that has since been the stage of most Western thought.[5]

Clearer yet, perhaps, is George Gaylord Simpson:

> Although many details remain to be worked out, it is already evident that all the objective phenomena of the history of life can be explained by purely naturalistic or, in a proper sense of the sometimes abused word, materialistic factors. They are readily explicable on the basis of differential reproduction in populations (the main factor in the modern conception

4. Stephen Gould, *Ever Since Darwin: Reflections in Natural History* (New York: W. W. Norton, 1979), 267.
5. Douglas Futuyma, *Evolutionary Biology*, 2nd ed. (Sunderland, MA: Sinauer Associates, 1986), 3.

of natural selection) and of the mainly random interplay of the known
processes of heredity. . . . Man is the result of a purposeless and natural
process that did not have him in mind.[6]

The same claim is made by Richard Dawkins:

> All appearances to the contrary, the only watchmaker in nature is the blind
> forces of physics, albeit deployed in a very special way. A true watchmaker
> has foresight: he designs his cogs and springs, and plans their interconnec-
> tions, with a future purpose in his mind's eye. Natural selection, the blind,
> unconscious automatic process which Darwin discovered, and which we
> now know is the explanation for the existence and apparently purposeful
> form of all life, has no purpose in mind. It has no mind and no mind's
> eye. It does not plan for the future. It has no vision, no foresight, no sight
> at all. If it can be said to play the role of watchmaker in nature, it is the
> *blind* watchmaker.[7]

These experts apparently believe therefore that Darwin, or science,
or both, or something else in the near neighborhood has shown that
theological or religious explanations of human life and behavior are
superfluous, that all of life can be explained on the basis of materialistic
factors, that human beings have not been designed by God, and that
the true explanation of all of life, including human life, is a blind process: the coupling of chance (random genetic mutation) with necessity
(natural selection). Accordingly, they apparently believe that Evolution
is incompatible with Design.

But are they correct? I don't think so. Dawkins, Simpson, and the rest
embrace *philosophical naturalism*. This is the view that there is nothing
but nature: there is no such person as God, or even anything at all like
God; there are no supernatural beings of any sort. Naturalism therefore
implies that we human beings have not been designed and created in
God's image (because it implies that there is no God); but science by
itself does not have this implication. Naturalism and evolutionary theory
*together* imply the denial of Design; but evolutionary theory *by itself*
does not have this implication. Evolution plays an important role in the
naturalistic way of looking at the world. It functions as a sort of myth,
in a technical sense of that term: it offers a way of interpreting ourselves
to ourselves, a way of understanding our origin and significance at the
deep level of religion. But evolutionary science by itself does not imply
that human beings, for instance, have not been created by God and cre-

6. George Gaylord Simpson, *The Meaning of Evolution*, rev. ed. (New Haven: Yale
University Press, 1967), 344–45.
7. Richard Dawkins, *The Blind Watchmaker* (New York: W. W. Norton, 1986), 5.

ated in his image, for God could, of course, have created human beings using evolution as a means. It is only evolutionary science combined with naturalism that implies the denial of Design. Since naturalism all by itself has this implication, it is no surprise that when you put it together with science or, as far as that goes, anything else—ancient Greek history or the *Old Farmer's Almanac* or the Apostles' Creed—the combination has these implications.

So it is naturalism, not science, that is really at issue here. Oddly enough, the eminent Harvard biologist Richard Lewontin let this particular cat out of the bag:

> Our willingness to accept scientific claims that are against common sense is the key to an understanding of the real struggle between science and the supernatural. We take the side of science *in spite of* the patent absurdity of some of its constructs, *in spite of* its failure to fulfill many of its extravagant promises of health and life, *in spite of* the tolerance of the scientific community of unsubstantiated just-so stories, because we have a prior commitment, a commitment to materialism. It is not that the methods and institutions of science somehow compel us to accept a material explanation of the phenomenal world, but, on the contrary, that we are forced by our *a priori* adherence to material causes to create an apparatus of investigation and a set of concepts that produce material explanations, no matter how counterintuitive, no matter how mystifying to the uninitiated. Moreover, that materialism is absolute, for we cannot allow a Divine Foot in the door.[8]

But perhaps we are being a little quick: isn't there a good reason for thinking Evolution and Design *are* incompatible? According to Darwinism, the main explanation of the structure of human beings and other organisms is that they have developed by way of natural selection operating on the genetic variation thrown up by random genetic mutation.[9] But if genetic mutation is really random, then the appearance of a mutation in a population is due to chance. And if it is due to chance, it is not due, of course, to design on the part of an intelligent agent—in which case Design is false. As Dawkins says, "Natural selection, the blind, unconscious automatic process which Darwin discovered, and which we now know is the explanation for the existence and apparently purposeful form of all life, has no purpose in mind."

8. Richard Lewontin, "Billions and Billions of Demons," review of Carl Sagan, *The Demon-Haunted World, New York Review of Books*, 44/1 (January 9, 1997): 31.

9. Some other factors are also sometimes cited: genetic drift, cataclysms of various sorts, and the like.

This suggestion raises warning flags: how could a sensible scientific hypothesis, part of empirical science, imply that life, human and otherwise, is not a product of divine design? Wouldn't that entail a slide into theology? In any event, there is equivocation here. It is indeed true, according to Darwinism, that what drives the whole process of evolution is (for the most part) natural selection operating on the results of random genetic mutation. But what is the sense of "random" here? And is this sense such that an event could not be both random and also intended and caused by God or some other intelligent agent? I don't think so. According to Darwin (or at any rate the neo-Darwinian synthesis), the sense in which variation is random is this: it is not called for by the design plan of the creature to which it accrues, and it does not occur because it is beneficial for that organism. Of course it might in fact *be* beneficial in the sense that it contributes to increase of reproductive fitness; but the needs of the organism to which it accrues play no part in its causation. But clearly a mutation could be both random in this sense and also intended and indeed caused by God. So the fact, if it is a fact, that human beings have come to be by way of natural selection operating on random genetic mutation is not at all incompatible with their having been designed by God and created in his image. Perhaps, for example, God orchestrates the whole process, causing the right mutations to show up at the right times, intending a certain result: the coming to be of us human beings.

Still, there may be a rejoinder. Consider a stronger sense of "random," a sense that implies what we might call deep chance, so that a mutation is random in this sense only if it is not caused by God; we could add, if we like, that if an event is random in this sense, it has no cause at all. Say that an event random in this sense is *genuinely* random. Now we can state Darwinism, or, if you like, Strong Darwinism, as follows: human beings and other organisms have come to be by way of natural selection operating on genuinely random genetic mutation. The empirical evidence, whatever exactly it is and however exactly it is to be understood, apparently doesn't distinguish between Strong Darwinism and Darwinism *simpliciter*. And therefore won't Strong Darwinism be just as successful and just as well confirmed as Darwinism taken the more modest way? If Darwinism *simpliciter* is more likely than not with respect to the relevant evidence, won't the same go for Strong Darwinism? If so, however, then perhaps Dawkins et al. are right after all: *Darwinism* is consistent with Design, but *Strong* Darwinism is not; furthermore Strong Darwinism is as well supported by the relevant empirical evidence as Darwinism, which is to say, very strongly supported indeed.

But is it true that Strong Darwinism is as strongly supported by the relevant empirical evidence as Darwinism *simpliciter*? Not necessarily.

Strong Darwinism, naturally enough, is stronger than Darwinism *simpliciter*; hence relative to given evidence, the former may be less well supported than the latter, even if both are consistent with that evidence. Indeed, it might be that Darwinism *simpliciter* is powerfully supported by the empirical evidence; whereas, Strong Darwinism is supported no more strongly than its denial. We can see this as follows. The relevant empirical evidence does not distinguish between Darwinism and Strong Darwinism: fair enough. But neither does it distinguish between Darwinism and Weak Darwinism: the theory that the genetic mutations in question, though random in the sense of Darwinism *simpliciter*, are not *genuinely* random. There is no reason to think that Strong Darwinism is more likely with respect to the relevant empirical evidence than weak; indeed, it looks as if Weak Darwinism is as likely, with respect to the relevant empirical evidence, as Strong Darwinism. But Weak Darwinism is incompatible with Strong. Clearly it is not possible that two incompatible propositions should both be more likely than not with respect to the empirical evidence; hence Strong Darwinism is not more likely than not with respect to this evidence.

So first, there is no reason to think Strong Darwinism is more likely than not with respect to the relevant empirical evidence; at any rate, the suggested reason is not a good one. But second, is it really true that Strong Darwinism is incompatible with Design? Not obviously. Here I'll simply draw on some excellent work by Del Ratzsch.[10] As Ratzsch points out, perhaps an intelligent agent could employ deep chance in order to pursue design. Suppose the outcome of a roll of fair dice is in fact a chance outcome; but suppose furthermore you know how the dice would fall if you were to throw them on a given occasion O. Perhaps you know that if you were to throw them on this occasion, they would come up snake eyes. Clearly, you could use this information to further your designs—winning some money, for example. Or you have a widget-producing machine with a randomizing element; the color of the widgets produced is a result of deep chance. You have always wanted to own the only widget in the world that is red, but is so as a result of deep chance. Now suppose you know that if, on a given occasion, you were to turn the machine on, it would produce a widget that was red as a result of deep chance. If so, you can bring it about that a widget of the kind you want is produced by deep chance.

Perhaps in the same way God could intend that there be creatures meeting a certain description—creatures just like us human beings, for example—and could bring it about that there are such beings by em-

---

10. Del Ratzsch, "Design, Chance, and Theistic Evolution," in *Mere Creation*, ed. William Dembski (Downers Grove, IL: InterVarsity, 1998), 303ff.

208                                                          CREATION

ploying deep chance. Perhaps, for example, God knew in advance what
sorts of genuinely random mutation would arise by chance in various
situations. God might know that if there was a certain population of
animals in a certain set of circumstances, then such and such mutations
would occur by deep chance. Using this kind of knowledge, he could
see to it that creatures of a certain type arise, but arise by virtue of the
workings of chance processes.

Critics might object that God could do this only if God knew *counterfactuals of chance*, counterfactuals akin to the counterfactuals of
freedom much discussed in treatments of the problem of evil. They
might add that although counterfactuals of freedom are bad enough,[11]
counterfactuals of chance are even worse; clearly enough, they might
say, there aren't any such things. More exactly, there aren't any *true*
counterfactuals of chance. Still more exactly (since clearly there are
such true counterfactuals as "If an event of kind K were to happen by
chance, then at least one event would happen by chance"), there aren't
any counterfactuals of chance that are nontrivially true. But I am not
convinced by the arguments against nontrivially true counterfactuals of
freedom, and if there is or could be such a thing as deep chance, I can't
see why there could not be true counterfactuals of deep chance. This is
not the place to argue this point, however, and for present purposes it
is not necessary to argue it. This is because Ratzsch also shows how it
could be that life is a result of design even if there aren't any nontrivially
true counterfactuals of chance:

> If no appropriate subjunctive is true (or even has a truth value), then a
> creator (if creating at all) would be in a position of having to give things
> the most promising-looking start and then having to take a subjunctive
> supervision stance of being prepared, if necessary, to intervene in order
> to keep things on a proper track. Should it turn out that things stay on an
> acceptable track—and that may well be in part a result of the way various
> undetermined, uncaused, random quantum events go—then no interven-
> tion would be necessary.[12]

And if no intervention is necessary, then the resulting process of evolution
could produce beings of a sort God intends in advance to produce, even
if this process involves deep chance and even if there are no nontrivially
true counterfactuals of chance.

11. See, e.g., Robert Adams, "Middle Knowledge and the Problem of Evil," in *The
Problem of Evil*, ed. Robert Adams and Marilyn Adams (Oxford: Oxford University Press,
1990), 116.
12. Ratzsch, "Design, Chance," 306.

## EVOLUTIONARY PSYCHOLOGY AND DESIGN

Those who accept Darwinism, naturally enough, often attempt to explain various features of contemporary organisms in Darwinian terms. One way to do this is to show how the trait in question does or did contribute to the reproductive fitness of the organism in question. Why do tigers have stripes? Because of their efficacy as camouflage, which, in turn, given the tiger's lifestyle, is fitness-enhancing. Or perhaps the trait in question is not itself adaptive, does not itself contribute to fitness, but is associated with a trait that does. As a special case, perhaps the trait in question is a spandrel, a trait that doesn't itself directly contribute to fitness but is a consequence of a mode of construction, for instance, that does. These explanations seem plausible, at least within limits: if you think the organisms in question arose in this way, then this seems a sensible way in which to explain at least some of their traits.

This sort of explanation has been extended to human beings as well; one enterprise of giving such explanations is evolutionary psychology. Formerly called "sociobiology," evolutionary psychology has been with us for at least the last twenty-five years, ever since the publication of E. O. Wilson's *Sociobiology*.[13] The heart and soul of this project is the effort to explain distinctive human traits—our art, humor, play, love, poetry, sense of adventure, love of stories, our music, our morality, and our religion itself—the heart and soul of this project is to explain all of these properties in terms of our evolutionary origin. This project is extremely popular and, I think, rapidly growing in popularity. About every other issue of the *New York Review of Books* carries a review of still another book intended to interpret ourselves to ourselves along these lines. A recent high (or maybe low) point is a book (also reviewed in the *New York Review of Books*) in which a new understanding of *religion* is proposed. At a certain stage in our evolutionary history, so the claim went, we human beings made the transition from being prey to being predators. Naturally, this occasioned great joy, and religion arose as a celebration of that happy moment! Granted, this sounds a little far-fetched: wouldn't we have needed the consolations of religion even more when we were still prey? Still, this was the claim. Some of these projects therefore are a little hard to take seriously, but others are attended with all the trappings of serious science, complete with models, mathematics, the fitting of models to data, and the sort of stiff, impersonal literary style in which science is properly written.

13. E. O. Wilson, *Sociobiology: The New Synthesis* (Cambridge: Belknap Harvard University Press, 1975).

Most of those who accept Design believe that human beings have been designed by God. Furthermore, most who think human beings have been designed by God think that human beings have been designed and created in the image of God. Still further, most who think human beings have been created in the image of God are Christian theists of one sort or another. And here we do encounter a conflict between Design, or some specification of it, and Evolution, or some applications of it. For some of the explanations offered by evolutionary psychologists do indeed seem to be incompatible with Christian theism. According to Steven Pinker, for example, the question here is, "How does religion fit into a mind that one might have thought was designed to reject the palpably not true?"[14] One answer he suggests: "Religion is a desperate measure that people resort to when the stakes are high and they have exhausted the usual techniques for the causation of success—medicines, strategies, courtship, and, in the case of the weather, nothing."[15] Another is a variant on the old canard that it's all because of the chicanery of priests: "I have alluded to one possibility: the demand for miracles creates a market that would-be priests compete in, and they can succeed by exploiting people's dependence on experts."[16] We trust such experts as dentists and doctors. "That same trust would have made me submit to medical quackery a century ago and to a witch doctor's charms millennia ago."[17] E. O. Wilson offers similar accounts of religious belief.[18]

Examples of this way of thinking are abundant, but I want to look at a particular example in just a bit more detail. According to Herbert Simon, there is a problem about *altruistic* behavior: why, he asks, do people such as Mother Teresa or the Methodist missionaries of the nineteenth century devote their time and energy and indeed their entire lives to the welfare of others? Not only the great saints of the world display this impulse; most of us do so to one degree or another. Simon addresses this problem.[19]

But first, why is it a problem? Why do we *need* to account for it? Why should altruism be a problem? Because, says Simon, we human beings have come to be by way of natural selection operating on some source of genetic variation. But then one would not expect altruistic behavior. What natural selection would select for, one thinks, would be behavior

14. Steven Pinker, *How the Mind Works* (New York: W. W. Norton, 1997), 554.
15. Ibid., 556.
16. Ibid., 557.
17. Ibid.
18. E. O. Wilson, *On Human Nature* (Cambridge: Harvard University Press, 1978); *Consilience: The Unity of Knowledge* (New York: Knopf, 1998); *Sociobiology.*
19. Herbert Simon, "A Mechanism for Social Selection and Successful Altruism," *Science* 250 (December 1990): 1665ff.

of a kind that promotes survival and reproductive fitness. Here fitness is not a matter of good physical condition, as with someone who can run ten miles; it is instead the probability that one's genes will be widely disseminated in the next and subsequent generation, thus doing well in the evolutionary derby. More plainly, says Simon, "fitness simply means expected number of progeny." Given our origin and development in terms of natural selection, what one would expect is that we human beings would always or usually try to act in such a way as to increase fitness: *this* behavior is what would be selected. People such as Mother Teresa and Thomas Aquinas, however, cheerfully ignore the short- or long-term fate of their genes. What, says Simon, is the explanation of this behavior?

The answer, he says, lies in two mechanisms: "docility" and "bounded rationality":

> Docile persons tend to learn and believe what they perceive others in the society want them to learn and believe. Thus the content of what is learned will not be fully screened for its contributions to personal fitness.[20]

> Because of bounded rationality, the docile individual will often be unable to distinguish socially prescribed behavior that contributes to fitness from altruistic behavior [i.e., socially prescribed behavior that does not contribute to fitness]. In fact, docility will reduce the inclination to evaluate independently the contributions of behavior to fitness. . . . By virtue of bounded rationality, the docile person cannot acquire the personally advantageous learning that provides the increment, $d$, of fitness without acquiring also the altruistic behaviors that cost the decrement, $c$.[21]

Apparently the idea is that people such as Mother Teresa and Thomas Aquinas display "bounded rationality"; they are unable to distinguish socially prescribed behavior that contributes to their fitness from altruistic behavior, that is, socially prescribed behavior which does *not* contribute to their fitness. They acquiesce unthinkingly in what society tells them is the right way to behave, and they aren't up to making their own independent evaluation of the bearing of such behavior on the fate of their genes. If they *did* make such an independent evaluation (and were rational enough to avoid silly mistakes), they would presumably see that this sort of behavior does not contribute to fitness, drop it like a hot potato, and get right to work on their expected number of progeny.

Now this account of altruism, like Pinker's explanation of religion, is incompatible with Christian theism. Clearly, no Christian could accept

20. Ibid., 1666.
21. Ibid., 1667.

this account as even a beginning of a viable explanation of the altruistic behavior of the Mother Teresas of this world. From a *naturalistic*
perspective, perhaps, this Simonian way of thinking about us human
beings and our altruistic propensities seems sensible. From a Christian
perspective, however, it is deeply mistaken and woefully inadequate. And
the next question I want to ask is this: How should those who accept
Christian theism respond to this sort of scientific project—"Simonian
science," as we may call it? Should they simply reject it? Should they
instead bracket or soft-pedal or reject the elements of Christian belief
that conflict with it? We could put the question like this: does Simonian
science give Christian theists a *defeater* or partial defeater for one or
more beliefs they hold as Christian theists?

That is the question, but we need a couple of initial qualifications.
First, we must note the swirling controversy and discussion among scientists and others as to the viability, scientific character, and respect-
ability of Simonian science;[22] here science—or, at any rate, scientists
and those who think about science—hardly speaks with a single voice.
So I want to idealize my question somewhat: let's suppose, for present
purposes, that science really does speak here with a single voice, one
that endorses Simonian science; let's suppose that Simonian science is a
deliverance of contemporary science in the way in which, for instance, the
doctrine of universal common ancestry is. And this leads to my second
qualification. Christian theists, I think, are committed to a high view of
science. Modern science arose within the bosom of Christian theism;
it is a shining example of the powers of reason with which God has
created us; it is a spectacular display of the image of God in us human
beings. So Christians are committed to taking science and the deliverances of science with the utmost seriousness. And now my question is
this: given the respect and even deference Christian theists owe science
and supposing Simonian science to be a deliverance of contemporary
science, if some of these deliverances contradict elements of Christian
belief, would this fact furnish Christian theists with a defeater or partial
defeater for those beliefs?

I think the answer is, "No, it would not." Why not? We can begin to
see the answer by considering a widely noted feature of science: *methodological naturalism*. Science, so the claim goes, does not presuppose
or endorse or require what I called *philosophical* naturalism; but it does
require *methodological* naturalism. Science is neutral with respect to the
former, but the latter is widely taken to be a constraint either on science
itself or on how science is properly done. What exactly is methodological
naturalism, and how shall we state the indicated constraint? This is not

22. See, e.g., Philip Kitcher, *Vaulting Ambition* (Cambridge: MIT Press, 1987).

an easy question, but for present purposes we will take methodological naturalism to be at least two connected ideas. First, in doing science, one cannot properly explain anything by appeal to God's action or the action of any other supernatural being. Propositions about the behavior or character or properties of such beings cannot be employed as scientific hypotheses. And second, in science one cannot properly use or appeal to anything known only by faith. For example, one cannot appeal to anything learned only from the Bible. One therefore could not explain altruism by appealing to the image of God in us human beings, or to the work of the Holy Spirit in human hearts. Even if this is where the true explanation ultimately lies, this explanation would be theology rather than science.

Much has been written about methodological naturalism; it is a large and important subject, and there are many good questions to ask about it,[23] but we shall have to leave those questions unanswered. For present purposes, I want to concede or assume that methodological naturalism really is *de rigeur* for science, in the sense that it is either a condition for science itself, is part of the very standpoint of science, or is at any rate a requirement for good science. And there is one more assumption: let us assume that from the scientific standpoint, the standpoint of methodological naturalism, Simonian science is the correct way to think about human beings. From this standpoint, we human beings are a product of evolution by natural selection. But then the most plausible way to think about ourselves, again from this standpoint, is one that explains our possession of those important human traits—mother love, love of learning, morality, religion, altruism, and so on—in broadly Darwinian terms.

So assume that science requires methodological naturalism, that methodological naturalism requires Simonian science, and that Simonian science contradicts Christian belief. Does this conflict give Christian theists a defeater or even a partial, potential, or incipient defeater for the beliefs involved? This is an epistemological question, so naturally enough we shall need a little epistemology. As I have noted, Christians are committed to respect for science. And science, we may say, is a product of *reason*, a battery of cognitive faculties prominently including perception, memory, rational insight, and so forth. But Christians typically think they know or rationally believe some propositions that are not among the deliverances of reason. They believe what Jonathan Edwards calls "the great things of the gospel": that God has created us human beings in his image; that human beings have fallen into sin,

23. See Alvin Plantinga, "Methodological Naturalism?" in *Facets of Faith and Science*, ed. Jitse van der Meer, 4 vols. (Lanham, MD: University Press of America, 1996), 1:177–221.

thus requiring redemption and renewal; that God has provided a means for this redemption by way of the suffering, death, and resurrection of the Second Person of the divine Trinity, who emptied himself, became incarnate, and took on our nature. The main point here is that faith is a source of knowledge or rational belief *in addition to* reason.

So from the point of view of Christian theism there are these two distinct sources of knowledge: faith and reason. Now return to our question: does Simonian science give Christians a defeater for the Christian beliefs incompatible with it? To get at the answer, note first that there are various *epistemic bases*, as we might call them, bases from which inquiry is conducted. I don't have the space to characterize epistemic bases properly; but an epistemic base would include background beliefs as well as directions for the pursuit of the inquiry in question. There is, for example, the *scientific* epistemic base. When you do science from this epistemic base, you use everything you know by way of reason. But the scientific epistemic base is also constrained, as we are presently assuming, by *methodological naturalism*. So, in doing science from this base, you explicitly exclude, from what you use, any beliefs about God and anything you know just by faith or revelation.

This is the scientific epistemic base; but there is also the Christian epistemic base, which comprises *everything* Christians know or believe, including what they know, as they think, by way of faith. The Christian epistemic base therefore has the scientific epistemic base as a proper part. And this means that learning that Simonian science is proper science need not provide the Christian theist with a defeater for the Christian beliefs with which the former is incompatible. For it often happens that a proposition probable or likely with respect to *part* of an epistemic base is unacceptable from the point of view of the *whole* epistemic base. You tell me you saw me at the mall yesterday; I remember that I wasn't there at all but spent the entire afternoon in my office. Then, with respect to part of my epistemic base—the part that includes your telling me that you saw me there—it is likely that I was there; but this fact does not give me a defeater for my belief that I wasn't there. My knowledge of your telling me that you saw me there does not constitute a defeater for my belief that I wasn't there.

Another example. Imagine that a group of whimsical physicists try to see how much of physics would be left if we refused to employ, in the development of physics, anything we know by way of memory. Perhaps something could be done along these lines, but it would be a poor, paltry, truncated, trifling thing. And now suppose that relativity theory, or some other established part of physics, turned out to be dubious and unlikely from this point of view. Consider physicists who do physics from the scientific epistemic base and furthermore believe the results: would they have a defeater for some of these beliefs upon learning that they were unlikely from the perspective of truncated physics? Surely not. They would note, as a reasonably interesting fact, that there was indeed a conflict: the best way to think about the subject matter of physics from the standpoint of the *truncated* epistemic base is incompatible with the best way to think about this subject matter from the perspective of the *whole* scientific epistemic base. But of course they take the perspective of the scientific epistemic base to be normative here; it is the right perspective from which to look at the matter. As a result, their knowledge of the way things look from the truncated base doesn't give them a defeater for the beliefs appropriate with respect to the whole scientific base.

Something similar goes for Simonian science and the Christian epistemic base. For the Christian, Simonian science is like truncated physics. Concede that from the point of view of the scientific epistemic base, constrained as it is by methodological naturalism, Simonian science is the way to go. But the scientific epistemic base is only a part of the total Christian epistemic base. When the Christian adds to the scientific epistemic base what she thinks she knows by faith—that God has created us human beings in his image, for example—what she gets is an epistemic base that does not support the conclusions of Simonian science at all. Thus the fact that Simonian science is proper science but incompatible with Christian belief—that fact does not automatically give the Christian theist a defeater for those of her beliefs controverted by Simonian science.

But isn't this just a recipe for intellectual irresponsibility, for hanging on to beliefs in the teeth of the evidence? Can't the Christian always say something like this, no matter what proposed defeater D presents itself? Can't she always say: "Perhaps D is probable or likely with respect to part of what I believe, but it is improbable with respect to the totality of what I believe, that totality including B itself, the candidate for defeat"? No, of course not. Defeaters are perfectly possible. According to Isaiah 41:9, God says, "I took [you] from the ends of the earth, and called [you] from its farthest corners, saying to you, 'You are my servant, I have chosen you and not cast you off.'" One who believes, on the basis of this text, that the earth is a rectangular solid with ends and corners or who holds pre-Copernican beliefs on the basis of such a text as "You set the earth on its foundations, so that it shall never be shaken" (Ps. 104:5) will have a defeater for these beliefs when confronted with the evidence from reason against them. The same goes for someone who believes, on the basis of the Genesis account, that the earth or the universe is only about ten thousand years old. But then what is the difference? Why is there a defeater in these cases but not in the case of Simonian science?

How is it that you get a defeater in some of these cases but not in others? Exactly what makes the difference?

I do not have the space here to work out the answer in any detail, as one says when he doesn't really know the answer. Still, we may be able to see the general outline of an answer. To do so, we must consider the result of deleting the proposed defeatee from the epistemic base in question. Suppose I delete from my epistemic base those beliefs incompatible with Simonian science, such propositions as that Mother Teresa, in acting as she did, was certainly not displaying limited rationality but was acting with maximal rationality. Now consider the remaining, reduced evidential base.[24] This reduced evidential base includes whatever empirical evidence the Simonian in fact appeals to, and it does not include D, the proposed defeatee, that is, the proposition that the way in which Mother Teresa lived was perfectly rational.

The question we must ask is this: are the conclusions of Simonian science, and hence the denial of B, warranted, or supported, or more likely than not with respect to this reduced evidential base? I should think not. For this reduced evidential base includes not only the empirical evidence appealed to by the Simonian but also the proposition that we human beings have been created by God and created in his image, along with the rest of the main lines of the Christian story. But with respect to *this* body of propositions, it is not likely that if Mother Teresa had been more rational, smarter, or functioning more properly, she would have acted so as to increase her reproductive fitness rather than live altruistically. But then the proposed defeatee—namely, that Mother Teresa was perfectly rational living in the very way she did live—is not improbable on this evidential base, this body of propositions. Hence the fact that Simonian science is more likely than not with respect to the scientific evidential base does not give the Christian theist a defeater for what she thinks about Mother Teresa or for any other part of her Christian belief.

Now compare the case of the person who thinks the earth is a rectangular solid on the basis of the verse mentioned above. Consider her evidential base reduced with respect to the proposed defeatee—the proposition that the earth has corners. With respect to this reduced evidential base, the proposition that the earth has no corners is very likely. For this reduced evidential base contains or includes all of our reasons for supposing that in fact the earth does not have corners. In this case, unlike the case of Simonian science, the reduced evidential

24. This has to be defined much more carefully: e.g., conjunctions of D with other propositions also have to be deleted, as well as disjunctions of D with other propositions that are in the base just because they are entailed by those disjuncts. Perhaps we could put it like this: my evidential base ($EB_{me}$ reduced with respect to D) is a set of propositions that does not entail D and is otherwise maximally similar to $EB_{me}$.

base provides evidence, indeed powerful evidence, against the proposed defeatee. Not so in the case of Simonian science. This is an important difference between these two cases, and this difference implies that the Christian theist has a defeater in the corners case but not in the case of Simonian science.[25]

By way of conclusion, Evolution, taken as including all five of those initial theses, is not, just in itself, incompatible with Design, although the conjunction of Evolution with naturalism is. Some theses from evolutionary psychology, however, *are* incompatible with Design, or at any rate with one important specification of Design, namely, Christian theism. But even if these theses are part of proper science, even if they are among the deliverances of science, they do not constitute defeaters for Christian belief.

25. The proposed defeatee's being probable with respect to the reduced evidential base is sufficient for its not being in fact defeated. It is not necessary, however, for the proposed defeatee could have *intrinsic* warrant, warrant it does not get by way of its relation to the members of the evidential base.

# 10

# THEOLOGY, PHILOSOPHY, AND EVIL

## Keith E. Yandell

T HE ESSAY THAT FOLLOWS CONSIDERS specific presentations of the logical and evidential problems of evil in the context of two contrasting views of human origins and destiny, distinctions among kinds of intrinsic worth, and the dilemma posed in the Platonic dialogue *Euthyphro*.[1]

## ORIGINS, DESTINY, AND A BROAD ACCOUNT OF THE PROBLEM OF EVIL

Here is one account of human origins:

God said, "Let us make humankind in our image, according to our like-ness; and let them have dominion over the fish of the sea, and over the

---

1. The essay that follows makes many controversial claims. In most cases, they appear as assumptions—undefended theses that are relevant to the line of reasoning presented. I think that they can be defended and, indeed, that they are true. But doing everything at once, or everything one would like in a brief essay, is not a viable option. Also, I am not assuming that all value is metaphysical or moral or that all human value is metaphysical or moral. I am simply concerned here with metaphysical and moral value.

birds of the air, and over the cattle, and over all the wild animals of the earth, and over every creeping thing that creeps upon the earth." So God created humankind in his image, in the image of God he created them . . . And it was so. God saw everything that he had made, and indeed, it was very good. (Gen. 1:26–27, 30–31)

In this scenario, an omnicompetent (omnipotent and omniscient) God creates human beings in God's image. Their intrinsic worth derives from this fact. There is an intrinsic worth to being alive, conscious, and self-conscious, and God gives these features to the humans that God creates. God is alive, conscious, and self-conscious in the most perfect manner; to have intrinsic worth is guaranteed by sufficient relevant resemblance to God, who possesses the greatest possible worth. Nothing happens that God does not permit to happen.

Here is another scenario regarding human origins:

That Man is the product of causes which had no prevision of the end they were achieving; that his origin, his growth, his hopes and fears, his loves and his beliefs, are but the outcome of accidental collocations of atoms; that no fire, no heroism, no intensity of thought and feeling, can preserve an individual life beyond the grave, that all the labors of the ages, all the devotion, all the inspiration, all the noonday brightness of human genius, are destined to extinction in the vast death of the solar system, that the whole temple of Man's achievement must inevitably be buried beneath the debris of a universe in ruins—all these things, if not quite beyond dispute, are yet so nearly certain that no philosophy which rejects them can hope to stand. Only within the scaffolding of these truths, only on the firm foundation of unyielding despair, can the soul's habitation henceforth be safely built.[2]

Here humankind has its origin in purposeless nonconscious processes. There being life, consciousness, and self-consciousness is nothing planned or purposeful. An uncreated material world exists that goes through a long series of unplanned processes and improbably gives rise to life, consciousness, and self-consciousness. Such beings have worth even given this origin. The cosmic environment is not friendly toward the existence of such creatures. There is no guarantee that any given life will be worth the having. There is no God to guarantee or permit anything.

2. Bertrand Russell, "A Free Man's Worship," in *Selected Papers of Bertrand Russell* (New York: Modern Library, 1927), 3. Russell adds, "A strange mystery it is that Nature, omnipotent but blind, in the revolutions of her secular hurryings through the abysses of space, has brought forth at last a child, subject still to her power, but gifted with sight, with knowledge of good and evil, with the capacity of judging all the works of his unthinking Mother." Russell here obviously does not appeal to his typical views on morality.

Here is one account of human destiny:

> Then I saw a new heaven and a new earth; for the first heaven and the first earth had passed away, and the sea was no more. And I saw the holy city, the new Jerusalem, coming down out of heaven from God, prepared as a bride adorned for her husband. And I heard a loud voice from the throne saying, "See, the home of God is among mortals. He will dwell with them; they will be his peoples, and God himself will be with them; he will wipe every tear from their eyes. Death will be no more; mourning and crying and pain will be no more, for the first things have passed away." And the one who was seated on the throne said, "See, I am making all things new." (Rev. 21:1–5)

In this account, all ends well for humanity.[3]
Here is another:

> Brief and powerless is Man's life; on him and all his race the slow, sure doom falls pitiless and dark. Blind to good and evil, reckless of destruction, omnipotent matter rolls its relentless way; for Man, condemned today to lose his dearest, tomorrow himself to pass through the gate of darkness, it remains only to cherish, ere yet the blow falls, the lofty thoughts that ennoble his little day; disdaining the coward terrors of the slave of Fate, to worship the shrine that his own hands have built; undismayed by the empire of chance, to preserve a mind free from the wanton tyranny that rules his outward life; proudly defiant of the irresistible forces that tolerate, for a moment, his knowledge and his condemnation, to sustain alone, a weary but unyielding Atlas, the world that his own ideals have fashioned despite the trampling march of unconscious power.[4]

Michael Scriven gives a less flowery account of this perspective: "We die, and then we rot."[5] In this account, all simply ends for humanity.

Christian theology offers a high view of humankind. Humans as created by God, in God's image, given the responsibility to be stewards of their physical environment, created to love God and one another—the picture is bright indeed. When one adds in the distinctively Christian doctrine of the incarnation—God becoming human in the person of Jesus Christ—one has a ringing affirmation of the depth of God's love for humanity. History nonetheless records tragedy after tragedy. Natural disasters, wars, genocide, disease, and crime take away peace, life, and dignity. One who was told that an omnipotent, omniscient, perfectly

3. This raises the question of whether universalism is true. I am not assuming universalism, nor do I take it that the claim that if God creates a person, that person's life is better to have had than not to have had entails universalism.

4. Russell, "A Free Man's Worship," 14–15.

5. Michael Scriven, *Primary Philosophy* (New York: McGraw-Hill, 1966), 177.

good God loves each human being and numbers the very hairs on every head and then learned of the Holocaust or an earthquake and tsunami that took more than 150,000 lives and left hundreds of thousands more homeless, without clean water, and exposed to disease would be baffled. The contrast between the actual world and the ideal of a world filled with flourishing human beings loved by God and maturing in their capacities to act nonselfishly in the interests of others as of themselves is stunning in its intensity. Who can count the ways in which the latter does not begin to describe the former or the former does not correspond to the latter? The problem of evil, put one way, is that there is this profound discrepancy between the ideal and the actual.

Christianity is quite aware of this fact and holds its views regarding God and humanity in the light of this knowledge. It affirms that human beings are sinners—moral agents who, knowing better, have acted wrongly. They have lied, cheated, and killed, and as their technology has improved, their wars have become more devastating. They have focused on their own misidentified interests and thus thwarted their own hopes of flourishing as persons, harming themselves and others; they have become experts at such matters. And "they" in this case are we. So the theme of human freedom and its consequent responsibility has been a large part of the Christian understanding of there being evil in the world. Specifically, this understanding holds that God highly values agents—persons who possess the capacity to freely make morally significant choices rightly or wrongly. Thus they have the power to do the sorts of good and evil that we actually possess. There are constraints on how far these powers go, but they go a long way indeed. We can deeply harm ourselves and others, including taking life and making life a horror to people whose lives we do not take. The notion of there being moral agents has traditionally, and rightly, been central to (though by no means exhaustive of) Christian reflections concerning the problem of evil.

Christianity has also held that this life is not all there is. God did not create us for the truncated development toward loving God and loving others as ourselves that we reach in our lives here under current conditions. Christianity offers a resurrection unto everlasting life, so that we live forever under quite different conditions from those even the most fortunate of us experience now—conditions without disease, pain and suffering, and war—in short, without sin and its effects. The relevance of this consideration will become evident shortly.[6] We have before us

6. Further, Christianity holds, in its most orthodox forms, that God has also created nonhuman agents—typically thought of as unembodied minds or spirits—who also affect the world, including humans, and can do so in highly negative ways. Further, the claim is that they have done so and that this fact is reflected in the existence of natural evils. Obviously, some of the powers of such agents will have to greatly exceed our own. The current

two broadly outlined perspectives concerning human origins and human destiny. In contemplating the problem of evil, it is worth asking what difference it makes to the problem, if any, if one of these perspectives is true rather than the other. In order to answer this question, we need to consider another set of distinctions.

## KINDS OF INTRINSIC WORTH

Here is one line of reasoning. Consider a person and a rock. The person is alive, conscious, and self-conscious. The rock is not. Being alive, being conscious, and being self-conscious are intrinsically valuable properties. It is thus better to be a person than it is to be a rock—better, period.[7]

Here is another line of reasoning. Consider a person and a rock. The person is alive, conscious, and self-conscious. The rock is not. It is, other things being equal, better to be alive rather than not, conscious rather than not, and self-conscious rather than not. But the "all things being equal" clause is not irrelevant. Suppose the rock and the person exist in a world in which every living thing is always, without hope of escape, at its pain threshold, where X's pain threshold is a level of pain such that, were it any higher, (i) if X were alive but not conscious, X would die; (ii) if X were alive and conscious but not self-conscious, X would lose consciousness; (iii) if X were alive, conscious, and self-conscious, then X would lose self-consciousness; or (iv) if X were conscious, X could not focus on anything save the pain; and (v) if X were self-conscious, X could not focus on anything save being in pain. Then, for a person who could choose whether to be under the conditions that obtain in this world or cease to exist, surely it would not be irrational to decline the privilege. It is at least defensible to say that it would not be worth living, to say that in such a world a rock would be better off than a person. (Nothing could be a rock in one world and a person in another, so to say that it would be better in such a world to be a rock than be a person, insofar as it suggests that it would be better oneself to be the one rather than the other, is to make an incoherent suggestion.)

---

acceptance rate of this view is nothing like universal, although the traditional idea that the world is a battleground between God and evil has sophisticated contemporary as well as traditional supporters. Cf. Gregory A. Boyd, *Satan and the Problem of Evil* (Downer's Grove, IL: InterVarsity, 2001).

7. There is a tradition that maintains that to exist is itself good—that insofar as an item exists, it is good that it does. Put theistically, to have been created by God is itself to be something possessing intrinsic value. A recent manifestation of this viewpoint is found in much of the environmental movement.

These lines of reasoning seem to lead to incompatible results regarding the intrinsic worth of being alive, conscious, and self-conscious. The *second* line of reasoning assumes this view: property Q is such that having Q is intrinsically valuable only if, under every possible circumstance, possessing Q is better than not possessing Q. On the basis of this criterion, few properties will be intrinsically valuable. Omniscience without omnipotence is probably not intrinsically valuable. Omnipotence (which entails omniscience) perhaps is, as perhaps is moral perfection. More plausibly, it is omnipotence plus moral perfection that is intrinsically valuable. I think it should be granted that being alive, being conscious, and being self-conscious are not, on the basis of this criterion, intrinsically valuable. Let us call value that is intrinsic according to this first criterion *unoutweighable*. There is another criterion for intrinsic worth assumed by the *first* line of reasoning: property Q is intrinsically valuable only if, under any circumstances in which something has Q, this something's flourishing in the way that possessing Q enables it to flourish is prima facie a good state of affairs, and this something's failing to flourish in this way is prima facie a bad state of affairs. On this criterion, it is much more plausible to think of being alive, being conscious, and being self-conscious as intrinsically valuable properties. Let us call value that is intrinsic according to this second criterion *outweighable*. We now have one of the distinctions that we need.

### Actual Intrinsic Worth

There is no such thing as existence—there is only something or other existing. There is no such thing as life—there is only something or other being alive. There is no such thing as consciousness—there is only something or other that is conscious. There is no such thing as self-consciousness—there is only someone's being self-conscious. What possesses intrinsic worth, outweighable or not, is not a property but something's having that property.

### Moral Agents

A moral agent is alive, conscious, self-conscious, and has libertarian freedom. This freedom is morally significant if it can be exercised relative to actions that matter morally. The more those actions matter morally, the more significance the freedom has. A central part of this significance is that, at least to a considerable degree, the moral character of an agent is determined by the morally significant choices that the agent makes.

Consider moral agent Algernon, who develops a highly dubious moral character. As a moral agent—a self-conscious (therefore living and conscious) person who is significantly free—Algernon has moral worth. This worth is not canceled by Algernon's dubious moral character. It would be wrong of anyone to eliminate Algernon on the ground that his character is bad. The reason for this is not merely—though it includes—the fact that the eliminator harms his own character by eliminating Algernon. Algernon's existence (which is simply Algernon) has a worth distinct from the worth of the moral character that Algernon develops. This worth is the basis for its being wrong to simply eliminate Algernon.

There are two types of intrinsic worth here. One is *metaphysical*—the worth of being a moral agent who is alive, conscious, self-conscious, significantly free, and determining his moral character. The other is *moral*—the worth of having whatever moral character is developed. The former is inherently positive. The latter is positive to the degree that the character is good.[8] This distinction between the metaphysical worth of a person and the moral worth of this person's character and life requires that a person is not identical to his or her character or life. That there is such a distinction follows from the fact that metaphysical identity is necessary and that any person could have had a different character or life than the one he or she actually has.[9] We now have the other distinction we need to make. We will shortly apply these distinctions to the problem of evil.

## THE LOGICAL PROBLEM OF EVIL

The problem of evil (as we will discuss it here) concerns whether the existence of evil is logically compatible with the existence of God. The logical problem of evil is concerned with whether "God exists" and "There is evil" are logically compatible claims. The presenter of the logical problem of evil argues along the following lines. It is a truth of modal logic that if some proposition P plus one or more necessary truths entail a proposition Q, then P itself entails Q. Symbolically, where P and Q are any propositions you like and N is one or more necessarily true propositions, it could be expressed this way: "If P and N entail Q, then P entails Q." One standard strategy for arguing that the existence of God and the existence of evil are logically incompatible is to apply this principle as follows. Begin with:

8. I am not claiming here that the only nonmetaphysical worth is moral worth or that the only nonmetaphysical worth a person has is entirely a function of his or her moral character. But there is not space here to discuss other sorts of worth.

9. I am not assuming that the intrinsic worth of a life is simply and only a function of the moral character that a person develops but only that its intrinsic moral worth is a function thereof. Any moral worth it has due to its effect on the lives of others is extrinsic.

(G)  God exists.

Find one or more necessary truths N that, together with G, entails:

(not-E)  There is no evil.

Then infer to not-E. The overall result is a proof of the proposition CS (for critic's success):

(CS)  If God exists, then there is no evil.

Since there is evil, the critic will then properly conclude that there is no God. If this application of what we can call *the modal strategy* is successful, then the critic has been successful. Proof of CS amounts to the critic's success.

Here are two concrete applications of the modal strategy by critics. Begin with:

(G)  God exists (= there is an omnipotent, omniscient, morally perfect Creator and providence).

Add:

(N1)  Necessarily, if a being is omnipotent, it has the power to prevent or eliminate any evil that it knows how to prevent or eliminate and wants to prevent or eliminate.

(N2)  Necessarily, if a being is omniscient, it knows how to prevent or eliminate any evil that it has the power to prevent or eliminate and wants to prevent or eliminate.

(N3)  Necessarily, if a being is morally perfect, it wants to prevent or eliminate any evil that it has the power to prevent or eliminate and knows how to prevent or eliminate.

G plus N1, N2, and N3 entail:

(GE)  God prevents or eliminates all evil.

Obviously, this entails:

(not-E)  There is no evil.

So statement G entails statement not-E; God exists only if there is no evil. But there is evil. So God does not exist.

The argument assumes that no evil has a logically necessary existence and that no evil could escape divine knowledge. But these assumptions seem obviously true, so the controversy rightly centers on whether one's having moral perfection entails preventing or eliminating all evils within one's power and ken.

Here is another critical application of the modal strategy. Begin again with:

(G) God exists (= there is an omnipotent, omniscient, morally perfect Creator and providence).

Continue with:

(N4) Necessarily, if God creates, then God creates the best possible world.

(N5) Necessarily, the best possible world contains no evil.

G and N4 entail:

(GC) God creates the best possible world.

N5 and GC entail:

(not-E) There is no evil.

Once again, if this strategy succeeds, we have a proof that God and evil cannot coexist.

The problem with these arguments lies not in the modal strategy that they employ (it is logically impeccable) but with these particular applications of it. The first application requires that this be a necessary truth:

(N3) Necessarily, if a being is morally perfect, it wants to prevent or eliminate any evil that it has the power to prevent or eliminate and knows how to prevent or eliminate.

The second application requires that these be true:

(N4) Necessarily, if God creates, then God creates the best possible world.

(N5) Necessarily, the best possible world contains no evil.

But it is not at all clear that any of these are necessary truths. Consider the following arguments. It is, I take it, plainly logically possible that there are moral agents created by God, and it is also logically possible that every moral agent God might create would sometimes choose to act wrongly. This is also true:

(1) It is logically possible that in creating moral agents whom God knows will sometimes choose to act wrongly, God does nothing that is morally unjustified.

Acting wrongly is an evil. Thus statement 1 is equivalent to:

(1*) It is logically possible that in creating agents whom God knows will sometimes do evil, God does nothing that is morally unjustified.

But statement 1* entails:

(2) It is logically possible that God, in allowing evil, does nothing morally unjustified.

This is also true:

(3) The existence of an evil that God does nothing morally unjustified in allowing is not incompatible with the existence of God.

We can derive this conclusion from statements 2 and 3:

(4) The sheer fact that there is evil is not incompatible with the existence of God.

If this is so, then at least one of N1, N2, and N3 is false. Since N1 and N2 are true, N3 is false. But then the first application of the strategy fails.

The second application of the moral strategy requires that God create the best possible world and that the best possible world be one that contains no evil. It is not clear that there is any such thing as the best possible world; perhaps for any possible world, there is another possible world that would be better. Nor is it clear that even if there is a best possible world, God can create it; if such a world contained moral agents, the choices of these agents would be up to them and could not be just made by God to occur. Since a world without moral agents would have no moral worth, the best possible world cannot be one lacking moral agents. In addition, there is an argument concerning virtue and vice.

Virtue ethicists hold that the notion of a virtue is central and fundamental in ethics. A person is virtuous insofar as he or she has the virtues, which are character traits or habits that arise from deliberately choosing to act rightly on many occasions. In some varieties of virtue ethics, among the virtues one finds character traits available only to those who conquer evils. Courage, fortitude, and compassion are examples. (The same view is held regarding some religious, as distinct from moral, virtues.) Consider, then, the following argument:

(5) It is logically possible that virtue ethicists are right at least about this much: a mature, morally good person is such in virtue of having the virtues.

(6) It is logically possible that among the virtues are some the acquiring of which requires that one overcome evils.

But:

(7) If it is logically possible that virtue ethicists are right at least about this much, that a mature, morally good person is such in virtue of having the virtues, and it is logically possible that among the virtues are some the acquiring of which requires that one overcome evils, then it is logically possible that becoming a mature, morally good person requires that one overcome evils.

Then:

(8) It is logically possible that becoming a mature, morally good person requires that one overcome evils. (from 5–7)

Add:

(9) It is logically possible that if God creates persons, then God is justified in creating them in circumstances in which they can become morally mature persons.

(10) If it is logically possible that becoming a mature, morally good person requires that one overcome evils, and it is logically possible that if God creates persons, God is justified in creating them in circumstances in which they can become morally mature persons, then it is logically possible that God justifiably permits there to be evils that persons can overcome.

Hence:

(11)  It is logically possible that God justifiably permits there to be evils that persons can overcome. (from 8–10)

But statement 11, together with the previously noted statement 3,

(3)  The existence of an evil that God does nothing morally unjustified in allowing is not incompatible with the existence of God,

entails that:

(4)  The sheer fact that there is evil is not incompatible with the existence of God.

Although there are other versions of the logical problem of evil, none I know of fare better than these. If there is a successful argument from the existence of evil to the nonexistence of God, it is more subtle than that. The logical problem of evil is unsuccessful.

## THE EVIDENTIAL PROBLEM OF EVIL

As was the case with the logical problem of evil, so too with the evidential problem of evil—the claim that the existence of evil, even if logically compatible with the existence of God, is evidence that God does not exist requires argument. Impressionistic accounts, however helpful in giving a general sense of the issues, are not sufficient for careful assessment. We will consider some specific versions of the evidential problem.

### Lives Worth Living

Marilyn Adams has claimed that if God creates a person, then God will see to it that the person, insofar as objectively rational and relevantly informed, would see that the person's life is worth living. It is not obvious what this entails. Presumably, in the language used here, this entails that if God exists, then no person's intrinsic worth is outweighed by the evils that the person experiences. But does it entail that the intrinsic metaphysical worth of simply being a person plus the worth of whatever sort of moral character the person had together will outweigh the disvalue of the evils that the person suffers? Or does it have the stronger entailment that the positive worth of the person's moral character itself will outweigh whatever badness there is to that character plus the evil the person undergoes? However exactly this claim should be expressed, let us call it the *divine-kindness thesis*. We will be concerned with whether the existence of evil provides evidence against what might be called divine-kindness theism—a theism of which the divine-kindness thesis is an essential part.

If we consider only this life, there are cases in which the lives that persons have lived were not ones of which the divine-kindness thesis, in either its stronger or weaker form, was true. This suggests the following version of the problem of evil:

(1) It seems plain enough that there have been lives on this earth so nasty, brutish, and short that, were the persons who lived them given sufficiently keen objective rationality and sufficient information to make an informed judgment, they would correctly judge that their lives had not been worth living.

(2) If it seems plain enough that there have been lives on earth so nasty, brutish, and short that, were the persons who lived them given sufficiently keen objective rationality and sufficient information to make an informed judgment, they would correctly judge that their lives had not been worth living, then if this life is all there is, it seems plain enough that the divine-kindness thesis is false.

(3) If this life is all there is, then the divine-kindness principle is false. (from 1, 2)

(4) If God exists, then the divine-kindness principle is true.

So:

(5) If this life is all there is, then it seems plain enough that God does not exist. (from 3, 4)

Thus far, if the argument is right, it establishes a significant connection between the truth of theism (insofar as it includes the divine-kindness thesis) and the truth of the thesis that humans survive physical death. By itself, this is no criticism of theism. For that, it must be the case that we have sufficient reason to deny that humans do survive physical death.[10] The argument, then, continues as follows:

(6) This life is all there is.

So:

10. The notion of "burden of proof" has its conceptual home base in legal proceedings. Insofar as it has application in philosophy, it amounts to this: the burden of proof lies with whoever is arguing for a conclusion. If Abe is offering an argument for God's existence, the burden of proof is on Abe. If Ben is offering an argument that God does not exist, the burden of proof is on Ben.

(7) It seems plain enough that God does not exist. (from 5, 6)

When one asks something like "How good a thing is it that a given person exists?" the answer depends in part on what the person's destiny is. If we assume a secular perspective, then the answer may well be that the value of the existence of many people is outweighed by the evils that they undergo within the span of their existence. If it is theistic, then the answer may well be that the value of the existence of every person fails to be outweighed, but instead itself outweighs, the evils that the person undergoes. There are two factors here: the extent of life and the providence of God. If a person lives only the symbolic three score years and ten (or far less), lives plagued by horrendous evil are good candidates for yielding the answer that there are persons whose existence had better not have occurred. If life extends far beyond such limits, but under conditions of chance or of causality that is indifferent to its results, or if there is an evil controller of the world, then again it is enormously likely that there are lives that would have been better not lived, persons who had better not have existed. If life extends at least indefinitely beyond the grave and an omnicompetent good providence rules, then even the existence of those who do least well will not be such that it would have been better for them never to have been. I do not see how one can answer the question whether there are persons such that it would have been better had they not existed without considering the matter of their destiny—of whether and, if so, under what conditions they exist beyond physical death. No amount of talk about religions appealing to a doctrine of an afterlife as an escape from the realities of this life makes the slightest difference to that fact. I take it that the idea of an afterlife finds its Christian motivation in the purposes and love of God and in the intrinsic worth that arises from being made in God's image, not as an afterthought about the existence of evil. But even were it merely the latter, this would make no difference to my point here.

It is not part of the theist's view that human persons just automatically, without God doing anything, survive the death of their bodies. It is that at each moment of their existence, in this life and any other a human person may have, the person depends for existence on being sustained therein by God. In the theist's view, survival of physical death, as well as survival from one moment to the next, depends on God's continued grace.

Another relevant matter concerns our ability to make large-scale judgments relative to the scope and depth of evil. Each day some teenage driver loses his or her life in an accident, going from most of life ahead to all of life behind. No one with any sense pretends to be able to say specifically why God permitted this to happen—to fill in the blank in the sentence "God's reason for permitting Jane Doe to have a fatal accident on January 3, 2005, was . . ." Nor is there, so far as I can see, any reason to think that anyone should be able to fill in such blanks, no matter how clear and richly detailed a reason God might have for permitting it. Nor is there, so far as I can see, any reason to think that the fact that no one can fill in the blank is any reason at all to think that there is no way to fill it in that results in a true statement. Similarly, however rich and detailed the reasons an omnicompetent God has for permitting all the evils that God permits, there is no reason to suppose that any human being can do very much by way of specifying how that general story goes. Again, I can see no reason one should expect that any of us should be able to specify on what basis an omnicompetent God permits all the evils that occur.

### The Appeal to Mystery

The obvious objection is that my remarks are an appeal to mystery. This seems to me simply false. Human history has included an extremely large number of events, no matter what even remotely plausible account for individuating events is accepted. A great many events occurred before any were recorded, and most of the events of human history have never been recorded anywhere at all. So no human being can come even remotely close to specifying the history of the race in any detail that remotely resembles what there is to record. None of these remarks come anywhere close to appealing to mystery. They simply note an immense complexity relative to which our available information and our cognitive abilities are modest indeed. What the above comments about our knowledge of God's reasons for permitting the evils there are identifies another immense complexity relative to which our available information and our cognitive abilities are modest indeed. Nonetheless, granting all of the above, it still seems true to say the following:

(1) It seems plain enough that there have been lives on this earth so nasty, brutish, and short that, were the persons who lived them given sufficiently keen objective rationality and sufficient information to make an informed judgment, they would correctly judge that their lives had not been worth living.

(Consider the short life of an infant who has terrible pain and little else in its brief appearance in this life.) Thus the central issue concerning this argument seems to me to concern another premise. The specific version of the problem of evil just considered requires this premise:

(6) This life is all there is.

This premise expresses a metaphysical claim that needs independent justification. Considering it would require considering competing views concerning the nature of human persons, a fascinating and complex affair. But any argument that requires a premise such as 6, and thus assumes a controversial metaphysical thesis that in turn will rest on various complicated arguments in the philosophy of mind, is not by itself a proof of its conclusion.

Further, the problem of evil is not an isolated set of issues. A relevant question concerns how one is to understand there having come to be items that possess the particular sort of metaphysical and moral worth that belongs to moral agents. Russell adds to his remarks concerning human origins:

> A strange mystery it is that Nature, omnipotent but blind, in the revolutions of her secular hurryings through the abysses of space, has brought forth at last a child, subject still to her power, but gifted with sight, with knowledge of good and evil, with the capacity of judging all the works of his unthinking Mother.[11]

Theism does seem to be a much better explanation of there being living, conscious, self-conscious beings than is atheistic naturalism. This is highly relevant to the overall assessment of the two positions. But it does not deal directly with the problem of evil.

### The Argument from Horrendous Evils

Among the evils that occur, we call some horrendous, meaning by this that these evils exceed their more garden-variety cousins by so much that it is difficult to see how any life that includes them could be worth living. Enduring the horrors of war, watching one's children be tortured to death, seeing one's own flesh be eaten away by leprosy or cancer, observing one's mental capacities diminish until one can no longer notice even that—these are some candidates for the status of horrendous evil. Without trying here to further define the category or decide which evils are such, I shall take it that there are horrendous evils in earthly terms in the following sense: an evil is *horrendous in earthly terms* if its occurrence in the life of a person renders the life that the person lives from physical birth to physical death not one worth living. Let us suppose there might be evils that are horrendous in human terms in the follow-

11. Russell, "A Free Man's Worship," 3.

ing sense: an evil is *horrendous in human terms* if and only if it is horrendous in earthly terms and there is no afterlife in which the person's continued existence in community with other creatures, no matter how wonderful and even if everlasting, would render that person's overall life worth living. Consider, then, this argument.

(H1) There are evils that are horrendous in human terms.
(H2) If there are evils that are horrendous in human terms, then there is no God.

Hence:

(H3) There is no God.

If divine-kindness theism is in view, H2 is true and H1 is the most debatable premise in the argument.

Even the present requirements of the divine-kindness thesis are not strong enough. A life might be worth living but contain evils that no omnicompetent, morally perfect God would permit. Suppose, for example, that a person sincerely repents his or her sin, places trust in God, and God promises the person a place in heaven. Upon death, God causes the person to be in pointless, terrible agony for a billion years. Then the person is placed in heaven forever, enjoying fellowship with his or her Maker in a peaceful community of loving persons. This person's life overall might then be well worth the living, but it would have included an evil that no omnicompetent, morally perfect God would allow—a *divinely impermissible evil*. Thus an addition to divine-kindness theism is needed: *God not only owes the persons whom God creates lives that are worth living; God owes them—and owes Godself—the absence of divinely impermissible evils*. So there is also this argument:

(D1) There are divinely impermissible evils.
(D2) If there are divinely impermissible evils, then God does not exist.

So:

(D3) God does not exist.

The relentless critic can combine these arguments as follows:

(HD1) There are evils that are horrendous in human terms, or there are divinely impermissible evils.

(HD2) If there are evils that are horrendous in human terms, then God does not exist, and if there are divinely impermissible evils, then God does not exist.

So:

(HD3) God does not exist.

Has the believer a response worth making?

If we consider the distinctions noted above regarding intrinsic worth, summarizing at least some of their relevance to the problem of evil, we obtain something like this:

(1) God's existence (if God exists) is an unoutweighable intrinsic good.
(2) The having of a human life is an outweighable intrinsic good.
(3) The existence of a human person is an outweighable intrinsic good.
(4) If this life encompasses all of a human life, then there are lives the intrinsic worth of which are outweighed.
(5) If this life encompasses all of the time during which a human person exists, there are some persons the intrinsic value of the existence of whom is outweighed.
(6) If divine-kindness theism is true, an omnicompetent, morally perfect God would create no human being the intrinsic value of whose existence was outweighed.
(7) If divine-kindness theism is true, then an omnicompetent, morally perfect God would create no human life the intrinsic value of which was outweighed.
(8) An omnicompetent, morally perfect God would permit no divinely impermissible state of affairs.

Given statements 1–8, these conclusions follow:

(9) If divine-kindness theism is true, then life on this earth does not encompass all of the time during which a human person exists.

and

(10) If divine-kindness theism is true, then there are no evils that are horrendous in human terms.

Note as well:

(11) That divine-kindness theism is true does not entail that there is no event, no stretch of a life, or no whole life on earth such that the event, stretch, or whole life is evil in a manner such that the intrinsic value of the existence of a human person during life on earth or the intrinsic value of a human life on earth (or both) is not outweighed—that there are no evils that are horrendous in earthly terms.

Thus the existence of such evils is not incompatible with the truth of divine-kindness theism.

The relevance of these considerations to the logical problem of evil is obvious. Let the set of propositions 1–11 be set (S).[12] Then consider:

(D) Divine-kindness theism is true.

and

(E) There are evils that are horrendous in earthly terms.

The triad S, D, E is consistent. So the pair D, E is consistent. But how does it relate to the evidential problem of evil?

It does so in various ways. One reason for thinking that evils that are horrendous in *human* terms exist is that there are evils that are horrendous in *earthly* terms. That there are the latter does not entail that there are the former. The critic's claim is that the existence of the latter makes the existence of the former more probable or else provides evidence for the existence of the former. Let us label the evils that outweigh the intrinsic worth of being a human person and the intrinsic worth of having human life, if this life is all there is, *outweighing evils*. Then one suggestion is this: "There are outweighing evils" counts against divine-kindness theism if the probability of D, "Divine-kindness theism is true," is lower on O, "There are outweighing evils," than it is on O's denial, "There are no outweighing evils." A typical support for the idea that the probability of D on O is lower than it is on O's denial is that (as was noted earlier) one who considers Christian views regarding human origins and destiny will not expect that O be true. It has never seemed to me that this support is worth much unless these expectations are rationally grounded. I doubt, for reasons partially articulated above, that "our" expectations in this matter have that advantage. We lack both the cognitive powers and relevant information to have informed opinions on these matters.

12. S contains at least one logically contingent proposition, namely, proposition 4.

Nor is finding some proposition on which the probability of D is lower than it is on its denial, even if this proposition is true, the same as finding evidence in favor of D's falsehood. Suppose a machine is built that has the capacity to probe all of a person's beliefs and make them a million in number, at least 90 percent of which are true. It also has the feature that it works only if it is presented first with a theist and then with an atheist. After being presented with one of each, it unfortunately blows up. The theist (Al) has at least 90 percent true beliefs, and given this fact, the probability of theism is greater than the probability of atheism. But the atheist (Michael) also has at least 90 percent true beliefs, and relative to this fact, the probability of atheism is greater than the probability of theism. Waiving the question as to whether it is not more probable that theism be true than that atheism be true, given that there are possessors of beliefs, neither the belief status of Al nor that of Martin provides evidence for the truth of theism or for the truth of atheism. Then, too, the probability of "There are living, conscious, and self-conscious beings" is higher given divine-kindness theism than it is for atheism.

What presumably is needed is some sort of *objective* connection between the truth of O and the falsehood of D—for instance, if D is true, then the truth of O cannot be explained successfully. To know this would require that there be no set of true propositions constitutive of, or conjoined with, divine-kindness theism (enriched as just noted) the truth of which explains the truth of O. Even if we cannot offer any such set of truths, save perhaps at an extremely abstract level, this is no real objection to there being such an explanation; we would not likely know what it is if there is one. After all, there being some explanation of O, given D, is not dependent on our knowing what it is, and our not knowing what it is provides no reason to think there is not one unless it is true (as it is not) that if there is such an explanation, we would know what it is. (The primary sense of "explanation" here is metaphysical—the metaphysical explanation of something X being whatever it is in virtue of which X obtains rather than not. Having the explanation—in the epistemological sense of "explanation"—is a matter of knowing what the metaphysical explanation is. Only in the epistemological sense are there false explanations.) But if our not knowing, save perhaps in the most abstract of terms, why God would permit evils that are horrendous in earthly terms is not evidence that there is no omnicompetent, morally perfect God to permit them, then the existence of those evils themselves is not evidence against theism or evidence that there are evils that are horrendous in human terms. The same comments apply to alleged evils that are not divinely permissible.

The topic of the evidential problem of evil is wide and deep, and we have only scratched the surface here. The hope is that enough has been said to make clear that the resources of divine-kindness theology, including

THEOLOGY, PHILOSOPHY, AND EVIL                                             239

relevant reflections on the kinds of intrinsic goodness, are highly relevant
to the evidential problem of evil and that even the claim that there being
evils that are horrendous in earthly terms is not by itself evidence that
theism is false—neither evidence that there are evils that are horrendous in
human terms nor evidence that there are divinely impermissible evils.

The argument given here notes a strong conceptual link between divine-kindness theism and survival of the death of one's body. As stated
here, it does not do so for every human person but only for the persons
whose existence or life (or both together) is such that their intrinsic worth
is overcome unless they survive in conditions under which their lives become better to have than not. Even in these cases, all that strictly follows
is that the persons in question continue to exist long enough so that the
good of their existence and the particular lives that they have lived are not
outweighed by (and outweigh) the evil those lives included. The notion
of divine kindness, however, is naturally and easily expanded to include
an efficacious love that sustains persons in existence perpetually.

One final comment for present purposes. An honest theist must grant,
so far as I can see, that he or she does not know specifically—and has no
specific suggestion to make about it—why God permits, for instance, a
child to be killed as its mother watches. The theist can, as noted, point
out that if there is a divine justification for permitting this to happen, it
is not reasonable to think that he or she would know it. The theist can
add that, given the existence of God, a particular life need never end,
and it may include both life in a community where one loves others as
one loves oneself and where one loves and is loved by God—a life profoundly worth living by one who possesses an unoutweighed intrinsic
worth. The basic problem is not in seeing how even a life with evils that
are horrendous in earthly terms might in the longer run be worth living
but in seeing how the stronger candidates for divinely impermissible
evils might contribute to the worth of that life in a manner that makes
their permission by God not impermissible after all. So far as I can
see, this is an ignorance that the divine-kindness theist must live with.
What I deny is that this fact is evidence against divine-kindness theism.
Again, it is evidence only if, were there an account of how even the best
candidates for divinely impermissible evils are divinely permissible after
all, we would know what this account is; and that is false.


## THE EUTHYPHRO DILEMMA

Some philosophers have argued that there being a genuine distinction
between good and evil itself poses a problem for theism. This conclusion is based on an old and famous argument that is intended to raise

a certain unwelcome dilemma for theism—the Euthyphro dilemma.[13] In the Platonic dialogue *Euthyphro*, the question is raised as to whether (i) the gods approve something because it is good, or (ii) something is good because the gods approve of it. Monotheizing the question, we get: (i) is something good because God approves of it, or (ii) does God approve of something because it is (already) good?

From the Euthyphro question arises the *Euthyphro argument*, which goes as follows:

(1) Either (i) God approves of something because it is good, or (ii) something is good because God approves of it.
(2) If (i), the ground or basis of something's being good lies outside, and is independent of, God.
(3) If (ii), then something is good because God arbitrarily chooses it—what is good rests on mere divine voluntarism, sheer choice not constrained by reasons.

So:

(4) Either the ground or basis of something's being good lies outside, and is independent of, God, or something is good because God arbitrarily chooses it—what is good rests on mere voluntarism, sheer choice not constrained by reasons.

The proponent of the Euthyphro argument takes statement 4 to amount to this:

(4*) Either morality is independent of (monotheistic) religion, or morality simply amounts to what God arbitrarily chooses.

The Euthyphro argument nicely raises some issues, but it does not settle anything. There are alternatives in addition to the two that the Euthyphro argument considers. The argument would succeed only if there were not. Here are at least some of them: (iii) a necessarily existing God exists and

13. One effort to short-circuit the problem of evil considers an issue related to those arising in Euthyphro considerations: There is a problem of evil only if there is evil. There is evil only if morality is objective. Morality is objective only if God exists. Hence there is a problem of evil only if God exists. If there is a problem of evil only if God exists, then the problem of evil does not show that God does not exist. So the problem of evil does not show that God does not exist. This argument requires that true principles of morality are necessary truths and that they require, or their necessity is best understood in terms of, God's necessarily existing, God's nature being necessarily good and necessarily determining God's will, and God's necessarily thinking thoughts that have as propositional contents true moral principles or the like. These are controversial issues in metaphysics.

is perfectly good by nature; thus what God wills, God wills in accord with God's nature, not arbitrarily; (iv) God exists with logical necessity, and God necessarily has thoughts the propositional content of which is the true principles of morality; (v) God exists, though not with logical necessity, and God is good by choice; God wills in accord with God's character and not arbitrarily, and this character is what it is due to God's free choices.

So the Euthyphro argument should begin with a premise at least as complex as this:

(1*)  Either (i), (ii), (iii), (iv), or (v).

But then the rest of the argument will not follow. The conclusion would then be much more complex:

(4**)  Either morality is independent of (monotheistic) religion, or morality simply amounts to what God arbitrarily chooses; or a necessarily existing God exists and is perfectly good by nature; thus what God wills, God wills in accord with God's nature, not arbitrarily; or God exists with logical necessity, and God necessarily thinks thoughts the propositional content of which is true moral principles; or God exists, though not with logical necessity, and God is good by choice; God wills in accord with God's character and not arbitrarily, and this character is what it is due to God's free choices.

Since the response to the Euthyphro argument depends on alternatives (iii) through (v) being genuine, it seems appropriate to say a bit more about them. Let us begin with alternative (v), which is perhaps the most complex. Suppose there are abstract objects—propositions, for instance—such that it is their existence and truth that ground (or are) the truth of moral principles. These abstract objects enjoy necessary existence and exist independent of God. The principles in question will then be true in all possible worlds—they will be necessarily true. Suppose there is a set S of such propositions that define what it is for something to be good—a set of propositions that can be expressed in some such form as this: X is good if and only if each proposition in set S is true of X. Strictly, there will presumably be some set if anything is good rather than evil. Then several things will be true. It will not be the existence or nature of God in virtue of which whatever is good is good. It also will not be possible that the abstract objects in question not exist or that they not ground the truth of true moral principles; and even an omnipotent being cannot change what it is impossible to change. But then there is nothing inelegant for theism that it be necessarily true that the truth of true moral propositions is grounded in the existence of the relevant abstract objects. The relationship between theism and morality is to be thought of in these terms. Moral principles are conditional propositions, such as "If there are persons, then they ought to be respected." Such principles are true whether there are any persons or not. But were God not to create any moral agents, there would be nothing on which they had purchase, nothing to which they applied. Further, there would be nothing that was morally perfect, that was paradigmatically morally good. So God makes it the case that there actually is a moral realm—actually exist things to which moral principles apply—and a moral paradigm. God's existence, according to this account, is to be thought of as follows: it is necessarily true that God is not caused to exist by anything else and does not depend for existence on anything else.

Consider alternative (iv). Suppose that a necessarily existing, necessarily perfect God exists and that no abstract objects exist (or none that ground moral principles). Suppose further that true moral principles are grounded in the propositional content of thoughts that God necessarily has. There is nothing arbitrary about any of this, and nothing distinct from God on which the truth of moral principles depends. God does not choose what will be good, but what is good is determined by thoughts that God necessarily has.

Consider alternative (iii). Suppose a necessarily morally perfect being exists, though with logical necessity. What this being wills is always good, and the divine will determines what is good. But there is nothing arbitrary here and nothing distinct from God on which morality depends.

Discussing whether there are still other alternatives to (iii) through (v), or deciding which of these is rationally preferable, is beyond anything we can attempt here. It is sufficient to note that the Euthyphro argument fails to establish the intended dilemma for theists.

## CONCLUSION

We have noted the general context in which the problem of evil arises by considering some relevant views of human origins and destiny and some considerations regarding kinds of intrinsic worth. We have argued that the logical problem of evil fails to refute theism; that divine-kindness theism has the resources to make strong replies to the evidential problem of evil: and, finally, that the Euthyphro dilemma is bogus.

# II

# PHILOSOPHICAL CONTRIBUTIONS TO THEOLOGICAL ANTHROPOLOGY

≫| William Hasker |≪

Wꜰ HAT IS AT STAKE FOR theology in the philosophy of human nature? Quite a lot, actually. After the nature and attributes of God, no other topic is so central for theology as the nature of human beings.[1] It is we humans who have sinned and rebelled against our Creator, alienating ourselves from God and placing upon ourselves a burden of guilt and shame. It is our humanity that the Son of God has taken upon himself for our redemption. And it is we humans who are to be transformed into the image of Christ and raised again in glory in the resurrection of the last day. Granted, philosophy can give only limited help with topics such as these; an adequate account of any of

---

1. Calvin said it well: "Our wisdom, in so far as it ought to be deemed true and solid wisdom, consists almost entirely of two parts: the knowledge of God and of ourselves" (John Calvin, *Institutes of the Christian Religion*, trans. Henry Beveridge, 2 vols. [Grand Rapids: Eerdmans, 1957], 1:37).

them must draw deeply upon the resources of biblical revelation. But there are certain *philosophical presuppositions* that are required if the theological assertions are to make sense, and these presuppositions are either imperiled or denied outright by widely held philosophical views about human nature. It is these presuppositions that will be the focus of our attention in this essay.

One such presupposition is *rationality*: humans must be creatures of reason. "Come now, let us reason together, says the LORD" (Isa. 1:18 NIV); this is a divine demand that can be met only by creatures that are inherently capable of reason. We must be able to apprehend the message God has delivered to us, recognize its merits as compared with all competing perspectives, and respond with whole-hearted belief, leading in turn to trust in the Lord and the Lord's promises. This is not to say that we are purely rational or anything of the sort, nor is it to deny that there is much more to us than our reasoning ability or that our reasoning itself has been distorted and corrupted by sin. But the capacity for reason must be there, however impaired in our present sinful state.

A second presupposition is that we are *responsible* beings—that we are rightly held accountable by God for our compliance with the moral law and for fulfilling God's purposes insofar as they have been disclosed to us. This presupposes the rational capacity to apprehend what it is that we ought to do. It also seems to presuppose that we are able to do what we are held accountable for doing (or not doing). Once again, both the reasonableness and the ability may have been damaged because of sin, but not, one would think, eradicated entirely; otherwise we should have sunk so low that morality, and therefore responsibility, would no longer apply to us.

Responsibility requires the ability to do what we are held responsible for doing, and this in turn requires *freedom*. Here we reach an area of intense controversy not only between attackers of Christianity and its defenders but also between those who are equally committed to the Christian vision but understand it differently. Some have been satisfied with what is known as a *compatibilist* view of free will, according to which our actions are free if we are able to do what we most strongly desire to do. Free will in this sense is compatible with causal determinism (thus the name); in particular, it is compatible with God's having so constructed us that our desires ineluctably lead us to act in the way God has foreordained for us to act. Others, however, insist on the importance of *libertarian* free will, meaning that when we choose freely, we are fully capable, given all our desires and everything else about the situation, of choosing something different from the thing we in fact choose. The main reason for this insistence lies in the conviction that if this is not so, if, when we choose, our choice is ultimately controlled by circumstances over which we had no control, then we properly deserve neither praise nor blame for what we have done.[2] Probably most Christians, if they carefully think through their views about this matter, will find that they subscribe to libertarian free will; this is certainly the strong majority view (though by no means unanimous) among contemporary Christian philosophers. For our present purposes, however, it is not necessary to make a definite decision on this point; from time to time, this essay will comment on the implications of both views of freedom.

Finally, Christians believe that human persons are *capable of everlasting life*, for this is what we have been promised. And in view of the teaching of Scripture as well as the fact of experience that all humans die and their bodies decay, this everlasting life is held to take the form of the resurrection of the body. But exactly what this entails and how we should think of God as acting to bring it about have become matters of controversy among Christian thinkers.

The Christian perspective on the nature of human beings, briefly outlined above, is under threat from multiple directions. Some of the most serious challenges at present, however, come from various forms of materialism and naturalism. *Materialism*, in the sense that is relevant here, holds that human beings are entirely composed of ordinary physical matter and that everything about them must be accounted for in material terms. According to *naturalism*, the world of nature is the sum total of what exists; there are no "supernatural" beings such as gods or angels, or any powers that can interfere with the uniform workings of natural processes. Naturalism and materialism tend to be closely allied, but they are not identical; not all naturalists are materialists, and (as we will see) there are some materialists who are not naturalists.

Typical versions of materialism call into question all aspects of the Christian view of human nature sketched above. If we consist of nothing over and above our physical bodies, the prospects for life after death seem anything but promising. The natural view to take, it would seem, is the one expressed by the philosopher Michael Scriven, who wrote, "We die, and then we rot."[3] (But see below for some thinkers who take exception to this judgment.) Free will and responsibility are both endangered, although relatively few philosophers are willing to deny outright that we are somehow responsible for our actions. According to materialism, we are wholly physical beings, and most materialists draw the logical conclusion that our actions are entirely the result of the

2. Granted, the immediate circumstances of our actions often consist at least partly of the results of earlier actions of our own. But if we ask about the causes of these earlier actions and continue to trace the causal chain backward, we quickly arrive at circumstances that obtained before we were born and were not in any sense under our control.

3. Michael Scriven, *Primary Philosophy* (New York: McGraw-Hill, 1966), 177.

operations of the elementary particles that make up our bodies, acting and reacting in accordance with the fundamental laws of physics. This leads to determinism (or quasi-determinism) and at best a compatibilist view of free will.[4] We may be "free" in that many of our actions are not constrained by external forces, but it is true all the same that those actions are merely the resultant of the physical behavior of the particles that constitute us. What we do is the consequence of what those particles do: they control us; we do not control them. It is a daunting task (to say the least) to reconcile this idea with a serious affirmation of a person's responsibility for his or her own actions. (Among Christian thinkers, even those who affirm God's universally determining decrees have usually wanted to avoid this sort of physical determinism.)

Even rationality is called into question by a consistent materialism— though this is a conclusion the materialists themselves are anxious to avoid. Materialists and naturalists tend to limit the reliable use of reason to the natural sciences and, in general, to what can be based fairly directly on sensory experience. But science would be impossible without logical and mathematical reasoning, and on materialistic assumptions, it turns out to be difficult or impossible to give an acceptable account of what reasoning entails. To reason properly (for instance, in a deductive argument) is, it would seem, to accept a conclusion because it is seen to follow from the premises; the logical relationship between premises and conclusion must play an essential role in determining the conclusion that is reached. But there is no place for this in the materialistic account of thinking. According to that account, the conclusion reached is purely the result of the actions and reactions of the elementary particles that make up our brains; principles of rational inference have no role to play. This argument against materialism is familiar to many through the writings of C. S. Lewis (though he did not originate it), and although it is sometimes claimed that it has been refuted, none of the refutations seem successful. If this argument works, materialism is in deep trouble.[5]

It should be clear by now that materialism poses a serious challenge to a Christian view of the nature of human beings. And the challenge

4. Contemporary quantum physics holds that there is an element of indeterminacy, of sheer randomness, in the behavior of the elementary particles of matter. It is debatable whether this indeterminacy would lead to indeterminism at the level of human actions. But even if it does, the indeterminism seems to be a matter of chance and randomness, not of free choice as this has normally been understood.

5. For a careful yet accessible presentation of the argument, see Victor Reppert, *C. S. Lewis's Dangerous Idea: In Defense of the Argument from Reason* (Downers Grove, IL: InterVarsity, 2004). Closely related to this argument is Alvin Plantinga's evolutionary argument against naturalism in *Warrant and Proper Function* (New York: Oxford University Press, 1993).

PHILOSOPHICAL CONTRIBUTIONS TO THEOLOGICAL ANTHROPOLOGY 247

cannot easily be ignored; the materialistic view, or something like it, is simply taken for granted in a great deal of contemporary discussion—as one *Newsweek* article put it, "The mind is what the brain does for a living." Christian teaching and preaching that pay no attention to this trend are in danger of being written off as irrelevant, tied to a view of the world that may have made sense in the past but can no longer be taken seriously in the light of modern scientific knowledge. The remainder of this essay discusses three Christian views, each of which attempts to respond to the challenges we have noted.

## TRADITIONAL DUALISM

Christians traditionally have rejected materialistic views of human nature, holding instead to *dualism*, according to which the mind or soul is something of a nature wholly distinct from the physical body—spirit, not matter. One influential form of dualism comes from the Greek philosopher Plato, but it is arguable that the Bible itself, though not philosophical in its approach, takes for granted a form of soul-body dualism.[6] In modern times the most influential variety of dualism has been *Cartesian dualism* (so called for René Descartes, 1596–1650), and it is this version of dualism that will be featured in the present section. According to Cartesian dualism, human bodies are ordinary physical things, made up of ordinary matter in complicated arrangements and bearing roughly the properties attributed to such bodies by contemporary science. Bodies, however, have no mental or psychological properties whatever; bodies as such do not even experience sensations such as pleasure and pain. Human minds or souls, on the other hand, are completely nonphysical; they possess no mass, extension, or location in space. These souls are the ultimate subjects of all mental and psychological properties; they sense colors, feel pains and pleasures, entertain plans, and decide upon courses of action. Under normal circumstances, each soul causally interacts with a particular body from which it receives sensory information and through which it executes its intentions. Bodies reproduce through the normal biological processes, but souls do not; instead they are individually created by God. As simple, indivisible substances, they are incapable of dissolution into parts and so possess a natural immortality.

Cartesian dualism does not occasion any of the conflicts with Christian belief that arise from a materialistic perspective. The soul, being nonmaterial, does not perish at death; instead it persists and is avail-

6. See John W. Cooper, *Body, Soul, and Life Everlasting: Biblical Anthropology and the Monism-Dualism Debate* (Grand Rapids: Eerdmans, 1989).

CREATION

able to be reunited with its body in the resurrection. Since the soul is not made of physical stuff, its operations do not lie within the scope of physical law; the threat of physical determinism is avoided, and free will becomes a real possibility. And since the soul interacts causally with the physical body, our bodily actions are not scientifically predictable any more than our thoughts. The soul, being created by God, has the capacity of reason and moral discernment given to it by its Creator. Furthermore, one may add, the soul has a natural longing and inclination for reunion and fellowship with God; as Augustine said, "Thou hast made us for Thyself, and our hearts are restless until they find rest in Thee" (*Confessions* 1.1).

It is easy to see why many Christians have felt (and some still feel) that a view something like Cartesian dualism provides a good option for a Christian understanding of human nature. This view allows science full scope in studying the body and its processes, but the mind or soul, the most crucial ingredient of the human person, lies beyond the purview of science and is to be understood rather in spiritual and theological terms. Nevertheless, this sort of dualism has suffered massive rejection in recent years, and we need to see why this has occurred. Some of the objections against dualism are thoroughly unsound and do not deserve to be taken seriously. It is often claimed that dualism must be rejected because interaction between a physical substance (the body) and a non-physical substance (the soul) is impossible. But it would be difficult to think of any other argument in philosophy that is so widely accepted and at the same time so completely lacking in merit. It is true that we do not understand how an immaterial soul can affect, and be affected by, a physical body. But it is equally true that we do not understand how causal processes operate even between physical things. Sometimes we can explain complicated physical processes by the simpler processes of which they are composed—the workings of a watch, for example, by the pushes and pulls of its springs and gears. But sooner or later we come to the end of such explanations, and we are left with merely a regular pattern in nature for which we have no further answer to the question "Why does it work this way?" It just does, that is all—but "It just does" is an answer that is equally available to the proponent of mind-body interaction.

Another objection of dubious merit is the complaint that dualism is an import from Greek philosophy, foreign to the thought world of the Bible. It is true that the Bible does not contain a worked-out philosophy of human nature (any more than it contains a worked-out philosophy on any other topic). The Bible does, however, assume throughout that a person can in some way survive the death of his or her body; this is true even in the parts of the Old Testament that do not contain a full-fledged view of life beyond the grave. And the separability of a person from his or her body is alien to materialism; it is in fact a key element in mind-body dualism.[7] More to the point is the objection that in Scripture the human person is seen as an integrated whole, not as the conjunction of the "good" and "noble" soul with the "bad" or, at best, unimportant physical form. And it is true that some versions of dualism have promoted an excessive separation of mind/soul from body, along with a low and demeaning view of bodily existence. But these tendencies are not essential to dualism; as Charles Taliaferro has shown, it is possible to embrace an "integrative dualism" according to which, in practical experience, mind and body form an integral unit, so that I live through my body and my body's life is my own life.[8]

So far, then, it may seem that dualism is faring well and that major objections raised against it can quite properly be dismissed. There are other objections, however, that are not so easily met. One of these is the *dependency problem*: Cartesian dualism would certainly not lead us to expect the detailed, fine-grained dependence of cognitive functioning on brain function that we find to be the case.[9] Once this dependency is spelled out in some detail, it becomes more and more difficult to maintain the independence of mind from brain and body that is the hallmark of Cartesianism. The mind is "the thing that thinks"—perhaps so, but only, it seems, when supported in a very intricate and detailed fashion by cerebral processes, with specific sorts of information-processing depending on very specific portions of the brain.[10] So far as I have been able to find out, Cartesians have no plausible explanation for this dependency, which goes far beyond anything their theory would lead us to expect.

Another important problem for Cartesianism is the *continuity problem*. Biology shows us clearly that in spite of the uniqueness of humans in certain respects, there is a great deal of similarity between us and other mammals in both structure and function. Furthermore, there is a fairly complete continuum stretching between humans, as the "highest" life form, and progressively lower forms such as fish, octopuses, insects, and bacteria. The challenge for the dualist is to say which, if any, of these

---

7. For a full discussion, with close attention to matters of biblical exegesis, see ibid.

8. See Charles Taliaferro, *Consciousness and the Mind of God* (Cambridge: Cambridge University Press, 1994), esp. 114–22, 226–47.

9. This dependency is a pervasive theme in the writings of neuroscientists. See, e.g., Malcolm A. Jeeves, *Human Nature at the Millennium: Reflections on the Integration of Psychology and Christianity* (Grand Rapids: Baker, 1997).

10. For more detail on this point (as well as on other difficulties for dualism), see William Hasker, *The Emergent Self* (Ithaca, NY: Cornell University Press, 1999), 151–57, and references given there.

other creatures possess immaterial souls. Unfortunately, it seems that any possible answer will be implausible, or embarrassing, or both at once. Descartes put the matter nicely when he said that if animals "could think as we do, they would have an immortal soul as well as we, which is not likely, because there is no reason for believing it of some animals without believing it of all, and there are many of them too imperfect to make it possible to believe it of them, such as oysters, sponges, etc."[11] Descartes's own solution was to limit souls to humans and consider all other animals as mindless automata, incapable even of sensation. This solution has few defenders today, and for good reason. (I sometimes tell my students, "If you can believe *that*, you can believe anything!") But to attribute souls only to "higher" animals—for instance, mammals and birds—still creates a strong impression of arbitrariness, not to say chauvinism. And on the other hand, the further down the scale we go, the more difficult it becomes to keep a straight face about the resulting picture. Remember that beings that have Cartesian souls—rather, that *are* Cartesian souls—are essentially immaterial and nonspatial and are only contingently embodied. So we have the prospect of an earthworm that is akin to us in this regard—"brother Worm," as Charles Taliaferro once remarked. Furthermore, we will have to say that God specially creates individual souls for worms, gnats, and even intestinal parasites! Once we have spent some time pondering these and similar implications of Cartesian dualism, I suspect that most of us will find ourselves looking, or at least hoping, for some other solution.

## A CHRISTIAN MATERIALISM?

Although dualism has traditionally been the mind-body theory of choice for theology, a number of contemporary Christian thinkers are striking out in a different direction. Impressed with the difficulties for dualism noted in the previous section and with the strong scientific evidence showing a close connection between the functioning of our brains and our mental lives, these thinkers conclude that the best prospects for a Christian understanding of human beings lies in some form of materialism.[12] They recognize that the weight of

11. René Descartes, letter to the marquis of Newcastle, in David M. Rosenthal, ed., *Materialism and the Mind-Body Problem* (Englewood Cliffs, NJ: Prentice-Hall, 1971), 21.
12. A representative set of papers promoting this viewpoint may be found in Warren S. Brown, Nancey Murphy, and H. Newton Malony, eds., *Whatever Happened to the Soul? Scientific and Theological Portraits of Human Nature* (Minneapolis: Fortress, 1998). Materialism is also the predominant view taken in Joel B. Greene, ed., *What about the Soul? Neuroscience and Christian Anthropology* (Nashville: Abingdon, 2004).

tradition is against them, but they do not regard this as decisive for what a contemporary Christian view ought to look like. Among the views available in the Greek philosophy that was prevalent in the early centuries of the church, some form of Platonic dualism was rather clearly the best option. But Scripture does not mandate any particular mind-body theory, and we Christians of the twenty-first century may well conclude that materialism is the better way to go. Undoubtedly, the predominance of materialist and physicalist views in present-day science and philosophy plays a role here. These thinkers rightly hold that we should avoid unnecessarily tying the Christian faith to outmoded ways of thinking that can easily result in its being dismissed without a fair hearing.

The success of these materialist versions of theological anthropology depends on whether they can satisfy the requirements for a Christian view sketched at the beginning of this essay. Can a materialist view show how humans can be rational, responsible creatures, endowed with free will and capable, assisted by divine grace, of everlasting life? If this can be done, the case for accepting such a view may well outweigh the force of tradition on the other side. So this is the question we need to examine.

It should be noted at the outset that these "Christian materialists" affirm only that human beings are fully material, not that everything that exists is material. These thinkers are materialists but not naturalists; in particular, they affirm that God is a nonmaterial being who has created the physical world of nature and also acts causally on things and persons within that world. (Thus the argument that interaction between physical and nonphysical is impossible must be rejected.) But within the natural world, everything that exists is material. Given this, can the essentials for a Christian view of human nature be maintained?

A key question here is whether a Christian materialism should affirm, with most other materialist views, that (as stated above) "our actions are entirely the result of the operations of the elementary particles that make up our bodies, acting and reacting in accordance with the fundamental laws of physics." The view that this is the case is known in philosophy as the *causal closure of the physical domain*; briefly stated, this is the view that every physical event has a physical cause.[13] This is unquestionably the predominant view in contemporary philosophy of mind; indeed, it has often been regarded as a requirement for physicalism or material-

---

13. As noted above, Christian materialists must recognize the exception that God, who is nonphysical, is nevertheless able to cause physical events. For them, then, causal closure must be qualified as holding that every *purely natural* physical event has a physical cause.

ism.[14] A materialist view that adheres to this assumption is causally reductionist in that it holds that "higher-level" causal connections (such as those between thoughts in our minds) can ultimately be explained in terms of the "lower-level" laws of particle interaction.

Opinions are divided on this point; some Christian materialists affirm causal closure whereas others reject it. The constraint of space limits me here to what may appear to be a rather dogmatic statement: if causal closure is affirmed, the essential requirements for a Christian view of human beings cannot be satisfied. In this case, the difficulty for a materialist view of reasoning—that the conclusions reached are determined by the laws of physics and not by whether the conclusion of the reasoning is supported by the premises—applies to a Christian materialist view as much as to any other. Rational inference, as we ordinarily understand the concept, simply has no role to play in our mental lives. But as has often been pointed out, undermining reason has the effect also of undermining whatever rational support we may have thought we had for materialism itself as well as for any other views we may hold. A worldview that cannot provide an adequate account of the very reasoning on the basis of which it is accepted is not a serious candidate for acceptance. Causal closure also implies that we cannot have free will if this is understood in the libertarian sense, that we are really capable, when we make a free choice, of deciding in any of two or more different ways. At best, we may have "compatibilist" free will, meaning that nothing prevents us from doing whatever it is we most want to do—although, as we have seen, both our wanting and our choosing are themselves causally determined by factors over which we have never had any control. This might be acceptable to those who hold to a deterministic or "Calvinist" theology, but even this is doubtful; most Calvinists, though welcoming universal determination by divine decrees, have shied away from the sort of mechanistic, physical determinism implied by causal closure.

So a viable Christian materialism must reject causal closure. Instead it must affirm the existence of "emergent" properties and causal powers

14. Thus Jaegwon Kim states, "This [causal closure] is the assumption that if we trace the causal ancestry of a physical event, we need never go outside the physical domain. To deny this assumption is to accept the Cartesian idea that some physical events need nonphysical causes, and if this is true there can in principle be no complete and self-sufficient physical theory of the physical domain. If the causal closure failed, our physics would need to refer in an essential way to nonphysical causal agents, perhaps Cartesian souls and their psychic properties, if it is to give a complete account of the physical world" ("The Myth of Nonreductive Materialism," in *Supervenience and Mind: Selected Philosophical Essays* [Cambridge: Cambridge University Press, 1991], 280). Kim also states, "If this is what you are willing to embrace, why call yourself a 'physicalist'?" ("The Nonreductivist's Troubles with Mental Causation," ibid., 356).

in complex material things such as human and animal bodies. This view must hold, in other words, that *certain complex objects have properties and causal powers that do not exist in their simpler constituents and cannot be predicted on the basis of the properties manifested by those constituents.* Among these emergent properties will be such items as consciousness, rationality, and free will, none of which (as best we can tell) are properties of the elementary constituents of matter[15]—nor can they be predicted or explained on the basis of the properties and behavior manifested by those constituents when they are not arranged in the complex configurations characteristic of organisms. Such a view will need to affirm, then, that the ordinary laws of microphysics do not fully describe the behavior of matter as it exists in living organisms, that under these special circumstances, the behavior of the elementary particles can and does deviate from what would be predicted on the basis of the microphysical laws. Such an *emergent materialism* is actually rather similar to dualism in that it acknowledges a whole range of distinctively mental properties quite different from the properties normally ascribed to material things and does not try to explain or "reduce" the mental properties in terms of ordinary physical properties. The difference from dualism is that emergent materialism does not invoke a soul, specially created by God, as the locus of these mental properties. Instead the mental properties are properties *of the material configuration itself,* but properties of this very special (emergent) kind, which are not found in simpler arrangements of physical stuff.[16]

Such an emergent materialism has many virtues, considered from the standpoint of a Christian view of human beings. It is able to acknowledge human rationality and free will in a full-blooded sense of these terms. It is also able to take morality seriously, as well as the human capacity for a relationship with God, and need not give the sorts of reductive explanations of these matters characteristic of naturalism. On the other hand, this view does face certain objections. One group of objections will come from the proponents of more standard materialist views, who will regard such an emergent materialism as an unacceptable compromise, far too close for comfort to "spooky" views such as dualism. Certainly, Christian philosophers and theologians may not be greatly moved by objections such as this. But often at least part of the motivation for a

15. Note that, according to the view here proposed, these properties will be grounded in the properties of the elementary constituents; otherwise their appearance in the composite object would be miraculous. But the particles never display such properties unless combined into an organism.

16. An excellent statement of such an emergent-materialist view (although he does not so label it) is found in Timothy O'Connor, *Persons and Causes: The Metaphysics of Free Will* (New York: Oxford University Press, 2000).

Christian materialist view is to present a picture of human beings that does not clash with the prevailing scientific orthodoxy. An emergent materialism such as is described here is unlikely to achieve much success in this endeavor.

Another difficulty for emergent materialism (indeed, for any sort of materialism) appears when we ask, In this view, exactly what is it that does the thinking? The inevitable reply is that it is the brain. But how is this supposed to work? How are we to make sense of the idea that thinking is something done by a complex physical object? The philosopher Leibniz put the problem thus:

> In imagining that there is a machine whose construction would enable it to think, to sense, and to have perception, one could conceive it enlarged while retaining the same proportions, so that one could enter into it, just like into a windmill. Supposing this, one should, when visiting within it, find only parts pushing one another, and never anything by which to explain a perception. Thus it is in the simple substance, and not in the composite or in the machine, that one must look for perception.[17]

To see the force of this, imagine yourself walking around in Leibniz's supersized "brain machine," and ask yourself, "Which of these pushes, pulls, and so on within the machine is a *thought*?" It does not seem that any answer to this question can make much sense. The difficulty here does not lie, as some have thought, in the fact that Leibniz's example was limited by seventeenth-century technology. If, instead of his "parts pushing one another," we fill the machine with vacuum tubes, transistors, or, for that matter, neurons, exactly the same problem remains. The problem does not lie in the pushes and pulls but rather in the complexity of the machine, the fact that it is made up of many distinct parts, coupled with the fact that *a complex state of consciousness cannot exist distributed among the parts of a complex object*. The functioning of any complex object such as a machine, a television set, a computer, or a brain consists of the coordinated functioning of its parts, which working together produce an effect of some kind. But where the effect to be explained is a thought, a state of consciousness, what function shall be assigned to the individual parts, be they transistors or neurons?

Even a fairly simple experiential state—for instance, your visual experience as you look at the page upon which this argument is set down—contains far more information than can be encoded in a single transistor or a single neuron. Suppose, then, that the state is broken up into bits in such a way that some small part of it is represented in each

17. Gottfried Wilhelm Leibniz, *Monadology* 17, in *Monadology: An Edition for Students*, ed. Nicholas Rescher (Pittsburgh: University of Pittsburgh Press, 1991), 19.

of the parts of the computer or the brain. Assuming this to be done, we have still this question: who or what is aware of the conscious state as a whole? For it is a fact that *I am aware* of my conscious state, at any given moment, as a unitary whole. Leibniz, in the passage quoted above, implies that the seat of consciousness must be something simple and indivisible—in other words, the soul. The materialist, who rejects this, needs to face this question: when I am aware of a complex conscious state, what *physical entity* is it that is aware of that state? This question, I am convinced, does not and cannot receive a plausible answer. But if materialism cannot answer the question, it is in deep trouble.

Yet another problem concerns the matter of life after death for persons who are wholly material. Traditionally, theology has assumed that after the death of the body the immaterial soul still persists, to be united with a transformed and glorious body in the resurrection. During the period between death and resurrection, therefore, one lives on as a soul; the soul is, so to speak, the connecting link between the body that died and the one that will rise again. According to materialism, however, there simply is no soul to provide this link. So, how can we survive our inevitable deaths? What, if anything, "binds together" the resurrection life with the one that has gone before, so that they are both part of the life of the very same person?

What is typically asserted by materialist views of the resurrection is that at some time after my death, God will re-create an assemblage of atoms (it probably does not matter whether they are the very same atoms or not) that is extremely similar (though probably not exactly similar; some repairs and improvements will be needed) to me as I was before I died. And, the story goes on, this re-created individual will be I, myself. But suppose that at the same instant someone were to create another individual, either exactly like the re-created Hasker or slightly more similar to the Hasker who perished?[18] In either of these cases, the re-created Hasker would not be identical with the one who had died. At best, we would have two presently existing individuals with an equal claim to be so identical—but since both cannot be identical with Hasker-who-died, neither is so. (Two things that are different from each other cannot both be identical with some third thing.) But this means that the identity of Hasker re-created with Hasker who died depends on the nonexistence of another equal or superior claimant to this status. But the identity of an individual simply cannot depend on anything like this—this would

18. It is not an answer to this to assert that God, being good, would not (and perhaps could not) create such duplicates or near duplicates. What is needed for the objection to go through is only the metaphysical possibility of a situation in which the appropriate atoms are arranged in the right configuration. It is hardly a necessary truth that only God would be able to do this.

amount to saying that as things stand, you are indeed the person you are, but if something else, having no direct connection with you as you now are, were different, then you would not be that person. If you found the last sentence a bit difficult to follow, do not worry: the problem is that the described situation simply does not make sense. But if it does not make sense, then neither does the materialist view of the resurrection make sense. "No soul, no life after death" is a slogan you can count on. And this means that the prospects for a Christian materialism are really quite bleak.

This section has pointed out difficulties for a Christian version of materialism, but in fairness it must also be said that all of these objections continue to be matters of controversy. And if the objections can be met, materialism may after all be a viable and attractive answer for Christians to the question about the nature of human beings.

## EMERGENT DUALISM

By this time it is likely that some readers are experiencing a degree of frustration. You may have found Cartesian dualism an initially plausible and attractive view, only to learn that it faces serious difficulties. This may have led you to greet materialism—perhaps especially emergent materialism—with a sense of relief as the perplexities of dualism are left behind. But materialism also seems to be confronted with severe difficulties, so where are we to turn for a viable answer to our questions?

We now examine another view, one that, if successful, might provide a resolution of your perplexities. *Emergent dualism*, as this view is called, claims to combine many of the advantages of both Cartesian dualism and materialism and at the same time avoid the major difficulties that afflict these views. Certainly, emergent dualism brings with it problems of its own—in philosophy, nothing is free.

In order to arrive at emergent dualism, we begin by accepting one of the cardinal tenets of materialism—that a human person, like all other organisms, initially consists of nothing but ordinary physical matter, arranged in structures of remarkable complexity. Next, we avail ourselves of the concept of *emergence*, already somewhat familiar to us from our consideration of emergent materialism. The core idea of emergence is that, when elements of a certain sort are assembled in the right way, something new comes into being, something that was not there before. The new thing is not just a rearrangement of what was there before, but neither is it something dropped into the situation from the outside. It "emerges," comes into being, through the operation of the constituent elements, yet the new thing is something different and often surprising; we would not have expected it before it appeared. In the case of the human person, what emerges must include such distinctively mental properties as consciousness, sensation, emotion, and thought, as well as the capacity for rational inference, moral awareness, and a relationship with God.

So far, emergent dualism agrees with emergent materialism. But emergent dualism takes the concept of emergence one step further: what emerges is not merely new properties but a *new individual*—an entity, or substance, that was not there before at all, namely, the person's mind or soul. In order to get a grip on this, an analogy may be of help. Think of an ordinary electromagnet, of the kind that is present in dozens of household appliances. In essence, the electromagnet is just a coil of wire, normally wound around a core of some kind. While the magnet is off, that is all there is to it. But pass a current through the wire, and a new thing appears—a magnetic field. This field exerts causal powers that were not there before it was created, enabling it to activate a switch, turn the armature of a motor, or lift a massive object. In talking about the field, we are not just using a manner of speaking; the field is a real thing, having an existence of its own distinct from that of the generating magnet. This is shown, for instance, by the fact that the field extends out in space well beyond the coil of wire that generates it. Furthermore, physical theory has shown that, in principle, a sufficiently strong magnetic field could become self-sustaining; it could have the capacity to continue to exist, all on its own, even if the magnet that generated it were to be destroyed. And now consider the following analogy. *As a magnet generates its magnetic field, so an organism generates its field of consciousness.* Corresponding to the current passing through the wire that generates the electromagnetic field, there are the processes in the neurons of the brain and nervous system that generate conscious awareness. This consciousness—the mind or soul, as we call it—is a real thing in its own right, distinct from the generating organism. The mind thus generated plays much the same role as the soul in traditional dualism; it is the ultimate subject of thinking, of emotions, and of the decisions we make and the actions we perform.

So much, then, for an initial statement of emergent dualism. How does it compare with other views we have considered? Unlike the reductive varieties of materialism, it is fully able to exhibit human persons as free, rational, and morally responsible. In this it resembles emergent materialism, but it differs from that position in that now we have not merely emergent properties but also an emergent individual, the mind/soul/consciousness. This is important because it gives us a way to answer the question of what is the "thing that thinks"—a question to which, if the unity-of-consciousness argument is sound, the materialist

CREATION

has no satisfactory answer. It is also able to give a coherent account of the resurrection of the dead: as in traditional dualism, the mind/soul continues in existence after the physical organism perishes and is united with a new body in the resurrection.

The topic of resurrection, however, raises further questions that need to be discussed. One might think that emergent dualism supports the mortality of the soul rather than its immortality. Destroy the magnet and the magnetic field disappears; does it not follow that the death of the generating organism should also lead to the disappearance of the field of consciousness? This is indeed a plausible inference, but it should not lead us to a denial of the life to come. We are not limited to considering what the conscious field in itself is able to do and likely to do; our question, rather, is, What is in God's power to bring about? Since divine power is limited only by logical consistency (even God cannot make a round square or a married bachelor), the question we must ask is whether it is logically coherent to suppose that the emergent mind/soul continues to exist after the death of the organism that generated it. And here, it seems, the answer must be "Yes." The magnetic field is a real thing in itself, distinct from the generating magnet—and as we have noted, phys-ical theory indicates that such a field would be capable, under the right circumstances, of continuing to exist on its own after the magnet has been destroyed. Following the analogy, may we not suppose that God is able to maintain our souls in existence after the death of our bodies and to furnish them with gloriously transformed bodies in the resurrection? Note, however, that not just any body would do; the resurrection body must be precisely tailored to fit the soul that, from that time on, it will sustain and support. (Random body switching, regarded as possible by some dualists, is not a possibility according to emergent dualism.) So, for emergent dualism, eternal life is entirely possible, but it will come about through an amazing and miraculous act of God, not as a natural attribute of our "immortal souls." (Christian materialists also stress that resurrection and eternal life are possible only through God's power. But if the argument given in the previous section is sound, they cannot give a logically coherent account of this possibility. And it is no solution to appeal to divine power if the thing that God is supposed to do is inher-ently self-contradictory.)

Emergent dualism must be compared also with traditional dualism. On the face of it, emergent dualism matches traditional dualism in what it has to offer for Christian theology; all of the desiderata identified at the beginning of this essay are fully satisfied. Granted, emergent dualism is a less traditional view, but this in itself is hardly of great weight.[19] It might also be suggested that postulating the creation of the soul directly by God is a good deal simpler than invoking a difficult doctrine of emergence. This also is true but of questionable importance. Only a little study of the natural sciences should be enough to convince us that the ways in which God has made the world are far more complex and subtle than anything we could have imagined before detailed investigation. (One of my favorite cartoons shows an ancient Greek scientist-philosopher standing in front of a board on which he has written, in large letters, "EARTH—AIR—FIRE—WATER," the four elements of ancient science. In answer to a comment from the audience, he replies indignantly, "What do you mean, 'That's a good start'? This is IT!")

On the other hand, emergent dualism has virtues that traditional dualism lacks. It can readily account for the pervasive dependence of our mental life on the condition and functioning of our brains, something that for Cartesian dualism is unexpected and lacks any natural explanation. Since consciousness is generated by the brain and nervous system, there is a close connection between specific types of brain activity and corresponding forms of mental processing—a connection that contemporary neuroscience is spelling out in detail. Emergent dualism also avoids the continuity problem; the similarities between humans and other animals cause it no embarrassment whatsoever. Other animals have souls, just as we do; their souls are less complex and sophisticated than ours because generated by a less complex and sophisticated nervous system. The animals' souls, however, are not "naturally immortal" any more than ours are, so we need not be concerned with Descartes's worry about "immortal oysters." If God sees fit to preserve certain of the beasts for life in heaven, they will be so preserved and resurrected; if not, not. One further point: emergent dualism does not strictly require a theory of evolution, but it has the merit that it fits nicely with such a theory, quite unlike Cartesian dualism in this respect. An emergent dualist will likely hold that minds/souls evolve along with the bodies that generate them; the minds, like the bodies, are subject to selection pressures that tend in the direction of more effective thinking as well as better bodily responses.

So far, emergent dualism seems to be faring well, but what are its costs? There really is just one major cost involved in this theory, but to some this cost may seem pretty steep. It is that we will have to attribute to ordinary, everyday matter, the stuff of sticks and stones and baseball

19. Note that there is in the history of theology, in addition to the predominant creationist view, a traducian view, according to which souls, like bodies, are produced through natural reproduction. Emergent dualism can legitimately claim a place in this traducian tradition.

bats, truly remarkable powers—the powers, that is, to produce, when arranged and functioning in certain complex structures, emergent minds with the capacity to seek truth, enjoy beauty, perceive good and evil, and enter into a relationship with God. One critic simply lays it down that the existence of an emergent substance is impossible—and of course, if he is right about this, emergent dualism is likewise impossible.[20] But no argument is given for this claim, so the objection is hardly decisive. Timothy O'Connor states, somewhat more modestly, that this sort of emergence "would involve the generation of fundamentally new substance in the world . . . That's a lot to swallow."[21] He may be right; perhaps this view *is* a lot to swallow. I would point out to O'Connor, though, that a lot of what is surprising about this view has to be swallowed anyway by anyone who buys into his own theory of emergent materialism. We still are going to have ordinary matter behaving in ways quite different from anything we have been led to expect from the rest of our experience with it, whether in the laboratory or in everyday life—except for its behavior when assembled into those remarkable contrivances known as organisms. The fact is, however, that in spite of remarkable scientific progress, our grasp on the ultimate nature of matter remains tenuous in the extreme. What we do know is that this ordinary matter is the creation of a Mind of incredible wisdom and subtlety. When this Being chose to make humans and other sentient creatures out of the dust of the earth, we may well suppose that this Being had the foresight to endow that dust with the powers that would enable such a creation.

In the final analysis, it may not be absolutely crucial which mind-body theory we choose to embrace. We want to know and affirm the truth, of course—but theories do not come with a label tied around them telling us which of them is "the truth." In view of this, we can only seek the best answers available in terms of all the knowledge that is accessible to us. Whichever view we accept—or even if we decide to remain agnostic on the question—we need to be aware that there are plausible alternatives, alternatives that can be accepted and defended with a degree of reasonableness. I would suggest that we also need to gain some awareness of the scientific work that is playing such a large role in shaping the attitudes of our contemporaries in these matters. And we need to keep a firm grasp on the nonnegotiable requirements that are essential for any properly Christian view of the nature of human beings. "Thou hast made us for Thyself . . ."

20. See Keith Yandell, "Mind-Fields and the Siren Song of Reason," *Philosophia Christi* 2/2 (2000): 183–95.
21. Timothy O'Connor, "Causality, Mind, and Free Will," in *Soul, Body, and Survival: Essays on the Metaphysics of Human Persons,* ed. Kevin Corcoran (Ithaca, NY: Cornell University Press, 2001), 50.

# INDEX